D0003598

Teach Yourself VISUALLY

Photoshop® Elements 13

Richard Wentk

Visual

A Wiley Brand

Teach Yourself VISUALLY™ Photoshop® Elements 13

Published by
John Wiley & Sons, Inc.
10475 Crosspoint Boulevard
Indianapolis, IN 46256

www.wiley.com

Published simultaneously in Canada

Copyright © 2015 by John Wiley & Sons, Inc., Indianapolis, Indiana

No part of this publication may be reproduced, stored in a retrieval system or transmitted in any form or by any means, electronic, mechanical, photocopying, recording, scanning or otherwise, except as permitted under Sections 107 or 108 of the 1976 United States Copyright Act, without either the prior written permission of the Publisher, or authorization through payment of the appropriate per-copy fee to the Copyright Clearance Center, 222 Rosewood Drive, Danvers, MA 01923, 978-750-8400, fax 978-646-8600. Requests to the Publisher for permission should be addressed to the Permissions Department, John Wiley & Sons, Inc., 111 River Street, Hoboken, NJ 07030, 201-748-6011, fax 201-748-6008, or online at www.wiley.com/go/permissions.

Wiley publishes in a variety of print and electronic formats and by print-on-demand. Some material included with standard print versions of this book may not be included in e-books or in print-on-demand. If this book refers to media such as a CD or DVD that is not included in the version you purchased, you may download this material at http://booksupport.wiley.com. For more information about Wiley products, visit www.wiley.com.

Library of Congress Control Number: 2014945052

ISBN: 978-1-118-96466-8 (pbk); ISBN: 978-1-118-96471-2 (ebk);
ISBN: 978-1-118-96467-5 (ebk)

Manufactured in the United States of America

10 9 8 7 6 5 4 3 2 1

Trademark Acknowledgments

Wiley, Visual, the Visual logo, Teach Yourself VISUALLY, Read Less - Learn More and related trade dress are trademarks or registered trademarks of John Wiley & Sons, Inc. and/or its affiliates. Adobe and Photoshop are registered trademarks of Adobe Systems Incorporated. All other trademarks are the property of their respective owners. John Wiley & Sons, Inc. is not associated with any product or vendor mentioned in this book.

LIMIT OF LIABILITY/DISCLAIMER OF WARRANTY: THE PUBLISHER AND THE AUTHOR MAKE NO REPRESENTATIONS OR WARRANTIES WITH RESPECT TO THE ACCURACY OR COMPLETENESS OF THE CONTENTS OF THIS WORK AND SPECIFICALLY DISCLAIM ALL WARRANTIES, INCLUDING WITHOUT LIMITATION WARRANTIES OF FITNESS FOR A PARTICULAR PURPOSE. NO WARRANTY MAY BE CREATED OR EXTENDED BY SALES OR PROMOTIONAL MATERIALS. THE ADVICE AND STRATEGIES CONTAINED HEREIN MAY NOT BE SUITABLE FOR EVERY SITUATION. THIS WORK IS SOLD WITH THE UNDERSTANDING THAT THE PUBLISHER IS NOT ENGAGED IN RENDERING LEGAL, ACCOUNTING, OR OTHER PROFESSIONAL SERVICES. IF PROFESSIONAL ASSISTANCE IS REQUIRED, THE SERVICES OF A COMPETENT PROFESSIONAL PERSON SHOULD BE SOUGHT. NEITHER THE PUBLISHER NOR THE AUTHOR SHALL BE LIABLE FOR DAMAGES ARISING HEREFROM. THE FACT THAT AN ORGANIZATION OR WEBSITE IS REFERRED TO IN THIS WORK AS A CITATION AND/OR A POTENTIAL SOURCE OF FURTHER INFORMATION DOES NOT MEAN THAT THE AUTHOR OR THE PUBLISHER ENDORSES THE INFORMATION THE ORGANIZATION OR WEBSITE MAY PROVIDE OR RECOMMENDATIONS IT MAY MAKE. FURTHER, READERS SHOULD BE AWARE THAT INTERNET WEBSITES LISTED IN THIS WORK MAY HAVE CHANGED OR DISAPPEARED BETWEEN WHEN THIS WORK WAS WRITTEN AND WHEN IT IS READ.

FOR PURPOSES OF ILLUSTRATING THE CONCEPTS AND TECHNIQUES DESCRIBED IN THIS BOOK, THE AUTHOR HAS CREATED VARIOUS NAMES, COMPANY NAMES, MAILING, E-MAIL AND INTERNET ADDRESSES, PHONE AND FAX NUMBERS AND SIMILAR INFORMATION, ALL OF WHICH ARE FICTITIOUS. ANY RESEMBLANCE OF THESE FICTITIOUS NAMES, ADDRESSES, PHONE AND FAX NUMBERS AND SIMILAR INFORMATION TO ANY ACTUAL PERSON, COMPANY AND/OR ORGANIZATION IS UNINTENTIONAL AND PURELY COINCIDENTAL.

Contact Us

For general information on our other products and services please contact our Customer Care Department within the U.S. at 877-762-2974, outside the U.S. at 317-572-3993 or fax 317-572-4002.

For technical support please visit www.wiley.com/techsupport.

Sales | Contact Wiley/at (877) 762-2974 or /fax (317) 572-4002.

Credits

Acquisitions Editor
Aaron Black

Project Editor
Martin V. Minner

Technical Editor
Paul Sihvonen-Binder

Copy Editor
Gwenette Gaddis

**Manager, Content Development
& Assembly**
Mary Beth Wakefield

Publisher
Jim Minatel

Editorial Assistant
Claire Johnson

Project Coordinator
Sheree Montgomery

About the Author

Richard Wentk has been writing professionally about technology and creativity since 1993. He is a regular contributor to numerous magazines including *British Journal of Photography*, *Computer Arts*, and *Total Digital Camera*. He is an associate member of the Royal Photographic Society and exhibits work regularly in the United Kingdom. He is also an app developer and the author of a number of books for developers and Mac users including *iOS App Development Portable Genius*. For the latest news and information, visit www.zettaboom.com.

Author's Acknowledgments

All books are a collaboration, and this one is no exception. I'd like to thank Aaron Black for commissioning the project, and Martin V. Minner for shepherding it from electronic copy to printed item as painlessly as possible.

Special thanks are due to Hans Peter Blochwitz, Rees Clements, and Fiona Tanner Oliver-Smith for permission to use their superb photos.

Extra special thanks to Annette Saunders for contributing further outstanding photos, and for everything else.

How to Use This Book

Who This Book Is For

This book is for the reader who has never used this particular technology or software application. It is also for readers who want to expand their knowledge.

The Conventions in This Book

① Steps

This book uses a step-by-step format to guide you easily through each task. Numbered steps are actions you must do; bulleted steps clarify a point, step, or optional feature; and indented steps give you the result.

② Notes

Notes give additional information — special conditions that may occur during an operation, a situation that you want to avoid, or a cross reference to a related area of the book.

③ Icons and Buttons

Icons and buttons show you exactly what you need to click to perform a step.

④ Tips

Tips offer additional information, including warnings and shortcuts.

⑤ Bold

Bold type shows command names, options, and text or numbers you must type.

⑥ Italics

Italic type introduces and defines a new term.

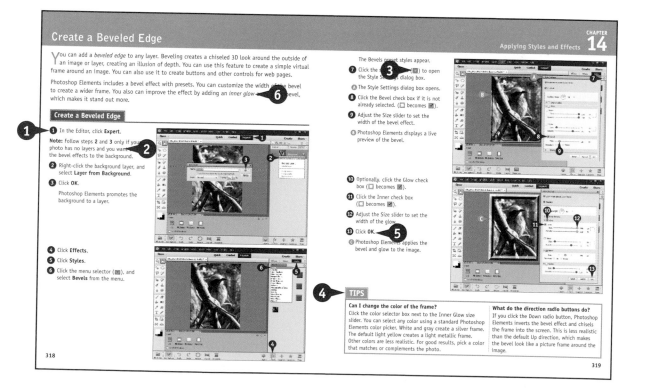

Create a Beveled Edge

You can add a *beveled edge* to any layer. Beveling creates a chiseled 3D look around the outside of an image or layer, creating an illusion of depth. You can use this feature to create a simple virtual frame around an image. You can also use it to create buttons and other controls for web pages.

Photoshop Elements includes a bevel effect with presets. You can customize the width of the bevel to create a wider frame. You also can improve the effect by adding an *inner glow* to the bevel, which makes it stand out more.

Create a Beveled Edge

① In the Editor, click **Expert**.

Note: Follow steps **2** and **3** only if your photo has no layers and you want the bevel effects to the background.

② Right-click the background layer, and select **Layer from Background**.

③ Click **OK**.

Photoshop Elements promotes the background to a layer.

④ Click **Effects**.

⑤ Click **Styles**.

⑥ Click the menu selector (▤), and select **Bevels** from the menu.

The Bevels preset styles appear.

⑦ Click the ▤ to open the Style Settings dialog box.

Ⓐ The Style Settings dialog box opens.

⑧ Click the Bevel check box if it is not already selected. (☐ becomes ☑).

⑨ Adjust the Size slider to set the width of the bevel effect.

Ⓑ Photoshop Elements displays a live preview of the bevel.

⑩ Optionally, click the Glow check box (☐ becomes ☑).

⑪ Click the Inner check box (☐ becomes ☑).

⑫ Adjust the Size slider to set the width of the glow.

⑬ Click **OK**.

Ⓒ Photoshop Elements applies the bevel and glow to the image.

TIPS

Can I change the color of the frame?
Click the color selector box next to the Inner Glow size slider. You can select any color using a standard Photoshop Elements color picker. White and gray create a silver frame. The default light yellow creates a light metallic frame. Other colors are less realistic. For good results, pick a color that matches or complements the photo.

What do the direction radio buttons do?
If you click the Down radio button, Photoshop Elements inverts the bevel effect and chisels the frame into the screen. This is less realistic than the default Up direction, which makes the bevel look like a picture frame around the image.

Applying Styles and Effects

CHAPTER **14**

318

319

Table of Contents

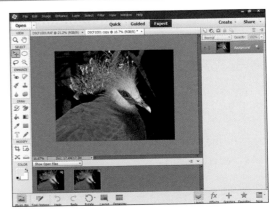

Chapter 3 Organizing Your Photos

Chapter 4 Using Advanced Organizing Tools

Table of Contents

Table of Contents

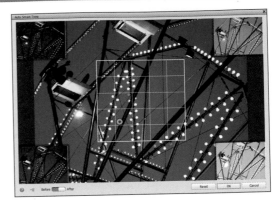

Chapter 11 Painting and Drawing on Photos

Chapter 12 Applying Filters

Table of Contents

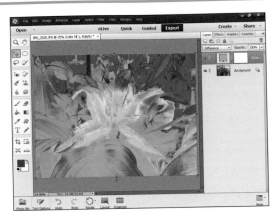

Chapter 15 — Saving and Sharing Your Work

CHAPTER 1

Getting Started

Are you interested in working with digital images? Do you want to improve or transform your photos? This chapter introduces Adobe Photoshop Elements 13, a popular photo editor and organizer.

You can use Photoshop Elements to edit, improve, and organize digital images. The product is split into two parts: the *Organizer* and the *Editor*. Use the Organizer to collect photos into albums; tag them; search them by place, tag, or date; and create slideshows. Use the Editor to improve the color and exposure of your photos, apply corrections, crop them, and transform them with creative effects. For example, you can add a virtual frame, make a photo look like a painting, add captions and other text, and decorate your photo with clip-art shapes and objects. The Editor supports layers, which make it easy to combine multiple images into a collage and experiment with changes without having to alter your original image. When you are finished with your images, you can use Photoshop Elements to print them or share them on the web or on photo-sharing and social-media sites such as Flickr and Facebook.

Fix Photos

The Editor is packed with features you can use to make simple and quick improvements to your photos. You can apply one-click fixes for color and contrast, correct color and exposure manually, and stretch and shrink your photos in many different ways to correct perspective and composition. You can crop photos to remove unwanted features and eliminate clutter. As you gain more experience, you can begin to select objects in your photos — including people — and move them within the photo or even delete them completely. You can also combine photos to create group shots and panoramas, and you can blend multiple photos of the same scene to remove unwanted moving objects.

Retouch and Repair

You can use Photoshop Elements to edit new photos to make them look their best as well as retouch and repair older photos that suffer from aging problems. For example, you can restore a faded photo by using saturation controls to make it more vibrant, or you can use the Clone Stamp tool to repair a tear or stain. You can also use the program's exposure commands to fix lighting problems as well as edit out unwanted objects with the Healing Brush.

Add Decoration

The painting and drawing tools in Photoshop Elements make the program a formidable illustration tool as well as a photo editor. You can apply colors or patterns to your images with a variety of brush styles. And you can also add text, captions, and speech or thought bubbles.

Create a Digital Collage

You can combine parts of different images in Photoshop Elements to create a collage. Your compositions can include photos, scanned art, text, and anything else you can save on your computer as a digital image. By placing elements on separate layers, you can move, place, and edit them independently.

Organize and Catalog

As you bring photos into Photoshop Elements, the Organizer keeps track of them. You can preview photos from one convenient window, group photos into theme-specific albums, tag photos with keywords, and search for photos based on time and date, location, and any tags you added. You can even find photos that are visually similar, and put names to faces in your photos.

Put Your Photos to Work

After you edit your photographs, you can print them out or share them, individually, in groups, or even in animated video slide show. You can share your photos online on Facebook or Twitter directly from the Organizer. You can also print photos on your own printer, or create photo books, calendars, and other projects.

Understanding Digital Images

Digital images are made of millions of tiny squares called *pixels*. When you take a photo with a digital camera or scan a photo with a scanner, the hardware converts the scene or the source image into a grid of pixels. This section introduces you to some important basics about how computers store images in digital form.

Acquire Photos

You can acquire photographic images to use in Photoshop Elements from a number of sources. You can download photos to Photoshop Elements from a digital camera, memory card, or photo CD. You can scan photographs, slides, or artwork and then import the images directly into the program. You can also bring in photos that you have downloaded from the web or received via e-mail.

Understanding Pixels

Each pixel is a single color. If you zoom in to your photo, you can see the pixels as a colored grid. If you have too few pixels, your image looks small on the screen and is soft if you try to print it. If you have too many pixels, your photos takes up lots of disk space when you save them and lots of computer memory as you edit them. Photoshop Elements works its magic by rearranging and recoloring these pixels. You can edit specific pixels or groups of pixels by selecting the area of the photo you want to edit.

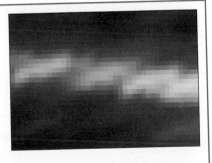

Bitmap Images

Images composed of pixels are known as *bitmap images* or *raster images*. The pixels are arranged in a rectangular grid, and each pixel includes information about its color and position. Most of the time when you are working in Photoshop Elements, you are working with bitmap content.

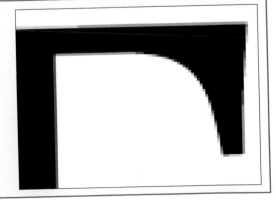

Vector Graphics

Text and shapes in Photoshop use a different format called *vector graphics*, which are mathematical recipes that draw shapes and letters. You can stretch or shrink vector graphics as much as you want without losing sharpness. You do not need to know math to work with vector graphics. You can add text by typing, and you can resize text and shapes by dragging your mouse. Photoshop Elements hides all the math that makes this possible.

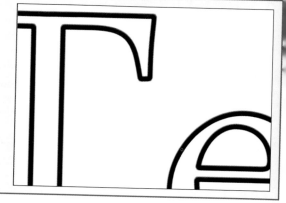

Supported File Formats

Photoshop Elements supports a variety of files, including BMP, TIFF, JPEG, GIF, PDF, PNG, and PSD, which stands for Photoshop Document. The PSD, TIFF, and PDF formats can include layers. Other formats cannot. The most common formats for images published on the Internet are JPEG and PNG.

```
Photoshop (*.PSD;*.PDD)
BMP (*.BMP;*.RLE;*.DIB)
CompuServe GIF (*.GIF)
Photo Project Format (*.PSE)
JPEG (*.JPG;*.JPEG;*.JPE)
Photoshop PDF (*.PDF;*.PDP)
Pixar (*.PXR)
PNG (*.PNG;*.PNS)
TIFF (*.TIF;*.TIFF)
```

File Size

Different formats differ from one another in the amount of storage they take up on your computer. Formats such as PSD and TIFF take more space because they save a perfect copy of a photo. They can also include multiple layers. PNG

Ratings: ★ ★ ★ ★ ★

Size: 9MB 1922x2560

Date: 1/1/2003 1:42 AM

Location: \\LILBOX\main\Pictures\PSE\+ iPhoto\

Audio: <none>

files are perfect copies of a photo, but do not include separate layers. JPEG and GIF files sacrifice some quality for a smaller file size. Typically you save your work as PSD files while you are editing or printing at home, and you save a separate copy as a JPG or a PNG when you want to share the file on the Internet.

Start Photoshop Elements

You can install Photoshop Elements from a DVD or from a download. After installation, you can launch Photoshop Elements in the usual ways.

On a PC, you can click the Photoshop Elements icon in the Start Screen. On a Mac, you can access it through the Finder in the Applications folder or through Launchpad.

Start Photoshop Elements

1 Open the Windows Start screen.

2 Click the **Adobe Photoshop Elements 13** button.

Note: Your location of the Photoshop Elements button may be different depending on how the Start screen is configured.

The Photoshop Elements welcome screen opens.

You can open the Organizer or the Editor from the welcome screen.

3 Click **Photo Editor**.

The Photoshop Elements Editor opens.

A You can click **Organizer** to open the Organizer.

B You can click 🔧 to choose the screen that appears when you launch Photoshop Elements.

Explore the Editor Workspace

To open the Editor, click **Photo Editor** on the welcome screen. You can then use its tools, menu commands, and panel-based features to edit your digital photos. You can select Quick, Guided, and Expert editing modes to reveal different editing options. The main Editor pane displays the photos you are editing.

A Image Window

This displays the photo you are editing.

B Image Tabs

These tabs switch between images in the Editor.

C Organizer Button

This button closes the Editor and loads the Organizer, where you can catalog your photos.

D Mode Buttons

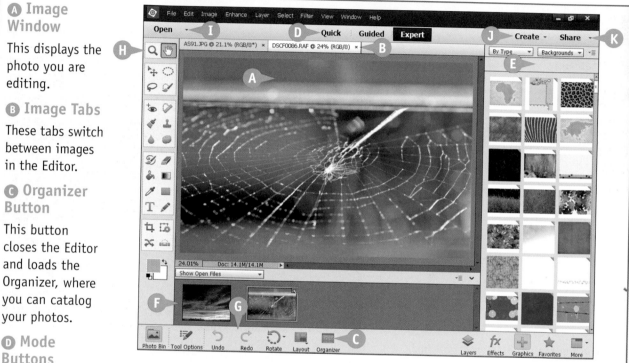

These buttons switch among the three Editor modes. (Expert mode is shown.)

E Panel Bin

This is an area for panels, which display information about layers, effects, graphics, and editing options.

F Photo Bin

This lists the loaded photos you can edit.

G Task Bar

These buttons select panels and various options. They also include important editing commands, including undo.

H Tools

These icons are the main editing tools in Photoshop Elements.

I Open Button

Click this button to select and load a photo for editing.

J Create Button

Click this button to create various photo-based projects such as calendars, CD/DVD jackets, and Facebook profile photos.

K Share Button

Click this button to share photographs by e-mail, on social networks, and on websites.

Tour the Organizer Workspace

In the Photoshop Elements Organizer, you can catalog, view, and sort your growing library of digital photos. The main Organizer pane, called the Media Browser, shows miniature versions of the photos in your catalog. To open the Organizer, click **Organizer** on the welcome screen.

Ⓐ Media Browser

This displays miniature versions, or *thumbnails*, of the photos and other media in your catalog.

Ⓑ Photo Details

This shows ratings information and the categories associated with each photo.

Ⓒ Editor Button

This button loads the Editor workspace, where you can edit your photos.

Ⓓ View Buttons

These buttons switch between views in the Organizer.

Ⓔ Panel Bin

This is an area for panels, which display quick fix, tagging, or photo information.

Ⓕ Import Button

Click this button to import photos from a camera, scanner, or folder.

Ⓖ Task Bar

These buttons select panels and various options. They also include important editing commands, including undo.

Ⓗ Time Line

Use this area to scroll through photos in date order.

Ⓘ Share Button

Click this button to share your photo by e-mail, on a social network, sharing via social networks, or through a private web page or slide show.

Switch between the Organizer and the Editor

Photoshop Elements has two main workspaces: the Organizer and the Editor. The Organizer lets you browse, sort, share, and categorize photos in your collection, and the Editor enables you to modify, combine, and optimize your photos. You can easily switch between the two environments.

You can use the Organizer to review your photos to find images for your projects. After you select your photos in the Organizer, you can open the Editor to adjust the colors, lighting, and other aspects of the photos, and then switch back to the Organizer to choose more photos to edit.

Switch between the Organizer and the Editor

① Start Photoshop Elements in the Organizer view.

Note: See the section "Start Photoshop Elements" for more on starting the program.

You can browse and sort your photos in the Organizer.

Note: For more about adding photos to the Organizer, see Chapter 2.

② Click a photo to select it.

③ Click **Editor**.

The photo opens in the Editor. If the Editor is not already running, it may take a few moments to launch.

Ⓐ The Editor opens in whatever mode you last used.

Ⓑ You can click **Organizer** to return to the Organizer.

Introducing the Photoshop Elements Tools

In the Editor, Photoshop Elements offers a variety of specialized tools that enable you to manipulate your image. You can select tools by clicking icons on the left side of the workspace or by typing a keyboard shortcut key. Keyboard shortcut keys are shown in parentheses. Many tools create *selections* — areas you can edit. Each Editor mode displays different tools. Expert mode displays all the tools, as shown here.

Ⓐ Zoom (Z)

Expand/shrink the image in the preview area.

Ⓑ Hand (H)

Drag the image when it is too big to fit into the preview area.

Ⓒ Move (V)

Move a selection.

Ⓓ Marquee (M)

Create a rectangular or round selection.

Ⓔ Lasso (L)

Draw a free-form selection shape with your mouse.

Ⓕ Quick Selection (A)

Create a selection by looking for similar colors or contrasting edges.

Ⓖ Red-Eye Removal (Y)

Correct red-eye problems.

Ⓗ Spot-Healing Brush (J)

Repair imperfections by copying nearby pixels.

Ⓘ Smart Brush (F)

Select and apply a "quick fix" collection of effects.

Ⓙ Clone Stamp (S)

Paint pixels from one area to another.

Ⓚ Blur (R)

Blur a selection.

Ⓛ Sponge (O)

Increase or decrease color *saturation* (intensity).

12

A Brush (B)

Paint on the image.

B Eraser (E)

Erase pixels by replacing them with the background color or making them transparent.

C Paint Bucket (K)

Fill a selection with a single color.

D Gradient (G)

Fill a selection with a blend of colors.

E Eyedropper (I)

Copy a color from the image.

F Custom Shape (U)

Draw various shapes.

G Type (T)

Add text to an image.

H Pencil (N)

Draw hard-edged lines.

I Crop (C)

Chop off unwanted parts of an image to improve it.

J Recompose (W)

Intelligently change the size of a photo while keeping elements intact.

K Content-Aware Move Tool (Q)

Move a selection and fill its old location with textures from the surrounding area.

L Straighten (P)

Straighten a crooked image or rotate it for special effects.

M Foreground and Background Color

Set the foreground and background colors used by the paint, draw, text, shape, and fill tools.

N Tool Options Panel

Display settings and options for the current tool.

Switch Editor Modes

The Photoshop Elements Editor has three modes: Quick, Guided, and Expert. Use Quick mode for simple, easy edits. This mode is perfect for beginners who are new to photo editing.

Guided mode offers step-by-step instructions for more complex edits and effects. Use it to experiment with what Photoshop Elements can do. Expert mode gives you full access to all the features in Photoshop Elements. Use it when you have more experience with the tools and feel more confident about working with them.

Switch Editor Modes

1 Open a photo in the Editor.

Note: See Chapter 2 for information about opening photos.

2 Click **Quick**.

Quick mode appears.

A Click the tool bar to select a tool.

Note: For more about tools, see the next section, "Work with Tools."

B Click here to select and apply one of the built-in quick adjustments and fixes.

3 Click a menu.

Photoshop Elements displays the menu commands.

C In Quick and Guided modes, some commands are grayed out and you cannot use them.

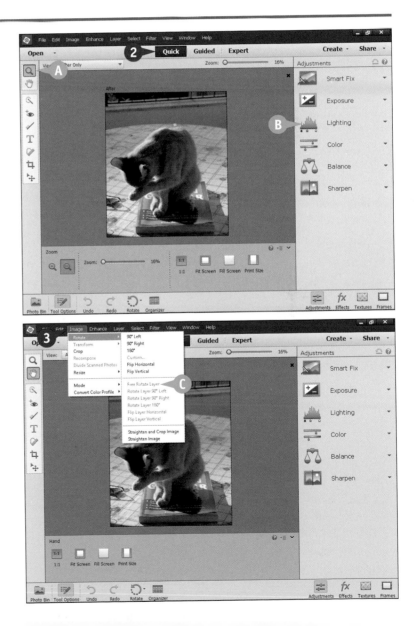

④ Click **Guided**.

Guided mode appears.

Ⓓ Click here to select a tool.

Ⓔ Click the headings in the panel bin to see step-by-step instructions for editing photos.

Note: Very few tools are available in Guided mode, but the step-by-step editing suggestions include tools and settings of their own.

⑤ Click **Expert**.

Expert mode appears.

Ⓕ Click a tool in the toolbar to select it.

Ⓖ Click an option to open its panel.

Note: See the section "Work with Panels" for more information.

TIPS

How do I view before and after versions of photos as I edit them?

In Quick mode and Guided mode, you can click the **View** menu in the upper left of the workspace. Select a Before & After view to display both versions of the current photo. You can choose horizontal and vertical versions, depending on the orientation of your photo.

How can I get extra help when learning about Photoshop Elements features?

Click the **Help** menu, and then click a help-related command. The Key Concepts, Support, Video Tutorials, and Forum commands take you to the Adobe website.

Work with Tools

You can use the tools in Photoshop Elements to make changes to an image. After you select a tool, the Tool Options panel displays controls and settings for the tool. For example, if you select the Rectangular Marquee tool, you can set the width and height of the selected area.

Some tools display a tiny mark in the upper-right corner when you position the cursor over them. This tells you can select related tools by clicking the tool icon again. For example, you can click the Lasso tool icon to select two further tools: Polygonal Lasso and Magnetic Lasso.

Work with Tools

Select a Tool

1 Click an Editor mode.

2 Position the mouse pointer over a tool.

Ⓐ A screen tip displays the tool name and shortcut key. You can click the tool name to access help information about the tool.

Click the tool to select it.

Ⓑ The Tool Options panel shows settings and options for the current tool.

Select a Related Tool

1 Click a tool that has a in the top-right corner.

Photoshop Elements displays the clicked tool and one or more related tools in the Tool Options panel.

2 Click one of the related tools.

You can also press a tool's shortcut key more than once to cycle through the related tools.

Close the Tool Options Panel

You can close the Tool Options panel to give you more space to view and edit your photos.

1 Click **Tool Options**.

The Tool Options panel closes.

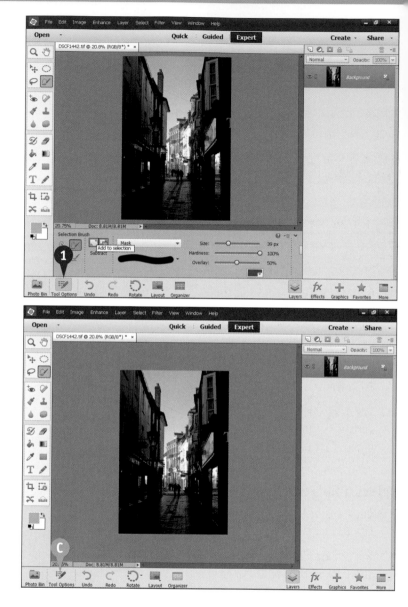

C You can click **Tool Options** again to reopen the Tool Options panel.

TIPS

How can I keep the Tool Options panel hidden?
In the Tool Options panel, click the panel menu (▣). By default, Auto Show Tool Options is selected and the panel is shown when a tool is clicked. Click **Auto Show Tool Options** to deselect the option and keep the panel hidden.

How can I reset a tool to its default settings?
With a tool selected, click the panel menu (▣) in the Tool Options panel and then click **Reset Tool**. You can click **Reset All Tools** to reset all the Photoshop Elements tools to their default settings.

Work with Panels

In the Photoshop Elements Editor, you can open *panels* to access different Photoshop Elements features. In Expert mode, shown in this example, most panels open in the Panel Bin at the right side of the workspace. Other panels open in a tabbed window. You can click this window to drag, click the tabs to select different features, and resize the window.

For example, the Layers panel shows the layers in your image, including the standard background layer available in all images. The Graphics panel displays clip-art and graphics you can add to your photos.

Work with Panels

Using the Main Panels

1 Open the Photoshop Elements Editor.

Note: For more on opening the Editor, see the section "Start Photoshop Elements."

2 Click one of the panel buttons.

Note: You can also access panels in the Window menu.

Ⓐ The clicked panel opens in the Panel Bin.

Ⓑ Many panels have buttons and sub-menus with further sub-options.

3 Click the panel button again.

The panel closes.

Ⓒ Closing the panels increases the size of the photo in the preview window.

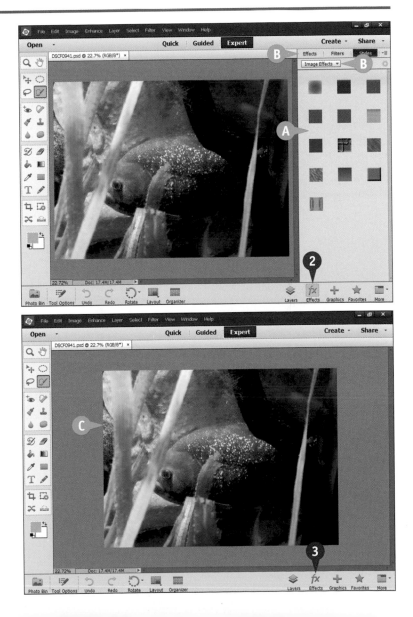

Open More Panels

1 Click **More**.

A window opens with tabbed panels.

2 Click any tab to display a panel.

D You can click and drag the panel header to move the window.

E You can click ⊠ to close the panel window.

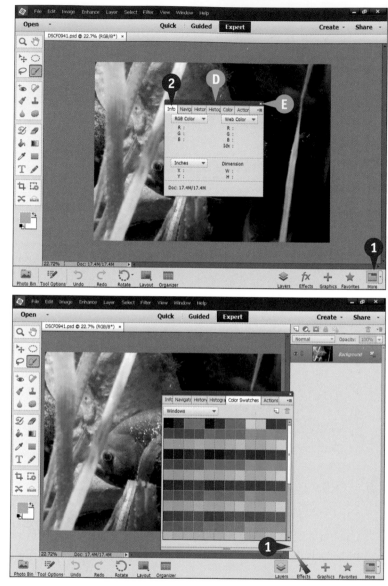

Resize Panels

1 To resize the panel window, click and drag the corner or edges. Not all panels in the panel window are resizable.

The panels resize.

TIPS

What do the tabs in the floating panel do?
Info shows color information for the pixel under the mouse pointer. **Navigator** is a combined zoom and drag tool. **History** shows a list of edits. **Histogram** shows a brightness/color graph. **Color** shows color presets, known as *swatches*. **Action** shows a list of ready-made edit operations.

How do I reset my panels?
Click **Window** and then **Reset Panels**. This resets the size of the panels and, in Expert mode, sets the Panel Bin to the Layers panel.

Set Program Preferences

You can use the Photoshop Elements Preferences dialog box to change various settings. For example, you can change image measurements from inches to centimeters or pixels, set how much memory is being used, control how many steps of Undo are remembered, and so on. You can make these changes from both the Editor and the Organizer.

Preferences are always saved to disk. Changes remain even if you quit and restart Photoshop Elements. In the Organizer, you can restore all preferences to their original state by clicking **Restore Default Settings** in the General preferences.

Set Program Preferences

In the Editor

1. In the Editor, click **Edit**. (On a Mac, click **Photoshop Elements Editor**.

Note: For more on opening the Editor, see the section "Explore the Editor Workspace."

2. Click **Preferences** ⇨ **General**.

As an alternative, you can press Ctrl+K (⌘+K on a Mac).

The Preferences dialog box opens and displays General options.

3. Select any settings you want to change.

A. For example, you can click the ⯆ to specify the shortcut keys for stepping backward and forward through your commands.

B. You can click this option (☐ changes to ☑) to open images in floating windows instead of tabbed windows.

4. Click any of the items in this list to select a different preference category.

C. You can also click **Prev** and **Next** to move back and forth between categories.

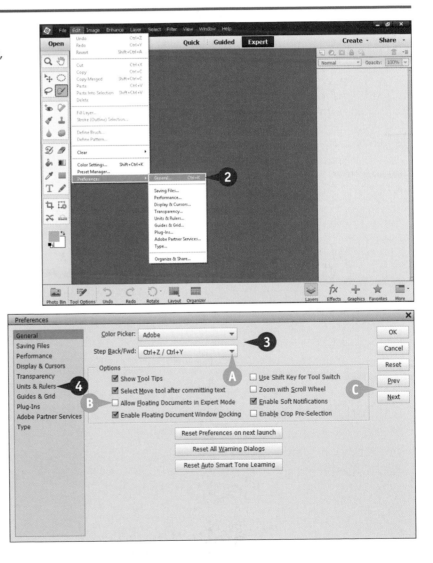

This example shows the Units & Rulers preferences.

5 Select any settings you want to change.

6 Click **OK**.

Photoshop Elements sets the preferences.

In the Organizer

1 In the Organizer, repeat steps **1** to **3** in the subsection "In the Editor," or press Ctrl + K (⌘ + K on a Mac).

Note: For more on opening the Organizer, see the section "Tour the Organizer Workspace."

The Preferences dialog box opens.

2 Select any of the preference groups.

Note: The groups and the settings are not the same as the Editor preferences.

3 Click and change any of the settings.

4 Click **OK**.

Photoshop Elements sets the preferences.

TIPS

What type of measurement units should I use in Photoshop Elements?

Typically, you use the units that match the output you want to produce. For web designs, use pixels. For print, use inches, centimeters, or millimeters. Percentage units are useful for general editing.

How do I give Photoshop Elements more memory so I can open work on more photos at once?

The Performance preferences show how much memory, or *RAM*, you have available and how much of it Photoshop Elements is using. Use the Scratch Disks preferences to use disk space instead of RAM.

View Rulers and Guides

I n Expert mode, you can turn on rulers and guides. Use rulers to measure widths and heights in your image. To change the units of measurement, see the previous section, "Set Program Preferences."

Guides are horizontal or vertical lines. You can add them in the Editor preview area to help you line up elements in your image. You can only see guides as you edit. They do not appear in printed images or in images saved for sharing.

View Rulers and Guides

Show Rulers

1 Click **Expert**

2 Click **View** ⇨ **Rulers**.

You can also press **Shift** + **Ctrl** + **R** (**Shift** + **⌘** + **R** on a Mac).

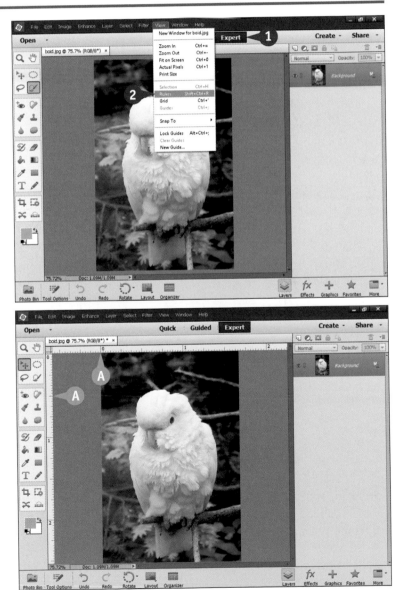

A Photoshop Elements adds rulers to the top and left edges of the image window.

Note: The left and top of the image always line up with 0 on the rulers.

Create a Guide

1 Click one of the rulers, and drag the cursor into the window (↘ changes to ↔).

Drag the top ruler down to create a horizontal guide.

Drag the left ruler to the right to create a vertical guide.

B A thin, colored line appears.

You can also click **View** and then **New Guide** to add a guide.

Move a Guide

1 Click the **Move** tool (✛).

2 Position the mouse pointer over a guide (↘ changes to ↔), and then click and drag.

A Photoshop Elements shows the guide position from the top or left of the image as you drag.

You can also press Ctrl + ; (⌘ + ; on a Mac) to display a grid on your image. The lines of the grid can help you align objects in your image.

TIPS

How do I make objects in my images "snap to" my guides when I move those objects?

The "snap to" feature is useful for aligning elements. Click **View**, **Snap To**, and then **Guides**. When you move an object near a guide, Photoshop Elements snaps it — pulls it — to the guide. Select **Document Bounds** to snap elements to the edges of a photo, and select **Layers** to snap to layer positions. Turn "snap to" off if you want to place elements by hand without automatic alignment.

Do guides work across layers?

Guides are for display only. They do not change an image or a layer. If you are working with layers, guides remain visible on top of the layer stack. For more about layers, see Chapter 13.

Importing and Opening Digital Images

Before you can start working with photos, you must import them. This chapter shows you how to import photos into the Organizer and open them in the Editor.

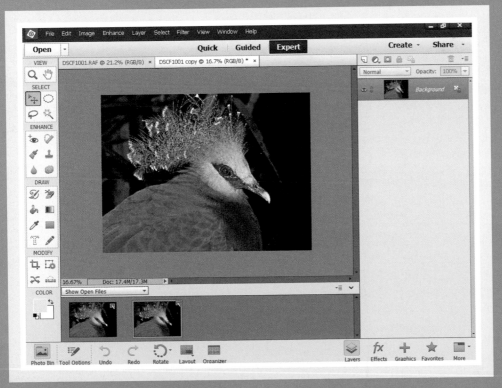

Get Photos for Your Projects

Photoshop Elements can accept images from various sources, including digital cameras, scanners, and photo-sharing sites. Before you can organize and edit your images, you must import them. Photoshop Elements imports different sources in different ways.

Digital Cameras

Photoshop Elements is compatible with the budget cameras built into mobile phones, with mid-range point-and-click enthusiast cameras, and with full-featured digital SLR (Single Lens Reflex) cameras at various price points. Some cameras support a direct USB connection, while others save their files to a memory card and need a *card reader* device, which also works over USB. Photoshop Elements supports both options and reads all the standard digital photo file types, including the RAW format used by better cameras to give the best possible image quality.

Scanned Photos and Art

You can use the Windows version of Photoshop Elements to scan photos and hand-drawn or painted art into your computer using an external scanner. Some scanners support transparency (slide) scanning, and you can use Photoshop Elements to crop, tidy up, and repair images from old slides. Note that scanning is not available on the Mac version, but you can use external scanning software to scan images and then import them manually as files.

Web Images

If you have photos or art stored on the web, you can save those image files to your computer and then open them in Photoshop Elements. In Internet Explorer on the PC, you can save a web image by right-clicking it and choosing **Save picture as** (**Save Image As** in Firefox or in Safari on a Mac). Inexpensive stock photo websites, such as iStockphoto, offer professional-grade images for download. On photo-sharing sites such as Flickr, users often allow noncommercial use of their photos.

Start from Scratch

You can also create your Photoshop Elements image from scratch by opening a blank canvas in the image window. You can then apply colors and patterns with the painting tools in Photoshop Elements, or you can cut and paste parts of other images to create a composite. See the section "Create a Blank Image" for more on opening a blank canvas.

Film Photos

Although most photography is now digital, cheap waterproof film cameras are still popular for vacation and sports photography. Some serious photographers continue to prefer the look of film. If you use a commercial film developing service, you can usually ask to receive your images pre-scanned to files on a CD or DVD. To import these images into Photoshop Elements, see the section "Import Photos from a Folder."

Working with Imported Photos

When you import images into Photoshop Elements, they appear in the Organizer. You can browse miniature versions of your photos, called *thumbnails*, sort them, group them into albums, and assign keyword tags to them. You can edit your photos by opening them in the Photoshop Elements Editor. You can open them in the Editor from the Organizer or open them directly from folders on your computer. See Chapter 1 for more on the Editor and the Organizer workspaces.

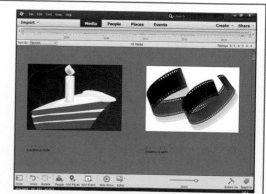

Import Photos from a Digital Camera or Card Reader

You can import photos into Photoshop Elements from a digital camera or from a memory card. To read from a camera, connect it to a USB port. To read from a card, connect a card reader — a small device with slots for different memory cards — and plug the card into a compatible slot. Some computers have a built-in card reader.

Every camera and card reader works differently. For example, you may need to set a special USB mode on your camera before you can read photos from it. Check your camera's manual for instructions.

Import Photos from a Digital Camera or Card Reader

1 In the Organizer, click **File** ➪ **Get Photos and Videos** ➪ **From Camera or Card Reader**.

The Photo Downloader dialog box opens.

Photo Downloader may automatically open when you connect your device to your computer, depending on the settings in Photoshop Elements.

2 Click ▼ to choose your camera or memory card from the Get Photos From menu.

A You can click **Browse** (**Choose** on a Mac) to set the import destination.

By default, Photoshop Elements downloads your photos into subfolders inside your Pictures folder. Each folder name includes the date of the photos.

B You can click ▼ to select a different naming scheme for subfolders.

Note: You can name subfolders with the shoot date in a variety of formats, the import date, and a custom name.

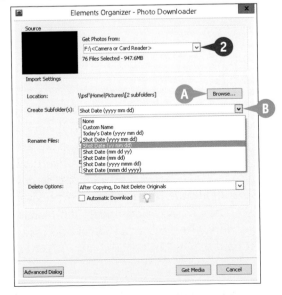

28

C You can click ▾ to set a naming scheme for your files.

D Click ▾ to choose whether to keep your photos on the device or delete them after downloading.

E On Windows only, you can click this option to set up Photoshop Elements to download your photos automatically using the current settings whenever a photo device is connected to your computer (☐ changes to ☑).

3 Click **Get Media**.

E Photoshop Elements downloads the photos from the device.

F You can click **Stop** to abort the download.

After downloading the photos, Photoshop Elements adds them to the current Organizer catalog.

TIPS

What can I do if I don't have a free USB port?

One option is to buy a *USB hub*. This optional extra provides additional USB ports that plug into a single USB port on your computer. There are three types. USB 1.0 hubs are cheap, but too slow for speedy downloading. USB 2.0 hubs are faster but more expensive, and are the best option for occasional photo downloads. USB 3.0 hubs work with all the most recent accessories, including fast hard drives, but are even more expensive.

How do I rename files automatically?

Select one of the many options from the Rename Files menu. You can combine a custom name, a shooting date, an import date, and a photo number. Use the box at the left under the menu to set a custom name. The Example line under the two boxes shows an example created using the settings.

Import Photos from a Scanner

You can import a photo into Photoshop Elements through a scanner attached to your computer in Windows. In Windows, the photo appears in the Organizer Media Browser after importing. On a Mac, you can use the Image Capture application to scan photos and send them to the Organizer. Some scanners include slide or film attachments that enable you to digitize slides or film.

Every scanner works differently. Consult the documentation that came with your scanner for more information. After scanning, you can rotate or crop the photo to fix any alignment issues. See Chapter 5 for details.

Import Photos from a Scanner

1 In the Organizer, click **File** ⇨ **Get Photos and Videos** ⇨ **From Scanner**.

The Get Photos from Scanner dialog box opens.

2 If your scanner does not appear here, click ☑ to select it.

By default, Photoshop Elements saves scanned photos in the Adobe folder inside your Pictures folder.

Ⓐ You can click **Browse** to choose another location.

3 Click ☑ to choose a file format.

Note: PNG is a good choice because it does not reduce image quality.

4 Click **OK**.

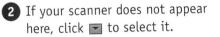

The software associated with your scanner opens. Different scanners have different software, so you may not see the options shown here.

5 Change your scanning settings as needed. You may need to specify whether the photo is black and white or color. You may also get to preview the scan.

6 If your software includes a Preview button, click it to see a preview.

B The preview may include a box that snaps around a photo, as shown here. If it does not, you can usually drag the corners of the preview box to the edges of the photo.

7 Click your scanner software's **Scan** button to scan your photo.

C Photoshop Elements scans the photo.

After scanning, the photo appears in the Organizer.

Note: Scanned photos often need to be cropped and/ or rotated. For details, see Chapter 5.

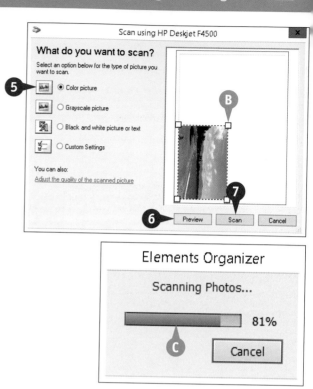

TIPS

How can I adjust the default settings for importing photos?
Click **Edit**, choose **Preferences**, and then click **Scanner**. In the Scanner Preferences dialog box that opens, you can adjust the default settings. If you scan photos to PNG files, you can ignore the quality slider. Click **OK** to save the settings. Photoshop Elements displays the updated settings the next time you scan a photo.

What resolution should I use while scanning?
Unless you have access to a commercial drum scanner, the maximum useful resolution of a typical scanner is around 600 dpi. Every time you double the resolution of your scan, the size of the file it creates increases by a factor of four. Scanning at a resolution of more than 600 dpi wastes disk space without increasing detail. If you are scanning photo prints, 300 dpi usually gives you all the detail you need. Slides/transparencies may need 600 dpi. For budget photo prints, 150 dpi is often enough.

Import or Search for Photos from a Folder

You can use the Organizer workspace in Photoshop Elements to import images from a folder. Select this option if you already have a collection of digital photos on your hard disk or if you want to import photos from shop-made CDs.

The Organizer also includes a search feature. You can use it to search your hard drives and find folders with photos. You can then choose which folders to import from.

Import or Search for Photos from a Folder

Import Photos by Selecting a Folder

1 In the Organizer, click **File** ⇨ **Get Photos and Videos** ⇨ **From Files and Folders**.

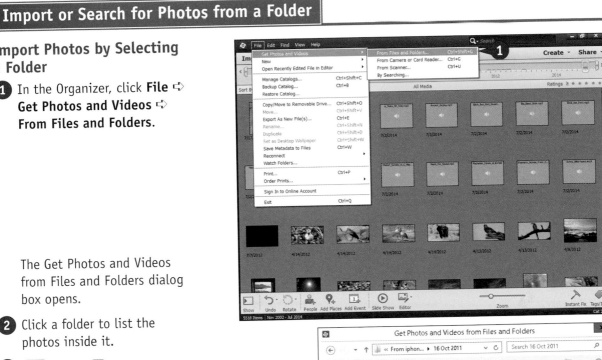

The Get Photos and Videos from Files and Folders dialog box opens.

2 Click a folder to list the photos inside it.

3 Ctrl +click (⌘+click on a Mac) to select the photos you want to import.

Ⓐ You can click this option if you want Photoshop Elements to fix photos with red eye (☐ changes to ☑).

Ⓑ You can select different file types, such as PDF documents or Photoshop Elements projects, by clicking ▾ and selecting a type.

4 Click **Get Media**.

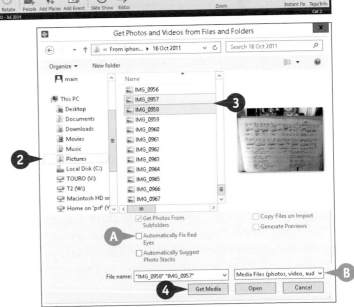

Photoshop Elements downloads the selected photos from the folder.

Ⓒ Photoshop Elements displays the imported photos by themselves in the Organizer.

5 Click **Back** to return to the previous Organizer view.

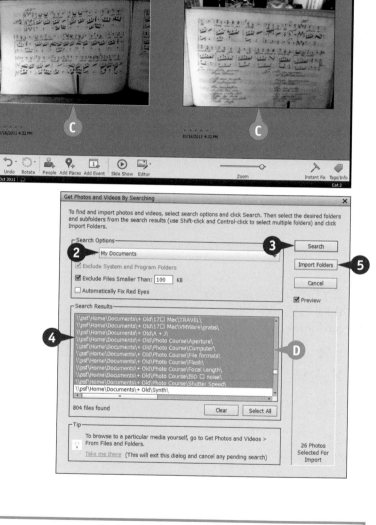

Import Photos by Searching

1 Click **File** ➪ **Get Photos and Videos** ➪ **By Searching**.

The Get Photos and Videos By Searching dialog box opens.

2 In the Search Options section, click the menu to choose all hard drives, a single hard drive, or to select a folder.

3 Click **Search**.

Ⓓ Your search results appear.

4 Select one or more folders. `Ctrl`+ click (`⌘`+click on a Mac) to select multiple folders.

5 Click **Import Folders** to get the photos.

TIP

How can I automatically add new images on my computer to the Organizer?
You can tell Photoshop Elements to watch certain folders on your computer. When you add new images to those folders, Photoshop Elements automatically adds them to the Organizer. Click **File** ➪ **Watch Folders**. Use the dialog box that appears to set the folders you want to watch. Use the Notify Me/Automatically Add radio buttons to tell Photoshop Elements to ask you whether to add the images, or to go ahead and add the images to the Organizer automatically.

Open a Photo

You can open a photo in the Editor to modify it or to use it in a project. After you open the photo, you can adjust its color and lighting, add special effects, and move objects in the photo to separate layers. You can also open photos from the Organizer for editing in the Editor.

You can open more than one photo at a time in the Editor. You can switch between photos using the window tabs. Open images also appear in the Photo Bin. For information about managing photos after you open them, see Chapter 5.

Open a Photo

Open a Photo in the Editor

1 In the Editor, click **Open**.

You can also press **Ctrl**+click (**⌘**+click on a Mac).

The Open dialog box appears.

2 Click the file selector menu to navigate to the folder containing the file you want to open.

3 Click the photo you want to open.

A If your file browser is set up for image previews, a preview appears.

4 Click **Open**.

Photoshop Elements opens the image.

B The filename and zoom (preview magnification) setting appear in the tab.

Note: Depending on your preferences, the image may appear in a floating window instead of a tab.

C If the Photo Bin is open in the Editor, the image also appears in the Bin.

D You can click **Window** to view a list of open photos at the end of the menu.

Open a Photo in the Organizer

1 In the Organizer, click the photo you want to edit.

2 Click **Editor.**

E You can also right-click the image and select **Edit with Photoshop Elements Editor.**

Photoshop Elements opens the photo in the Editor.

TIP

What types of files can Photoshop Elements open?

Photoshop Elements can open most of the image file formats in common use today. Here's a partial list.

File Type	Description
BMP (Bitmap)	The standard Windows image format
TIFF (Tagged Image File Format)	A format for print
JPEG (Joint Photographic Experts Group)	A format for web images
PNG (Portable Network Graphics)	An alternative web format to GIF and JPEG
PSD (Photoshop Document)	Photoshop's native file format

Create a Blank Image

You can start a Photoshop Elements project by creating a blank image and then adding a photo, text, or graphics. When you create a blank image, you specify the dimensions and the resolution. Photoshop Elements offers a number of useful preset sizes, including common paper sizes and web browser dimensions.

You can add content from other images to your blank image as separate layers. For more on layers, see Chapter 13. You can also use the Brush tool to add streaks of color. See Chapter 11 for information about using and customizing the Brush tool.

Create a Blank Image

1 In the Editor, click **File** ⇨ **New** ⇨ **Blank File.**

You can also press Ctrl + N (⌘ + N on a Mac).

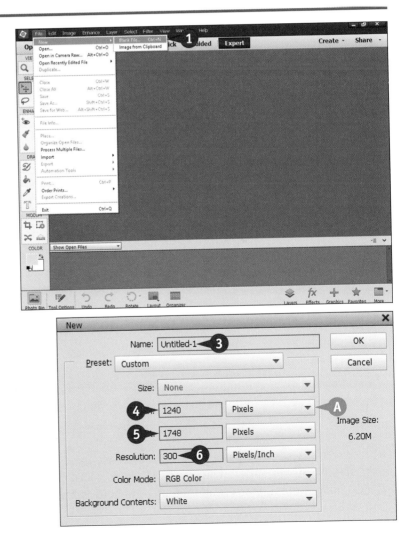

The New dialog box opens.

3 Type a name for the new image.

Ⓐ Click this menu to change the size units of the image.

Note: Changing the units for one dimensions also changes the units for the other dimension.

4 Type the width of your image.

5 Type the height of your image.

6 Set the resolution of the image.

Note: Use the default RGB color mode for color images.

Note: If you copy an image or selection before creating a new image, Photoshop Elements automatically copies its dimensions, unless you select a different size.

36

B You can click the Size menu to select one of the preset sizes.

C You can click the Background Contents menu to select a background color.

Note: By default, Photoshop Elements makes the background white.

7 Click **OK**.

Photoshop Elements creates a new blank image with the dimensions you selected.

Note: See Chapter 11 for information about adding text and Chapter 14 for information about adding frames and other graphics.

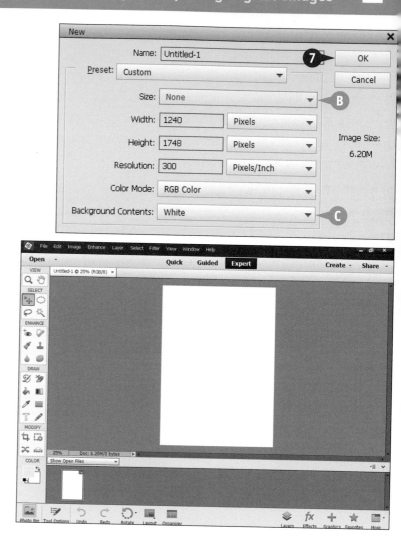

TIPS

What should I choose as a resolution for a new image?
For web or multimedia images, select 72 pixels/inch, the standard resolution for onscreen images. To output images on a typical inkjet printer, use a resolution of 240 to 360 pixels/inch.

How do I open a frame from a video clip?
Open a video frame in Photoshop Elements by clicking **File**, **Import**, and **Frame from Video**. In the dialog box, you can browse for and open a video clip, scan through the clip, and import a frame into the Editor. Photoshop Elements supports importing from WMV, MPEG, and AVI files; Mac users can import MOV files.

Save a Photo

Y ou can fix the changes you make to a photo by saving it. Photoshop Elements can save files in a number of formats. The default format is PSD. This includes useful project information, but it can be read only by a limited collection of Adobe-compatible products.

Use PNG for most applications and JPEG if you need very small files — example, to make a web page load quickly — and if you can afford to lose some image quality. You can save multiple versions of the same image as a *version set* in the Organizer.

Save a Photo

Save a New Photo

1 In the Editor, click **File** ⇨ **Save As**.

Note: For photos that you have previously saved, you can click **File** and then **Save**.

The Save As dialog box opens.

2 If you need to change the name, type it here.

A You can click the folder selector to choose another folder or drive for the file.

B You can click the Save as type menu (format menu on a Mac) to choose a different file format.

Note: Photoshop Elements adds the correct file extension automatically. You do not need to add it to the filename.

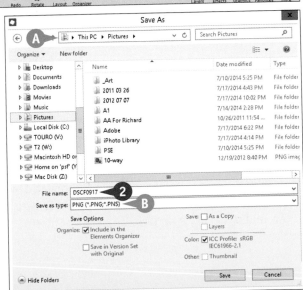

C Click this option to add the file to the current Organizer catalog (☐ changes to ☑).

D Click this option to save the file as part of a version set with other versions (☐ changes to ☑).

You can use this option only if a version set for the photo already exists.

3 Click **Save**.

Photoshop Elements saves the image file.

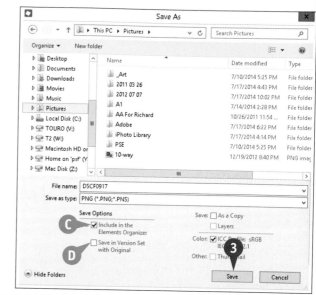

View a Version Set in the Organizer

1 In the Organizer, find a version set ().

A You can use the scroll bar to browse your photos.

2 Click ▶ to expand the version set so you can view all the photos in that set.

Photoshop Elements expands the version set.

TIPS

How can I save my open photos as an album in the Organizer?

In the Photo Bin, click the bin menu (▦). Click **Save Bin as an Album** (**A**). In the Save Photo Bin dialog box, type a name for the album and click **OK**. The photos are saved as a new album in the Organizer.

Duplicate a Photo

In the Editor, you can duplicate a photo to keep an unedited "safe" version before you begin changing it. When you make a duplicate, Photoshop Elements creates a new window for it. You can then save the duplicate to disk to create your backup. See the previous section, "Save a Photo," for more details. Note that creating a duplicate automatically creates a version set.

The Photoshop Elements editor includes a special side-by-side view for comparing original and edited versions of a photo. For more about working with different views and layouts, see Chapter 5.

Duplicate a Photo

1 In the Editor, click **File** ⇨ **Duplicate**.

The Duplicate Image dialog box opens.

A You can type here to change the name of the duplicate.

Note: The default adds "copy" to the original name.

2 Click **OK**.

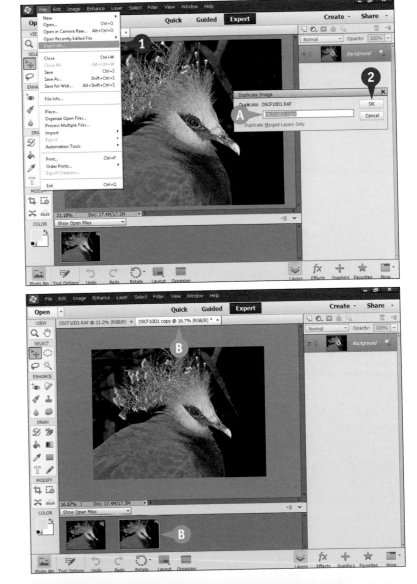

B Photoshop Elements opens a duplicate of the photo as another tabbed window.

Close a Photo

You can close a photo after you finish editing it. Although you can have more than one photo open at a time, closing photos can free up memory and make your computer work faster. It also reduces workspace clutter.

If you try to close an edited photo without saving it first, Photoshop Elements asks if you want to save it so you do not lose the changes. When you exit Photoshop Elements, it closes all open images and also warns you about unsaved changes.

Close a Photo

1 In the Editor, click **File** ⇨ **Close**.

You can also press `Ctrl`+`W` (`⌘`+`W` on a Mac).

A You can also click ⌧ to close a photo.

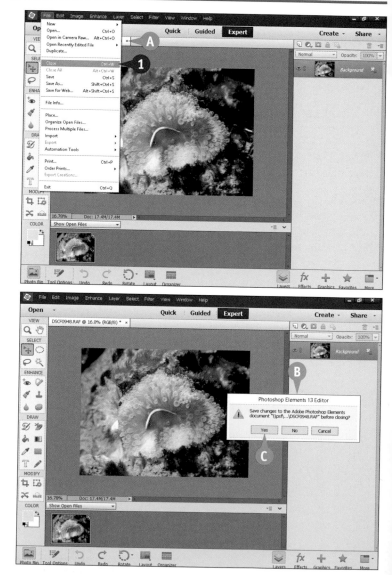

B If you have edited but not saved your photo, Photoshop Elements asks if you want to save it before closing.

C Click **Yes** to save your work or **No** to lose your changes.

Photoshop Elements closes the photo.

Note: If you open the Editor by selecting a photo in the Organizer and clicking the **Editor** button, closing the file also hides the Editor.

Organizing Your Photos

Are you ready to organize your digital photos? You can catalog, view, and sort photo files by using the Organizer. You can also use it to search your photo library, and to find people, places, and events. This chapter shows you how to take advantage of the many photo-management features in the Organizer.

Introducing the Organizer

You can use the Photoshop Elements Organizer to manage your photo library. When you import a photo or save an edited photo, Photoshop Elements adds it to the Organizer. To help you manage and search your photos, you can associate them with people, places, or events. You can also group photos into albums and tag them with descriptive keywords.

If you want to edit one or more photos, you can click the **Editor** button to launch the Photoshop Elements Editor. You can then correct the photo, cut and paste objects into it, or apply special effects. You can switch back to the Organizer when you are finished. The Editor disappears, and you can continue browsing and organizing your photos.

Virtual Browser

The Organizer acts as a virtual browser, showing you *thumbnails,* or miniature versions, of your pictures. You can preview many photos in a single window. The thumbnails you see in the Organizer are illustrated links to the original files. You can delete images from the Organizer without deleting them from disk.

Catalog

When you bring photo files into the Organizer, the program adds them to your catalog of images. Images are cataloged by date. You can keep all your photos in one catalog, or you can store them in separate catalogs. If you want to group your photos further, you can collect them into albums. See the sections "Create a Catalog" and "Work with Albums" for details. For more on grouping photos, see Chapter 4.

Keyword Tags

You can use keyword tags — short written descriptions — to help you sort and track your photos. You can assign more than one tag to each photo. You can then search for photos that match certain tags or sort your photos in tag order. The Organizer includes a set of ready-made tags to help you group photos by colors, activities, and photographic details. You can also create custom tags of your own. For more on keyword tags, see Chapter 4.

People, Places, and Events

We often group photos by the people in them, the places they were taken, and the events at which they were taken. Photoshop Elements 13 has special features to help you group your photos in these ways. You can automatically import your list of Facebook friends and match photos to their names. If your camera includes a GPS feature, you can find where your photos were taken on a map. You can also group photos into events by time and date.

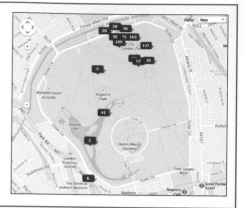

Find Photos

The Organizer also includes full-featured search tools for sophisticated searches. You can search your catalog by date, filename, or by the people, places, and events associated with your photos. You can apply ratings using a five-star system and then view photos that meet a certain rating criteria. See the sections "Find Photos" and "Rate Photos" for more information. You can even find photos that look like other photos by searching for visual similarity.

Create and Share

After grouping and organizing your photos, you can use Organizer to share them. For example, you can create a custom slideshow or photobook for friends and family. You can also select photos to share on social networks such as Facebook or Twitter and photo-sharing sites such as Flickr. And you can send images to others via e-mail, or upload them for safe-keeping to Adobe's Revel Cloud Service. See Chapter 15 for more about sharing.

Open the Organizer

You can organize and manage your digital photos in the Organizer in Photoshop Elements. The Organizer works alongside the Editor to help you keep track of your digital photos and other media. You can open the Organizer from the welcome screen that appears when you start up Photoshop Elements or switch to it from the Editor.

The main feature of the Organizer is the Media Browser, which features a grid of *thumbnails* or miniature versions of your photos. You can select a thumbnail and make basic changes to a photo directly in the Organizer or open the image in the Editor to make more complex changes.

Open the Organizer

From the Welcome Screen

1 Start Photoshop Elements.

Note: See Chapter 1 for more on starting Photoshop Elements.

The welcome screen appears.

2 Click **Organizer** to open the Organizer.

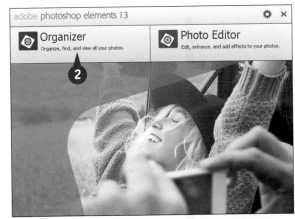

The Organizer opens.

To import photos into the Organizer workspace, see Chapter 2.

To create a new catalog for your photos, see the next section, "Create a Catalog."

From the Editor

 Start Photoshop Elements.

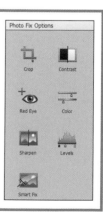 From the welcome screen that appears, click **Photo Editor** to open the Editor.

The Editor opens.

You can now load, edit, and save photos.

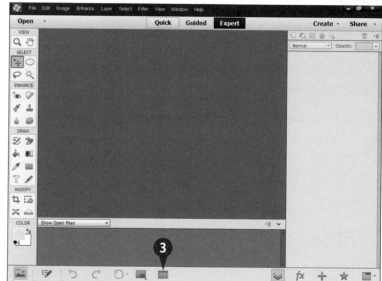 Click **Organizer** to open the Organizer.

Note: You can also close the Editor window, resize it, or hide it to reveal the Organizer behind it.

Note: If you select a photo in the Organizer and click the **Editor** button to edit it, the Organizer locks the file and displays an Edit in Progress message until you close the file in the Editor. You can continue using the Organizer while this message is visible.

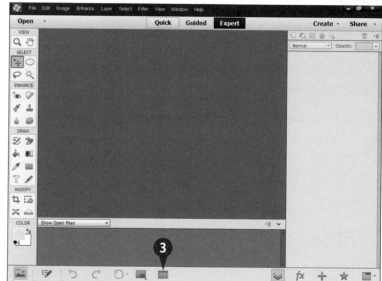

TIP

Can I edit photos in the Organizer?
The Organizer includes an Instant Fix feature for simple photo corrections and cropping. To use it, click **Instant Fix** in the Organizer. The editing options appear. Click a thumbnail in the Media Browser, and click an option to optimize the color or lighting in your photo, to crop it, or to remove red eye. You can also sharpen a photo or apply an overall Smart Fix, which makes a best guess about exposure and color corrections.

Create a Catalog

The photos you manage in the Organizer are stored in catalogs. You can keep your photos in one large catalog or separate them into smaller catalogs. When you launch the Organizer for the first time, Photoshop Elements creates a default catalog called My Catalog.

You can collect the photos in a catalog into smaller groups called albums. See the section "Work with Albums" for more. You can also combine similar photos into stacks to save space. See Chapter 4 for details.

Create a Catalog

1 In the Organizer, click **File** ⇨ **Manage Catalogs**.

A You can restore a catalog you have previously backed up by clicking **Restore Catalog**. See Chapter 15 for more on backing up photos.

The Catalog Manager dialog box opens.

Photoshop Elements lists the available catalogs.

2 Click **New**.

③ Type a name for the new catalog.

Ⓑ You can click this option (☐ changes to ☑) to import free music included with Photoshop Elements for use in slideshows.

Photoshop Elements creates the new catalog and opens it.

Ⓒ Photoshop Elements displays the name of the current catalog.

Ⓓ The number of files in the catalog appears here.

Ⓔ In this example, free music files have been imported.

Note: To import photos, see Chapter 2.

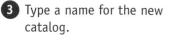

How do I switch to a different catalog in the Organizer?

Open the Catalog Manager by following steps **1** and **2** in this section. Select the catalog you want to open in the catalog list, and click **Open**. You can open one catalog at a time. As a shortcut, you can also click the catalog name in the lower-right corner of the Organizer window.

How can I keep others from viewing the photos in the Organizer?

You can change the security settings of a catalog so that only the user currently logged into your computer can access it. Open the Catalog Manager by following steps **1** and **2** in this section. Select the catalog you want to protect, and click **Move**. Use the radio buttons to change the security setting.

View Photos in the Media Browser

After you add photos to your catalog, you can view them in the Organizer's Media Browser. The Media Browser displays thumbnails (miniature versions) of your photos. It also shows selected details including a star rating, an optional caption, and the date and time the photo was created.

You can change the size of the thumbnails. To see more thumbnails at once, make them smaller. To see more detail in a single photo, make its thumbnail bigger. You can also filter and sort your photos in various ways to find specific photos in your collection. For details, see Chapter 4.

View Photos in the Media Browser

1 Open the Organizer.

The Media Browser displays the photos in the Organizer catalog.

A The Media Browser is the default view in the Organizer. You can click **Media** to switch to it from another view.

Photos are sorted by their capture date from newest to oldest by default.

2 Click and drag the Zoom slider.

As you drag to the right, the thumbnails become bigger. As you drag to the left, they become smaller.

B You can use the scroll bar to browse the thumbnails.

3 Click the **Sort By** menu, and select **Oldest**.

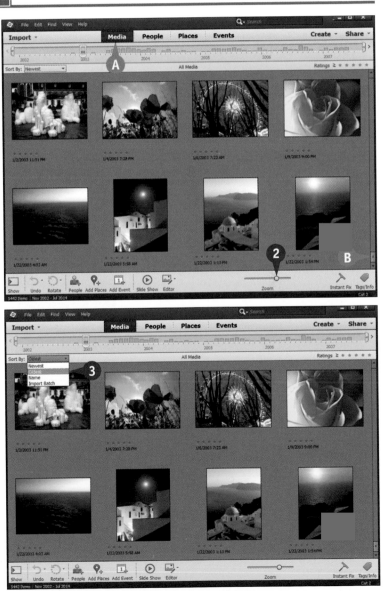

The oldest photos now appear first. The scroll bar moves to the top.

④ Click the **Sort By** menu, and select **Import Batch**.

Photoshop Elements groups the photos into batches imported at the same time from the same source.

TIPS

How can I hide certain file types in the Media Browser?

The Media Browser can display photos, videos, audio and music files, Adobe project files, and PDFs. Select View ➪ Media Types to control which files appear in the browser. You can show or hide each media type by clicking the corresponding menu.

Why does the display stay the same when I select Newest or Oldest?

For convenience, the Media Browser does not change the photos you are previewing when you switch between Newest and Oldest views. However, the scroll position changes. If you preview your newest photos in Newest mode and select Oldest mode, the scroll bar moves to the bottom of the window.

View Photos in Full Screen

You can switch to Full Screen mode in the Organizer to get a clearer view of your photos. Photoshop Elements expands the photo to fill the workspace and displays special panels for applying commands.

Full Screen mode is useful when you want to perform basic edits on a large version of your photo but do not want to switch to the Editor. You can access a film strip in Full Screen mode that displays image thumbnails from your current catalog. This enables you to switch to another image.

View Photos in Full Screen

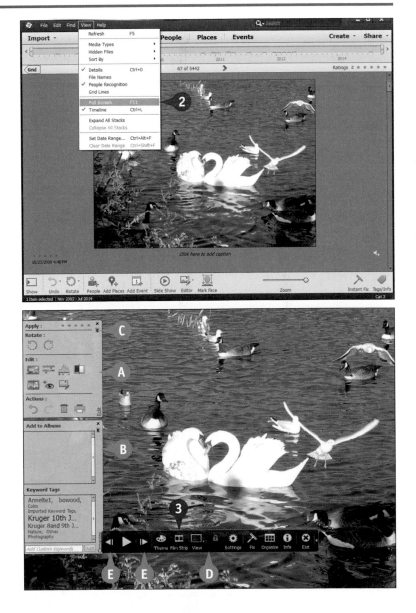

1 In the Organizer, click the photo you want to view in Full Screen.

2 Click **View** ➪ **Full Screen**.

Photoshop Elements opens the photo in Full Screen.

A You can use this Quick Edit panel to perform quick edits.

B You can use this Quick Organize panel to add images to albums and to manage keyword tags.

C The panels automatically hide if not used. You can click the pin icon (📌) to turn this hiding on and off.

D Controls for viewing different photos and managing panels appear here.

E You can click the **Next** (▶) and **Previous** (◀) buttons to view other photos.

Note: You can also press ➡ and ⬅.

3 Click **Film Strip**.

F The Film Strip opens, displaying thumbnail versions of your images.

G Click the left (◀) and right (▶) arrows to scroll through the thumbnails.

H You can also drag the slider (▥)

4 Click a thumbnail.

Photoshop Elements displays the photo.

5 Click **Exit** or press the `Esc` key to exit Full Screen mode.

Note: The control bar for full screen mode auto-hides if you do not move your mouse.

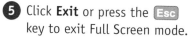

TIP

How do I zoom and pan the photo in Full Screen mode?

Roll the mouse wheel. The image zooms in or out, depending on your movement, and displays a zoom percentage. You can also click repeatedly to change between 100% zoom and a fit-to-screen zoom percentage calculated by Photoshop Elements. To pan the image, click and drag it with your mouse.

View Photo Information

You can use the Information panel to view general information about a photo, including the filename, file size, image size, and location. You can edit some of this data in an associated panel.

You can also view associated tags, creation and access dates, and *metadata* — detailed information about a digital photo. Metadata includes camera settings for the photo, so you can use this information to check the exposure time, flash settings, and f-stop/aperture.

View Photo Information

1 In the Organizer, right-click a photo.

2 Click **Show File Info**.

The Information panel opens.

A The General properties appear by default.

B You can add or edit a caption for the photo here.

C The rating, size, capture date, and other information for the photo appear in this area.

If you have assigned keyword tags to the photo, they also appear here. See Chapter 4 for details.

3 Click **Metadata**.

The Metadata properties appear. This includes the camera model and settings if the photo came from a digital camera.

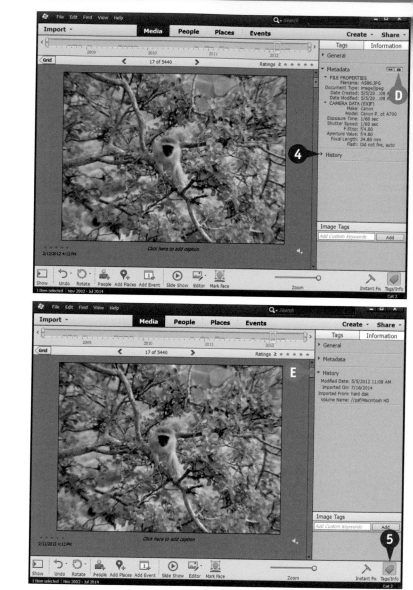

D You can click 🖽 to display extra detail.

4 Click **History**.

The History properties appear.

E Photoshop Elements displays information about the photo's file, including when the file was last modified and when it was imported.

Note: The History information does not include a detailed history of all the edits you make.

5 Click **Tags/Info** to close the Information panel.

TIP

Can I change the date and time of a photo?
Yes. Right-click the photo you want to edit. Select **Adjust Date and Time**. You can now change the date and time that Photoshop Elements uses when it sorts photos by date. You can either set the date and time by hand, change the date and time to match the file's creation date, or apply a time offset to correct for time zone errors. Use this option if you want to fix sorting errors — for example, because you copied a photo from an old collection and now it has the wrong date and time.

Add a Caption

You can add captions to your photos in the Organizer. Use captions as short notes about images. You can include location and content details for photos that do not already have them. This can make it easier to search for them later.

Captions appear below a photo when the image is viewed with details showing. You can display captions when viewing a slideshow in the Organizer; see the section "Display a Slideshow in Full Screen" in Chapter 15. You can also include caption information with photos when you print them; see Chapter 15.

Add a Caption

1 In the Organizer, right-click the photo you want to caption.

2 Select **Add Caption**.

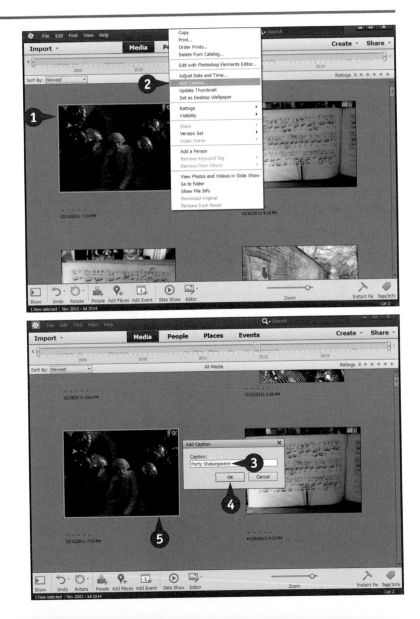

The Add Caption dialog box opens.

3 Type a caption for the photo.

4 Click **OK**.

The Organizer adds the caption to the photo's metadata. The caption appears in Photoshop Elements and other compatible photo editors.

5 Double-click the image.

A large thumbnail of the photo appears.

 Select **View** ⇨ **Details** if there is no check mark next to Details in the menu.

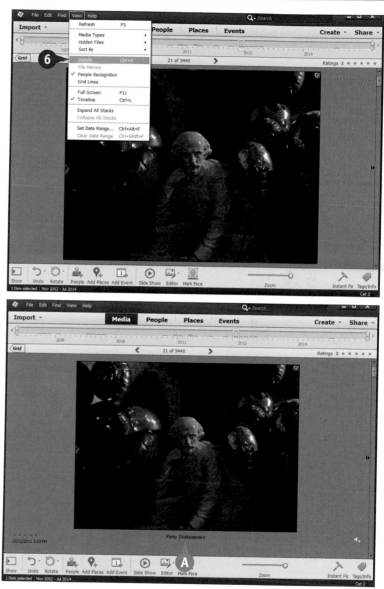

A The caption appears below the photo.

TIPS

Are there other ways to add captions to photos?

Yes. You can also add captions to your photos by using the Information panel. See the previous section, "View Photo Information," for details.

How do I edit a caption?

To edit a caption in the Media Browser, follow step **6**, click the caption, and make your changes. You can delete the caption completely, type a new caption, or make changes to the existing caption text. Click outside the text box to save your changes.

Work with Albums

You can use albums to group photos. You can group photos that feature specific people or which were taken on certain dates. For example, you could collect all your Christmas or Halloween photos into a single album, even though they were taken in different years.

Albums are also a convenient way to group photos before making a slideshow or photobook. You can create as many albums as you want. The same photo can appear in many albums. Local Albums use photos on your hard disk. Mobile Albums use photos stored in the Cloud. See Chapter 15 for details.

Work with Albums

Create a New Album

1 In the Organizer, open a catalog.

Note: For more on catalogs, see the section "Create a Catalog."

2 Click **Show** to access the Albums panel.

The button text changes to Hide.

The Albums panel appears.

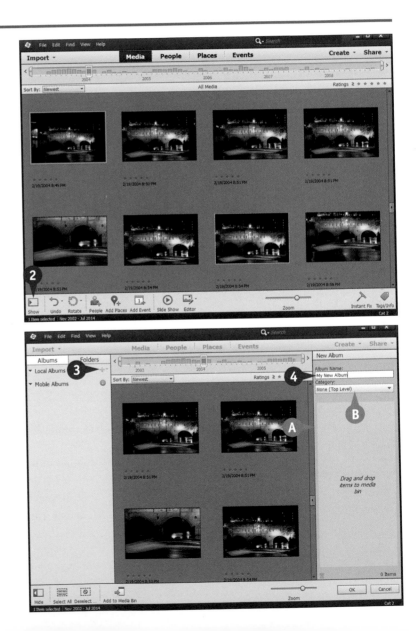

3 Click the plus sign (➕).

Ⓐ The New Album panel opens.

4 Type a name for the album.

Ⓑ If you have created at least one category, you can click this menu to assign the album to it. See the note for details.

5 Click and drag a photo from the Media Browser to the Content list box.

The Organizer adds the photo to the album.

6 Repeat step **5** for all the photos you want to add to the album.

You can `Ctrl`+click (`⌘`+click on a Mac) to select multiple photos and then click-drag them all to the album.

7 Click **OK** to close the Add New Album panel and save the album information.

View an Album

1 Click the album name in the list of albums.

C The Organizer displays all the photos in the album.

D Photos in an album are marked with an album icon (■).

Note: If you cannot see the icons, select **View.** Click **Details** if there is no check mark next to it.

D You can click **All Media** (hidden by the menu) to return to the entire catalog.

E To delete an album, right-click the album name and select **Delete** in the menu that appears.

TIPS

How do I remove a photo from an album?
You can right-click any photo and select **Remove From Album ⇨ [Album Name].** The album does not have to be open. You can also right-click an album, select a photo in the Content panel, and click the trash icon (🗑) at the bottom left of the media bin for the album.

What are album categories?
Album categories are like folders for albums. You can use them to group related albums. Click ▼ next to ➕, and select **New Album Category.** Enter a name, and click **OK.** You can now drag one or more albums into the new category. Categories can contain further categories.

Find Photos

The Organizer includes powerful search tools. You can look for photos by date, by filename, by location, or by finding custom tags. As you take more photos, these search options can help you find the images you want without scrolling.

These examples find photos in a date range, and by searching all the text associated with a photo, including captions, keyword tags, and album names.

Find Photos

Find Photos by Date

1 In the Organizer, click **View** ⇨ **Set Date Range**.

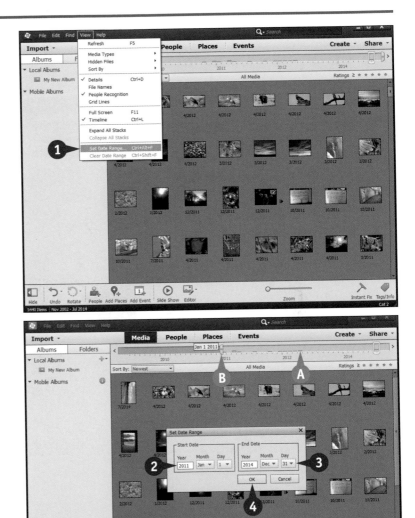

The Set Date Range dialog box opens.

2 Select the start date for your search.

3 Select the end date for your search.

4 Click **OK**.

Ⓐ The Organizer displays photos between those dates in the Media Browser.

Ⓑ The Timeline view shows the start date.

Note: You can reset the date search by clicking **View** and then **Clear Date Range**.

Find Photos with a Text Search

1 Type one or more keywords in the search box.

Photoshop Elements searches the filenames, captions, keyword tags, album names, and other text associated with your photos.

C Photoshop Elements displays photos that match your text as you type.

If you type multiple keywords, Photoshop Elements displays photos that match all the keywords.

2 Click **Back**.

Photoshop Elements cancels the search.

TIP

What other search options can I use?

You can search the Organizer using the Find menu.

Search Option	Function
By Caption or Note	Searches for text in the notes and captions of your photos
By Filename	Searches the catalog for a particular filename
By History	Finds photos from the print, e-mail, import, or creation dates
By Media Type	Searches for projects, photos, and audio or video files in your catalog

Rate Photos

You can add star ratings to your photos. Each photo can have no rating at all or a star rating between 1 and 5. You can use star ratings to mark important photos you want to keep and to hide less successful photos you do not want to see. You can also use them as a quick and simple grouping option.

You can search the Media Browser for photos with a specific rating or show images with a rating which is equal or better. To see ratings in the Media Browser, turn on the Details option.

Rate Photos

Apply a Rating

1 If details are not visible in the Media Browser, click **View ⇨ Details**.

2 Click a star (⭐) to apply a rating.

You can add a star rating from 1 to 5 by clicking the icons from left to right. After clicking a thumbnail to select it, you can also press a number key from **1** to **5**. Pressing **0** removes the rating.

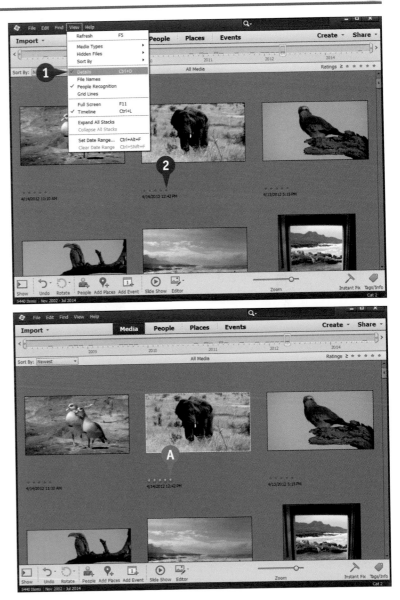

A Photoshop Elements assigns the rating and gold stars (⭐) appear.

You can also apply ratings in the Information panel. See the section "View Photo Information" for more.

Note: You can click the stars to change the rating.

Note: To remove a rating, click the first star twice.

Filter by Rating

 Click the ratings menu and select a filter setting.

2 Click a star to select the rating you are looking for.

Photoshop Elements displays photos that match your ratings.

To select a different rating, repeat steps **1** and **2**.

B To ignore ratings and turn off the rating filter, click the first star twice.

TIPS

How do I apply the same rating to multiple photos?

Ctrl+click (⌘+click on a Mac) to select the photos you want to rate. Apply a star rating to one of the selected photos. Photoshop Elements applies the rating to all the selected photos.

Does the rating filter work in the different Organizer views?

Yes. For example, if the People view is selected and the rating filter is set to greater or equal to three stars, only people in a photo with a three-, four-, or five-star rating appear. The Places and Events views work in a similar way.

View Versions of a Photo

As you make edits to a photo in Photoshop Elements, the Organizer can keep different versions grouped together. The group is called a *version set* and has a special icon. You can use version sets to keep an original unedited photo and compare it with one or more edited versions, and to try out different interpretations of a photo to see which works best.

To save an edited photo in a version set, click **Save in Version Set with Original** when saving. See Chapter 2 for more about saving photos.

View Versions of a Photo

1 Save a photo in Photoshop Elements in a version set. See Chapter 2 for details.

A Version sets appear with an icon (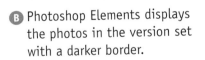).

2 Click ▶ to expand the set.

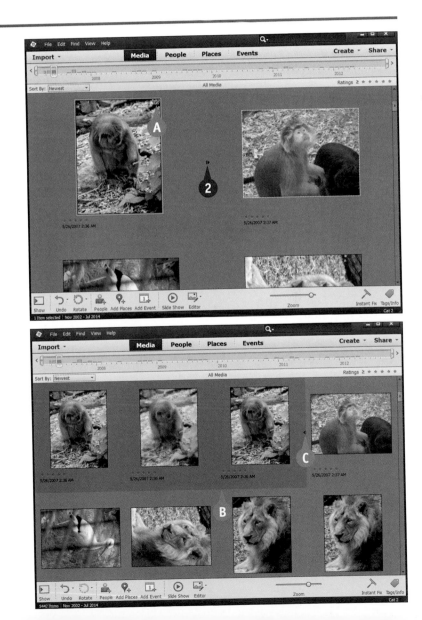

B Photoshop Elements displays the photos in the version set with a darker border.

C You can click ◀ to collapse the version set.

By default, the most recent version appears on top of the collapsed set.

To display a different version on top of the set, you can right-click a version, click **Version Set** in the menu, and then click **Set as Top Item**.

Remove a Photo from the Organizer

You can remove a photo from the Organizer. The photo disappears from the current catalog. Use this feature to eliminate unsuccessful photos, get rid of old photos you no longer want, and make a catalog less cluttered.

By default, removing a photo leaves the original file on your hard drive. You can delete the file permanently by checking a box in the confirmation dialog box, but you should usually leave the file on disk in case you change your mind.

Remove a Photo from the Organizer

1 Right-click a photo.

2 Click **Delete from Catalog**.

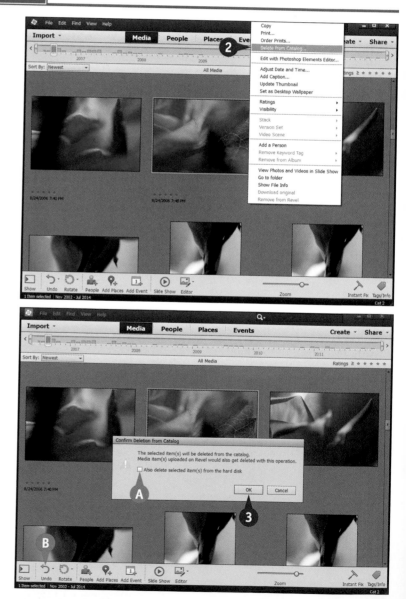

The Confirm Deletion from Catalog dialog box appears.

Ⓐ You can click this option to delete the photo from your hard drive (☐ changes to ☑).

3 Click **OK**.

Photoshop Elements removes the photo from the Organizer catalog.

Ⓑ You can click **Undo** to put the removed photo back in the catalog.

Using Advanced Organizing Tools

Photoshop Elements includes advanced tools for managing images. For example, you can associate tags with photos to help you identify their content. You can group photos based on where they were taken, the people in them, and with your own custom categories.

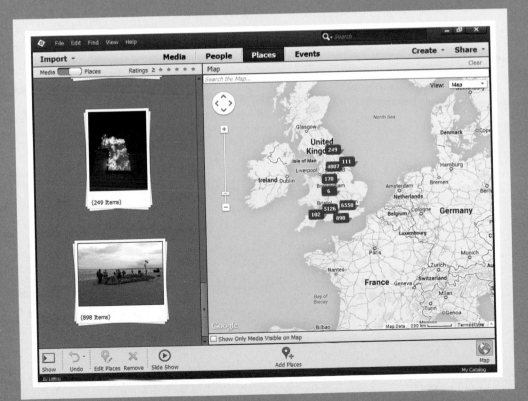

Find Duplicate Photos

You can use the Organizer to find all the duplicate photos in your collection. You can then *stack* them — collect them so they take a single space in the Organizer. For more about stacking, see the "Stack Photos" section in this chapter.

If you have many photos and a slow computer, a duplicate search can take minutes or even hours. To search for duplicates of a single photo, use the Visual Similarity search. For details see the Find by Visual Similarity section in this chapter.

Find Duplicate Photos

1 In the Organizer, click the search box (🔍) and select **Duplicate Photo Search.**

You may see an alert box about Visual Similarity search.

2 If this alert appears, click **OK,** deselect all photos in the Organizer, and repeat Step **1.**

B Photoshop Elements displays a progress bar as it searches for duplicates.

Note: You may see a second progress bar showing an automatic Visual Similarity search after the first progress bar completes.

C Photoshop Elements groups all similar photos into small collections.

D You can use the Zoom slider to make the photos bigger so you can see more detail.

 Review the collections.

Note: The search finds similar photos as well as duplicates. You must review the collections by eye to decide which photos you want to stack.

 Click **Stack** to group a collection.

5 Use the scroll bar to scroll through all the collections. Repeat Step **4** for every collection you want to stack.

6 Click **Done** when finished.

Photoshop Elements stacks the photos you selected as duplicates.

TIP

Is there a simpler way to find duplicates?
Unfortunately not. The Duplicate Search uses the Visual Similarity Search tool and looks for similar photos rather than exact duplicates. A key benefit is that the tool finds photos that have the same content, even after they have been resized. The disadvantage is that this feature does not provide a true duplicate search. However, it is still quicker than looking for duplicates by hand.

Work with Keyword Tags

Keyword tags help you categorize and filter your digital photos. For example, you can create a tag called *car* and apply it to all your photos of cars. You can assign the Organizer's preset tags or use tags that you have created. You can also assign more than one tag to a photo. For example, a photo of an automobile could have a *car* tag as well as a *convertible* tag.

The Organizer comes with several predefined tags, but the selection is limited. You should add your own tags to make searching easier.

Work with Keyword Tags

Create a Keyword Tag

1 In the Organizer, click **Tags/Info**.

2 Click **Tags**.

3 Click the plus sign (⊞).

The Create Keyword Tag dialog box opens.

4 Click the category menu, and choose a category for the new tag.

5 Type a name for the keyword tag.

Ⓐ You can add a note about the keyword tag here.

6 Click **OK**.

Assign Tags

1 Click and drag the tag from the Keyword Tags panel, and then drop it on the photo you want to tag.

B The Organizer displays a keyword tag (🖼️).

You can also drag a thumbnail image from the Media Browser to a keyword tag to assign a tag.

Note: If you cannot see a tag, select View ➪ Details in the main menu.

2 Click the Keyword Tags search box.

C Photoshop Elements lists all existing tags.

3 Click a tag in the list.

4 Click a photo you want to tag.

You can **Ctrl**+click (**⌘**+click on a Mac) to select multiple photos.

5 Click **Add**.

Photoshop Elements applies the tag (🖼️) to the selected photo.

TIP

How do I edit a keyword tag?

Right-click the keyword tag, and choose **Edit** (**A**). The Edit Keyword Tag dialog box opens. Type a new keyword tag name or make other edits to the tag, and click **OK**. Photoshop Elements applies the changes. Any images that have the keyword tag applied are updated.

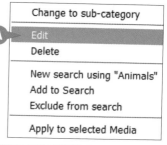

continued ▶

Work with Keyword Tags (continued)

After you assign keyword tags, you can tell Photoshop Elements to display photos with any combination of tags. For example, you can show photos with certain kinds of content, or which feature certain people.

To save you time, Photoshop Elements can tag faces automatically. For details see the next section, "Define People in Photos." This makes it easy to use tags to find people.

Work with Keyword Tags (continued)

Filter by Tags

1 Open the Tags/Info panel if it is not already visible.

2 Position your mouse pointer over the keyword tag you want to apply, and click the box (☐ becomes 🔲).

A You can click ▶ to expand a tag category.

B You can click ▼ to collapse a tag category.

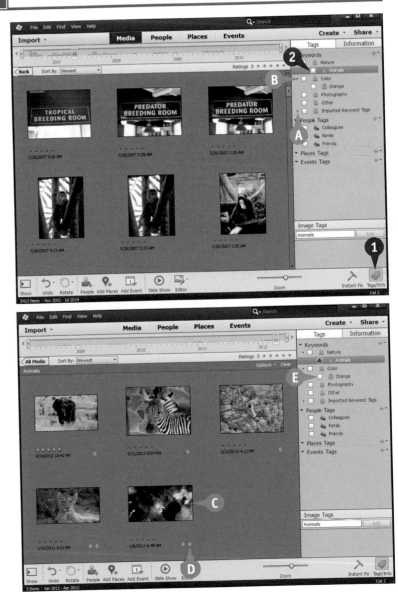

C The Organizer displays all the photos with the tag you selected in Step **2**.

D The Organizer displays a tag mark (🔲) for each tag associated with a photo.

Note: You can hover the mouse pointer over each tag to view the tag name as a tool tip.

E To filter by multiple tags, click additional tag boxes (☐).

If you check multiple tags, only photos that have all the tags appear. You cannot select photos with any other combination of tags.

Remove a Tag from a Photo

 Right-click a photo with a tag.

2 Click **Remove Keyword Tag**.

3 Click the keyword tag you want to remove.

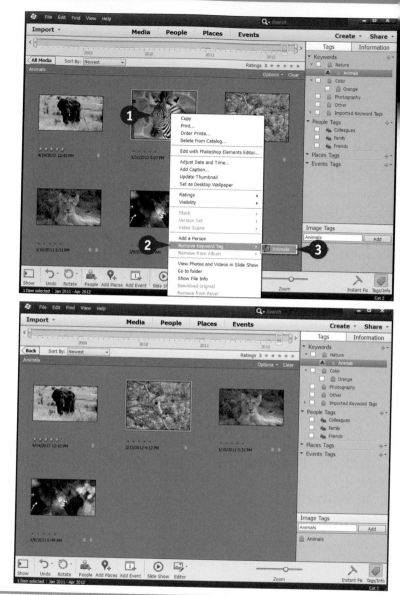

The Organizer removes the keyword tag from the photo.

If the tag was filtering the photo in the Media Browser, the photo disappears.

TIP

How can I create a new keyword tag category?

Photoshop Elements comes with several predefined categories such as Nature and Color, but you can define your own. Click the ⬛ next to ➕, and click **New Category** in the menu that appears. The Create Category dialog box opens. Type a name for the category (Ⓐ). Optionally, you can choose a color (Ⓑ) and icon (Ⓒ). Click **OK** to save the category.

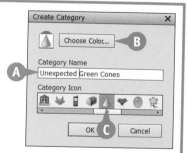

Define People in Photos

You can find people in your photos and tag them with names. The Organizer includes a feature that looks for human faces in your photos. You can view all the faces as a collection and tag them with names. Searching a catalog for faces can take a long time. The search is not perfect. It sometimes mistakes random objects for faces or misses people.

Click **People** at the top of the Organizer to see a grid of stacked photos with all the people you have named. You can double-click a stack to view photos that feature that person.

Define People in Photos

1 In the Organizer, select photos with people that you want to name.

If you do not select any photos, Photoshop Elements searches all the photos in the current catalog. This can take a long time.

2 Click **Add People**.

3 If you are you searching an entire catalog, click **YES** when an alert appears.

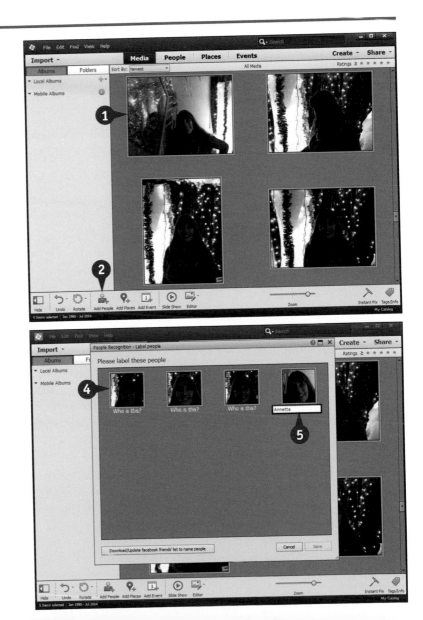

Photoshop Elements searches for faces and displays the results in a People Recognition dialog box.

4 **Shift**+click or **Ctrl**+click (**⌘**+click on a Mac) to select all the photos of one person's face.

5 Type a name for the face.

6 Press **Enter**.

A Photoshop Elements tags all the photos you select with the name.

If you selected photos of more than one person, you can repeat Steps **3** to **5** to label them.

7 Click **Save**.

Depending on how many photos you are analyzing, Photoshop Elements may present additional sets of faces to name or confirm. You can continue naming them and click **Save** or click **Cancel** to stop.

8 Click **People**.

Photoshop Elements displays the people you have defined.

B You can move your cursor across a thumbnail to preview the faces for a person.

C Double-click a face to display the photos for that person.

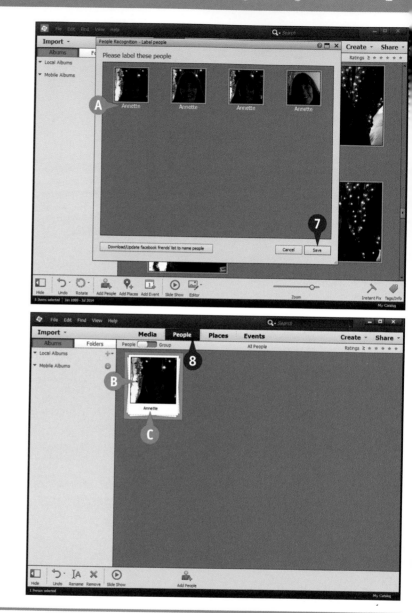

TIPS

How do I tag my friends on Facebook in my photos?
In the People Recognition dialog box, click **Download/Update facebook friends' list to name people**. Complete the steps to authorize Photoshop Elements to access your Facebook information. Complete Steps **4** and **5** to tag faces with names. As you type a name, Photoshop Elements suggests similar Facebook friends. Click a name, and Photoshop Elements links the tag to a Facebook friend.

What does the Faces/Photos switch do?
When you set the switch to Faces, Photoshop Elements shows cropped close-ups of faces. When you select Photos, Photoshop Elements shows the photos they appear in.

Define Places

You can use the Places feature in the Organizer to locate your photos on a map. To define places, click and drag photo thumbnails onto a Google map.

You can place a batch of photos at a single location, or specify different locations for each photo more precisely — for example, to spread photo locations around different parts of a park or a small city area. Placing individual photos takes more time. Placing photos in a batch takes less time, but is less accurate. You can choose either approach.

Define Places

1 In the Organizer, click the photo you want to place on the map.

Note: You can control Ctrl+click (⌘+click on a Mac) to select multiple photos.

Note: Skip this step if you want to map all your photos. (This is not recommended if you have many photos.)

2 Click **Add Places**.

The Add Places dialog box appears.

3 Use the map controls to pan and zoom to the location where the photos were taken.

You can also click-drag with your mouse to pan, and use the mouse wheel to zoom in and out.

4 Click and drag a thumbnail onto the map.

If you selected more than one thumbnail in Step **1**, you can drag them all to a single location. You can also click them to select them one by one and drag them to different locations.

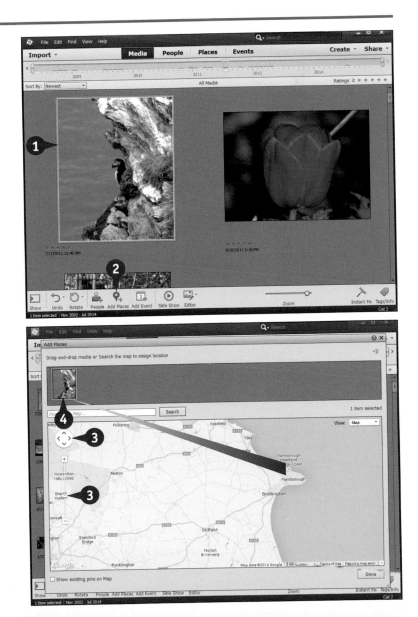

A Photoshop Elements displays an icon to mark the place.

5 Click ☑ to confirm the location.

You can click ⊘ or press **Esc** to cancel.

6 Click **Done**.

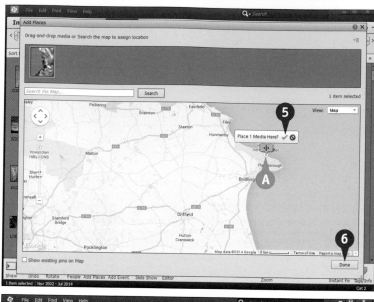

7 Click **Tags/Info** to view tags for your photos.

8 Click **Places Tags**.

D Photoshop Elements automatically tags your selected photos based on the place.

For more about tags, see the section "Work with People, Place, and Event Tags."

To view a map showing where you have placed all your photos in the Organizer, see the next section, "View Places."

TIPS

What happens if my photos have location information associated with them already?

Some cameras, including iPhones and other camera phones, assign a location to a photo automatically when you take it. This is sometimes known as *geo-tagging*. Photoshop Elements reads this information and adds the locations without being asked. So you do not need to add these locations manually.

How can I place the photos at a named location?

If you know the name of a location you can type the name into the Add Places search box and click **Search**. Photoshop Elements tries to find the location. If it succeeds, click ☑ to group the photos at that location.

View Places

You can view the Photoshop Elements map to see all the places linked to your photos. Click each icon on the map to view the photo or photos at that location.

You can use zoom and panning controls on the map to find photos that you have placed at certain locations. You can also search for places by keyword.

View Places

1 In the Organizer, click **Places**.

A map appears.

A Icons on the map represent defined places with numbers representing the number of photos at a place.

2 Use the map controls to pan and zoom to find a location of interest.

B You can also type the name of a location here press **Enter** to search for it.

C As you zoom out, Photoshop Elements groups photos at nearby locations together to avoid clutter.

D Photoshop Elements displays the matching photo groups here.

Note: To find a matching group, check the number of items.

E You can use the map controls or your mouse to zoom in if you want to see more detail on the map.

3 Click a place icon on the map.

4 Click **Show Media**.

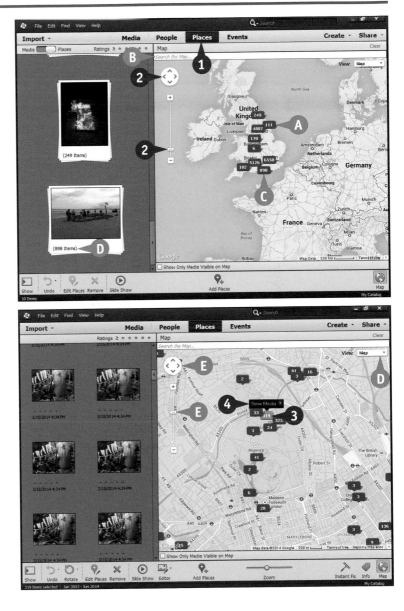

F Photoshop Elements shows only the photos associated with the place.

Note: The location icon does not remain highlighted in blue.

G You can click **Map** to toggle the map open and closed. Closing the map gives you a larger area for viewing photos.

5 Click **Clear**.

Photoshop Elements shows all the photos again and returns to the default view on the map.

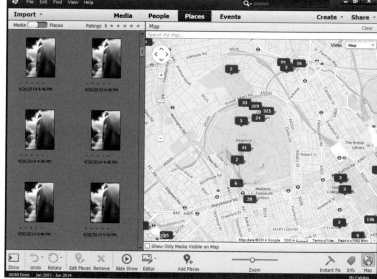

TIPS

How can I move a photo to a different place?
If you want to change the location associated with a photo, you can select the photo and click **Edit Places** at the bottom of the Organizer workspace. The Edit Place dialog box appears. You can now click+drag the photo to a different location on the map.

How can I remove a photo from a place?
Right-click the place icon (🔲) for the photo, and click **Remove** command in the pop-up menu. Because the tags are nested, you may need to remove multiple tags for each photo.

Define Events

You can group your photos into *events* to associate them with specific dates or time periods. This is a good way to organize photos taken on birthdays, holidays, and vacations. You must define an event before you can add photos to it. To view your events, click **Events** at the top of the Organizer.

Photoshop Elements also supports *Smart Events,* which group photos by date automatically. For more about Smart Events, see the "Using Smart Events" section in this chapter.

Define Events

1 In the Organizer, `Ctrl`+click (`⌘`+click on a Mac) to select the photos for your event.

To find photos that were taken during a specific time period, see Chapter 3.

2 Click **Add Event**.

The Add New Event pane opens with your photos added.

A You can click and drag to add more photos to your event.

3 Type a name for the event.

Photoshop Elements sets a start and end date for your event based on the timestamps associated with the photos.

B You can click the calendar icons to change the start and end dates of the event.

C You can type an optional description for the event here.

4 Click **Done**.

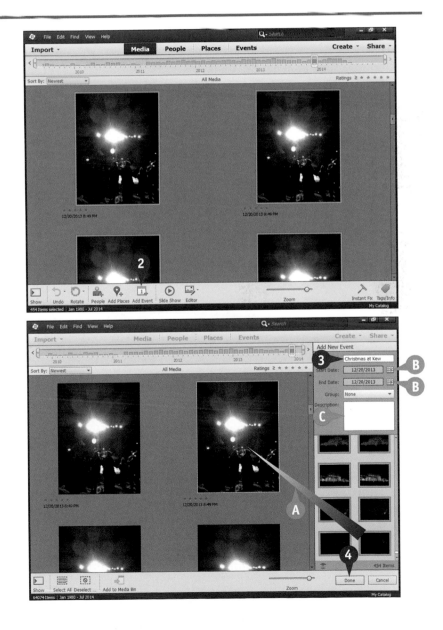

D Photoshop Elements adds event icons (⬜) to the photos. You can position your cursor over them to view the names.

You can right-click an event icon (⬜) to remove a photo from an event.

5 Click **Events**.

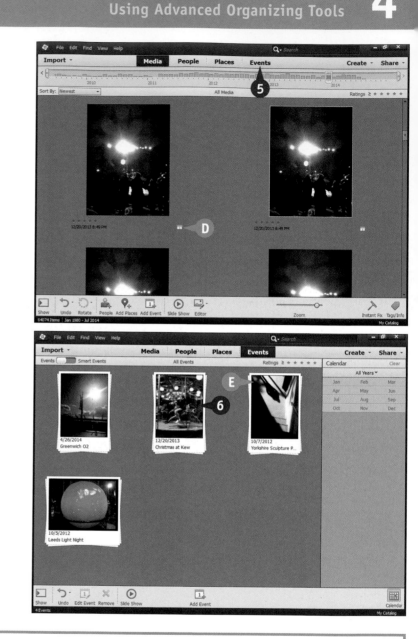

Photoshop Elements displays the events you have defined.

E You can move your cursor across a thumbnail to preview the photos for an event.

6 Double-click an event to display its photos.

Note: Every event you create has a tag associated with it. See the section "Work with People, Place, and Event Tags" for more.

TIPS

After saving an event, how do I add more photos to it?

Click **Events**, and then double-click an event to select it. Click **Add Media** at the bottom of the Organizer to add more photos to it.

How can I view my event photos as a slideshow?

Select an event, and click **Slide Show** at the bottom of the Organizer. Photoshop Elements creates a slideshow that cycles through the photos included in the event. If you position your cursor over the slideshow, a toolbar appears. Use this toolbar to change slide duration, background music, and other settings. The slideshow feature also works for **People** and **Places.**

Using Smart Events

You can use the Smart Event feature to group your photos by date automatically. You can use this feature as-is or as a starting point for custom events; you can select one or more Smart Events and collect them into a custom event.

When you work with Smart Events, Photoshop Elements groups photos imported on the same day or within a date and time range. When you group photos by time, you can click and drag a slider to set a time range. Note that photos are grouped by the time you imported them, not the time they were shot.

Using Smart Events

1 In the Organizer, click **Events**.

2 Click the virtual switch to select **Smart Events**.

Photoshop Elements groups your photos by date.

A Each group shows the date and the number of photos.

3 Click **Time.**

Photoshop Elements displays your photos in groups based on time and date.

Note: Photoshop Elements does not group photos by time of day. It groups photos by a time range within or around each date.

B You can click and drag the slider to set the time/date range used to create the groups.

Drag to the right to use shorter lengths of time. Drag to the left to use longer.

4 Click any group, or multi-select any group of groups with Ctrl +click (⌘+click on a Mac).

5 Click **Name Event(s)** to convert the group into a custom event.

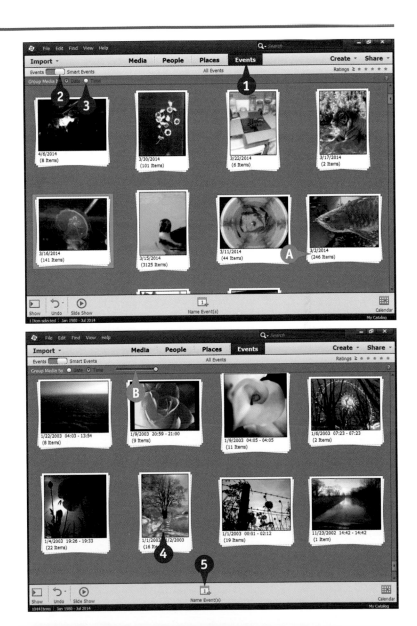

The Name Event dialog box opens.

6 Type a name for the event.

Photoshop Elements sets a start and end date for your event based on the import times of the photos.

C You can click the calendar icons to change the start and end dates.

D You can type a description of the event here.

7 Click **OK**.

Photoshop Elements saves the event.

8 Click here to view custom Events instead of Smart Events.

Photoshop Elements displays custom Events.

E The new event appears in the grid.

You can double-click the event to view its photos.

TIP

How can I filter my events by date?

1 In the Events view, click **Calendar** at the bottom of the Organizer workspace.

2 Click the year menu to select a year.

A To filter by month, you can click a month. Months with events are highlighted.

B To filter by day, you can click a day. Days with events are highlighted.

Photoshop Elements displays the events you select.

Work with People, Place, and Event Tags

When you create People, Places, or Events for your photos, Photoshop Elements automatically creates tags for you. You can use the Tags search panel to see which photos include them.

You can select more than one tag at once. For example, you can select a Place tag and then select People tags to see photos that include those people at that place.

Work with People, Place, and Event Tags

1 In the Organizer, click **Tags/Info**.

2 Click **Tags**.

3 Click **People Tags** if the people tag list is not already open.

People-related tags appear.

A You can click a tag to view photos tagged with that person's name.

B People tags are marked with ![icon].

Note: If you cannot see an icon, confirm that **View ⇨ Details** is checked and move the Zoom slider in the toolbar.

4 Deselect any People tags, and click **Places Tags** if the Places tag list is not already open.

Place-related tags appear.

Note: Place tags are pre-grouped by country, area, city, and specific location.

C Each place is associated with a set of location tags. Click through the closed tags to view a specific location tag.

D You can click any Place tag to view photos at that location.

E Place tags are marked by ![icon].

5 Deselect any Place tags, and click **Events Tags** if the Event tag list is not already open.

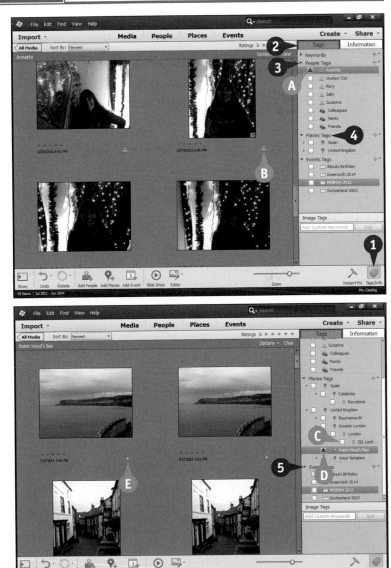

Event-related tags appear.

Each event defined in your photos is associated with a tag.

F You can click any Event tag to view photos of that event (□ becomes 🔍).

G Event tags are marked by an event icon 🔳.

H You can select more than one tag to find combinations of people, places, and events.

I Photoshop Elements displays photos that combine the tags you select.

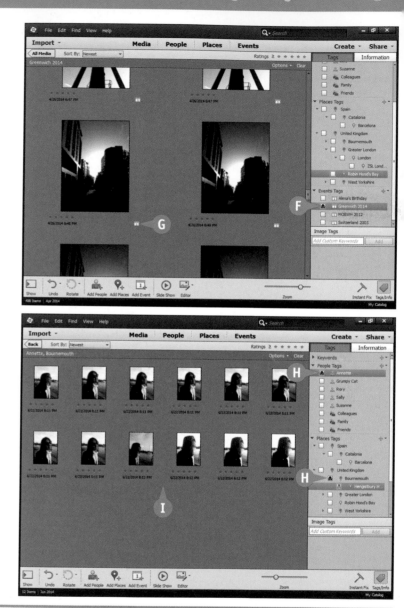

TIPS

How do I create a place shortcut?

You can make a shortcut for a place tag to replace a long address with a more descriptive name. For example, you can replace a tag named "123 South Main Street" with "Home." In the Tags panel, right-click a place name and click **Rename**. Type the new name into the dialog box that appears.

Why do I not see any place tags even though I have locations marked on my map?

Photoshop Elements creates Place tags when you drag a photo to a location on the map or when you search the map for a location and assign photos to it. It does not create Place tags automatically for photos with location information. To add tags manually, see the Define Places section earlier in this chapter.

Apply an Instant Fix

You can optimize color, lighting, and make other basic edits in the Organizer using the Instant Fix tools. This is a good way to make simple improvements without loading the Editor.

Most of the fixes are one-click improvements with no settings. They work on many photos, but may not give good results on photos with unusual lighting. After you apply a fix, the Organizer saves the photo with the original in a version set. See Chapter 3 for more about version sets.

Apply an Instant Fix

1. In the Organizer, click the photo you want to fix.

2. Click **Instant Fix**.

   The Photo Fix Options panel opens.

3. Click an instant fix, such as **Crop**.

The Crop Photo dialog box appears.

4. Click and drag the edges and corners of the crop tool to set the area of the photo you want to keep.

Ⓐ You can click the crop menu to select various standard width/height ratios.

5. Click **Done**.

Ⓑ You can click **Cancel** to exit the tool without cropping.

Photoshop Elements crops the photo.

Ⓒ Photoshop Elements adds the edited photo to a version set and displays the open version set icon (☒).

Note: For more on version sets, see Chapter 3.

❻ Click another instant fix such as **Color.**

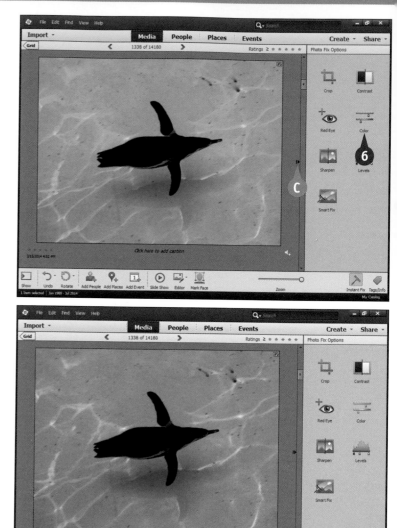

Photoshop Elements fixes the color.

TIPS

How do I rotate a photo in the Organizer?
You can click to select a photo and then click **Rotate** at the bottom of the Organizer workspace to rotate the photo counterclockwise. You can click the Rotate button's menu triangle (▾) to open a menu with a clockwise rotate command.

How do I undo Instant Fix changes?
You can click **Undo** at the bottom of the Organizer workspace. If you performed multiple changes in the Instant Fix panel, you must click **Undo** multiple times to undo them.

Stack Photos

You can save screen space in the Organizer by grouping related photos into stacks. The Organizer shows the top photo in a stack and hides the others. You can select photos manually before stacking them, or you can ask Photoshop Elements to suggest stacks by searching your collection for similar photos.

Stack Photos

Create a Stack

1 **Shift**+click or **Ctrl**+click (⌘+click on a Mac) to select the photos you want to stack.

2 Right-click one of the selected photos.

3 Click **Stack** ⇨ **Stack Selected Photos**.

Ⓐ You can click **Automatically Suggest Photo Stacks** to have Photoshop Elements suggest stacks based on photographic similarity.

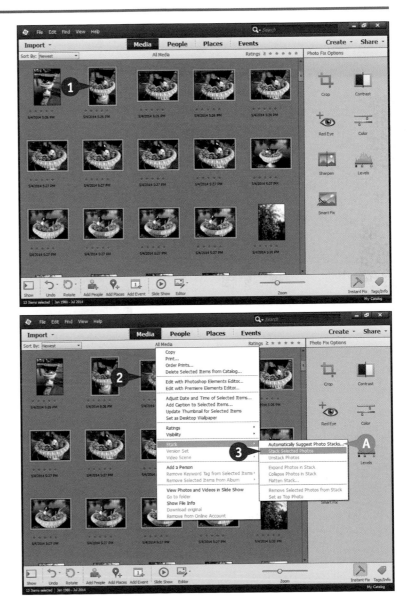

Ⓑ Photoshop Elements stacks the photos you selected. The photo you right-clicked appears on top of the stack.

Ⓒ The stack is marked with a stack icon (⬚).

Ⓓ You can click ▶ to expand the stack.

The Organizer shows the photos in the stack.

You can click ◀ to close the stack.

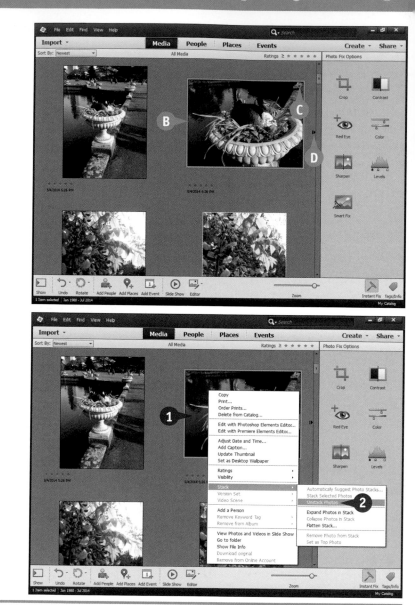

Unstack Photos

① Right-click a photo in a stack. If the stack is collapsed, right-click the top photo.

② Click **Stack** ⇨ **Unstack Photos**.

Photoshop Elements deletes the stack. The photos reappear as separate item in the Organizer.

TIPS

How do I automatically stack photos as I import them?

① In the main menu click **Get Photos and Videos** ⇨ **From Files and Folders**.

② In the dialog box that opens, click **Automatically Suggest Photo Stacks** (☐ changes to ☑).

When you import the photos, Photoshop Elements suggests groups of photos to be stacked based on their photographic similarity.

☑ Get Photos From Subfolders

☐ Automatically Fix Red Eyes

② ☑ Automatically Suggest Photo Stacks

Search for Similar Photos

You can search for photos with similar colors and shapes. This can be useful for finding related shots in a large catalog, or for more creative applications, such as finding similar images for a collage.

The search tool includes a slider that can be set to look for matching colors, matching shapes, or a mix of the two. Color searches are more accurate and take less time, but shape searches can produce some surprisingly close hits.

Search for Similar Photos

1 Click a photo to select it as a search target.

2 Click **Find** ➪ **By Visual Searches** ➪ **Visually similar photos and videos**.

Note: You can click **Objects appearing in photos** to search for images containing similar objects.

Note: If a dialog box appears asking if you want to index your photos, click **OK, Start Indexing**. Indexing makes searches faster and more accurate.

Photoshop Elements finds similar photos and lists them.

Ⓐ The target photo appears first.

Ⓑ Each photo includes a percentage to show how closely it matches the target.

3 Click and drag the slider to the left to look for similar colors.

Photoshop Elements finds photos with similar colors.

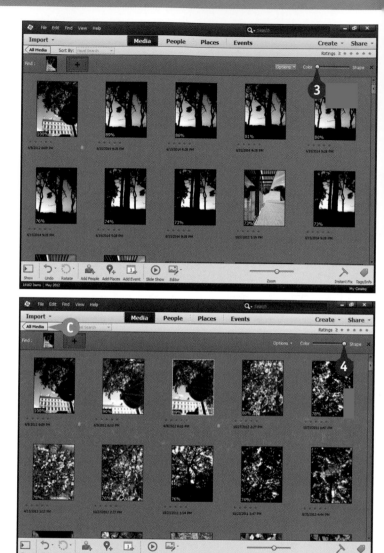

4 Click and drag the slider to the right to look for similar shapes and textures.

Photoshop Elements finds photos with similar shapes and textures.

Note: In this example, the search finds more photos with foliage after it runs out of photos with similar shapes. Color differences are ignored.

C You can click **All Media** to clear the search.

TIP

Can I search for more than one target at a time?
Yes. When the search results appear, you can drag another photo to the empty box (A) to add it as a target. If you drag the top few hits to the Find: area you can narrow a search and make it more precise.

Applying Basic Image Edits

Are you ready to start working with images? This chapter shows you how to fine-tune your workspace. You also learn how to resize your image, crop it to remove unwanted content, and make speedy edits in Quick mode.

Manage Open Images

Each image you open in Photoshop Elements appears in its own window. A single window gives you the maximum space for editing, but you can have many windows open at once to compare images or copy content between them.

In Expert mode, you can use tabs at the top of each window to switch between images. Each tab lists the name of the image file, the current magnification, and the image mode. You can also use the Photo Bin or Window menu to switch between different open images. This switching works in all three modes — Quick, Guided, and Expert.

Manage Open Images

Using Tabs

1 In the Editor, click **Expert**.

2 Open two or more images.

Note: For more on opening the Editor, see Chapter 1. For more on opening image files, see Chapter 2.

Ⓐ The Editor preview area shows the currently selected image ready for editing.

Ⓑ Tabs for each image appear here and show the filename and display magnification (zoom).

3 Click a tab to select a different image in the preview area.

The photo becomes active.

Using the Photo Bin

The Photo Bin usually displays thumbnails (small versions) of all the images open in the Editor.

Note: See the tip for more on how to display other images in the Photo Bin.

Ⓐ If the Photo Bin is closed, you can click **Photo Bin** to open it.

1 Double-click a thumbnail.

The photo becomes active.

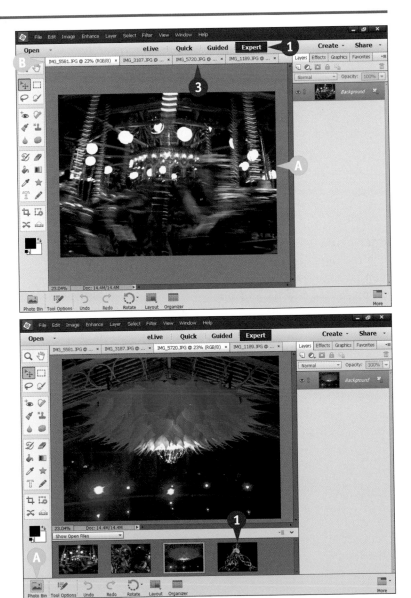

Using the Window Menu

1 Click **Window**.

2 Click an image filename.

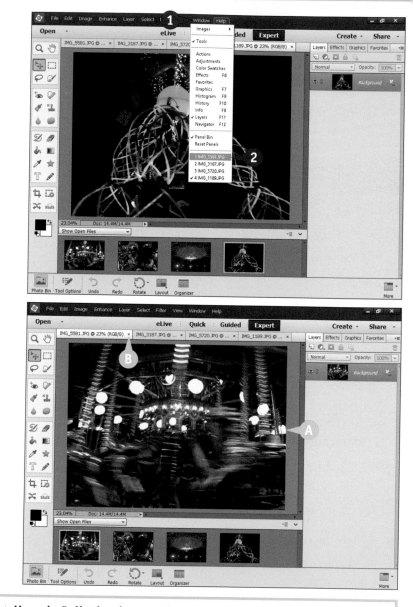

A The photo becomes active.

B You can click ☒ to close a tab.

Closing a tab also closes its image in the Editor.

Note: If you loaded the files from the Organizer, closing all open tabs closes the Editor. If you open files directly into the Editor, it remains open.

TIPS

How do I load more than one file at once?

You can use **Ctrl**+click (**⌘**+click on the Mac) or **Shift**+click to select more than one image in the Organizer. If you click the Editor button in the toolbar, all the images are loaded into the Editor.

How do I display images from the Organizer in the Photo Bin?

By default, the Photo Bin shows open files. Click the menu above the photo at the left of the bin to change this. Click an album name to load thumbnails of the photos in the album. Click **Show Files Selected in Organizer** to tell the Photo Bin to load files as soon as you as click them in the Organizer. This option can save a step, but it forces you to switch between the Organizer and Editor.

Using Layouts

You can use *layouts* to view more than one image at a time in the Editor. Layouts can arrange images in columns, in a grid, or in rows. You can use this option to compare images or to select and copy content between them.

When viewing multiple images at once, only one of the windows is active. Choose the active window by clicking its tab, clicking inside the window, or selecting the image from the Photo Bin or the Window menu.

Using Layouts

1 Click **Layout**.

Photoshop Elements displays a menu of layouts.

2 Select a layout from the menu.

Photoshop Elements displays multiple windows, each with a different image.

This example shows the **All Columns** option.

3 Click an image or a tab to select it.

Ⓐ You can use the scroll bars to position each image in its window.

Note: You can also change the image magnification and move images with the Zoom (🔍) and Hand (🖐) tools in the toolbar. For details, see the next two sections.

Click **Layout**.

 You can click **Column and Rows** or **Rows and Column** to display three images at a time.

 Click one of the combined row/column layouts.

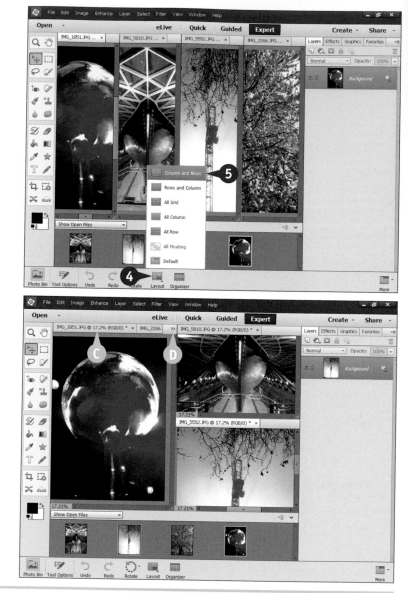

Photoshop Elements displays a split layout.

C You can click the tabs to select the image that appears in each layout area.

D You can click the arrows to see more windows.

TIPS

Why is the All Floating option grayed out?
Select **Edit** ➪ **Preferences** ➪ **General** (**Photoshop Elements** ➪ **Preferences** ➪ **General** on the Mac), and check the **Allow Floating Documents in Expert Mode** box. You can now select the All Floating option and move/float/resize windows independently. This is a good option to use with a large monitor. Note that if you now load files from the Organizer, they ignore the current layout and appear in floating windows.

Can I control how Photoshop Elements arranges tabs in a layout?
No. Photoshop Elements makes its own decisions about how best to distribute the photos in a layout. You cannot prioritize or group the photos differently.

Using the Zoom Tool

You can use the Zoom tool to change the preview magnification. You can zoom in to view/edit fine details or zoom out to see the complete image. You can click the tool to zoom in or out, or you can set an exact zoom by typing a percentage into a box.

Zooming changes the magnification in the Editor preview area. It does not resize the image or add/remove pixels.

Using the Zoom Tool

Increase Magnification

1 In the Editor, click the **Zoom** tool (🔍).

You can also press **Z**.

Note: For more on opening the Editor, see Chapter 1.

2 Click the image.

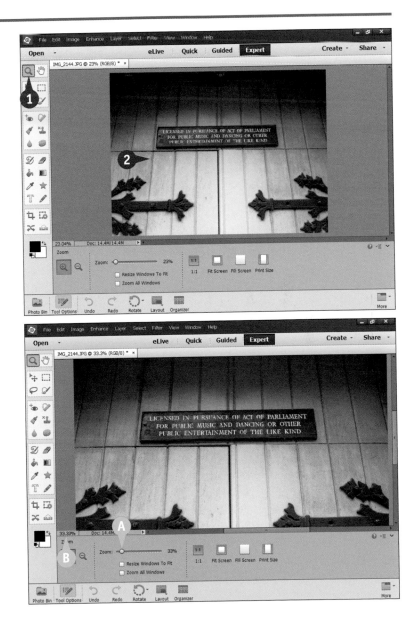

Photoshop Elements increases the magnification of the image. By default, the Zoom tool zooms in when you click the image.

The current magnification shows in the image title bar and the Tool Options panel.

The Tool Options panel is available only in Expert mode.

Ⓐ You can change the zoom by clicking and dragging the slider in the Tool Options panel.

Ⓑ You can change the zoom by clicking the percentage box and typing a new value, followed by **%**, followed by **Enter**.

Decrease Magnification

1 Click the **Zoom Out** button (🔍).

You can also press and hold **Alt** (**Option** on a Mac).

2 Click the image.

Photoshop Elements decreases the magnification of the image.

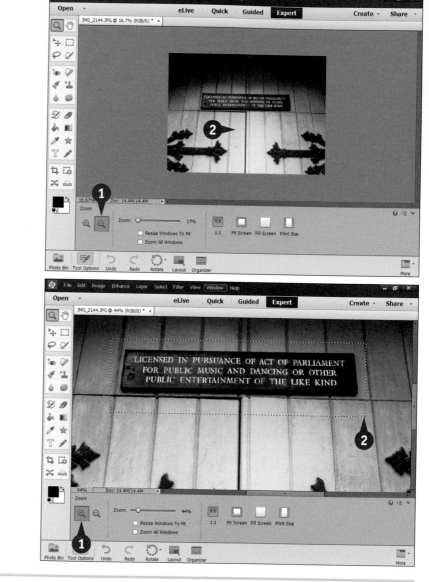

Magnify a Detail

1 Click the **Zoom In** button (🔍).

2 Click and drag with the mouse pointer to select an area.

The area appears magnified.

The more you zoom in, the larger the pixels appear and the less you see of the image's content.

TIPS

What is the quickest way to reset the magnification to 100%?

Double-click the **Zoom** tool. But you may find the Fit Screen option more useful. Click the **Fit Screen** button when the **Zoom** tool options are open. You can also click **Ctrl**+**0** (**⌘**+**0** on a Mac) on the numbers on your keyboard, not on the keypad.

Why do lines and details disappear at different magnifications?

The calculations Photoshop Elements uses to resize the image on the screen have to work very quickly. They are not as sophisticated as the slower math used to stretch or shrink an image when you resize the canvas. If an image has fine lines or text, they can vanish or double in thickness if the zoom factor is not 100%. If this happens in your image, set the zoom to 100% to check if the problem disappears.

Pan the Image

When an image is too big to fit into the Editor preview area, you can use the Hand tool to drag it within the window. You can also use scroll bars to move the image left and right or up and down. This is called *panning* the image.

Use the Hand tool to look at details in an image at high zoom. If you have a small monitor, you must use this tool to pan your images so you can see them with adequate detail.

Pan the Image

Using the Hand Tool

1 In the Editor, click **Expert**.

Note: For more on opening the Editor, see Chapter 1.

2 Click the **Hand** tool (⬚).

You can also press **H**.

Note: The Hand tool works only if the image is magnified and does not fit into the Editor preview area.

3 Click and drag inside the image window.

The view of the image shifts inside the window.

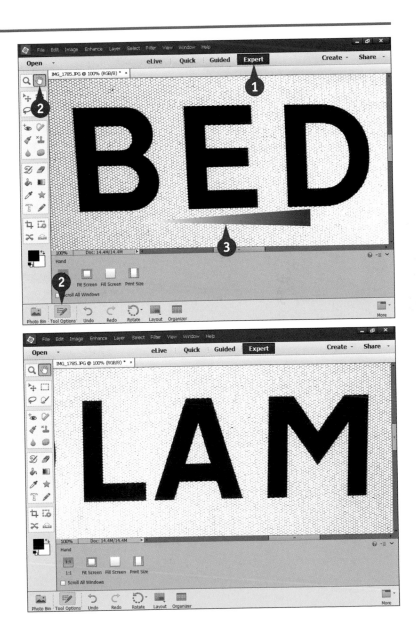

Using the Scroll Bars

1 Click and drag the horizontal scroll bar to move the image left or right.

2 Click and drag the vertical scroll bar to move the image up and down.

Resetting the View

1 Click the Fit Screen button.

Photoshop Elements resets the magnification to fit the entire image into the Editor preview area.

The Hand tool does not work at this magnification. Clicking and dragging has no effect.

TIP

What does the Scroll All Windows check box do?

When you have multiple windows open in a layout, you can select this option to drag all the photos at the same time. If all the windows have the same magnification and the same dimensions, corresponding areas appear in all the windows. This can make it easier to compare the images and copy and paste content between them. If the magnifications are not the same, the photos scroll at different rates.

Change the Canvas Size

You can change the canvas size to crop an image or add a one-color frame — sometimes called a *mat* or *matte (mount* in the U.K.) — around it. Changing the canvas size is like making a photo smaller by cutting off the edges with scissors or making it bigger by gluing card around it. The photo is not stretched or squashed.

Making the canvas smaller than the photo crops it by cutting away the edges. Photoshop Elements warns you when this happens. Making the canvas bigger adds colored space around it. The default color is white, but you can select some other color.

Change the Canvas Size

1 In the Editor, click **Image** ➪ **Resize** ➪ **Canvas Size**.

Note: For more on opening the Editor, see Chapter 1.

The Canvas Size dialog box opens.

A You can see the current photo/canvas dimensions here.

B You can click these menus to change the units of measurement.

C Check this box (☐ changes to ☑) to specify relative instead of absolute dimensions for the new canvas.

Note: In relative mode, you can specify how much you want the dimensions to change; Photoshop Elements works out the new dimensions for you. Negative numbers crop the canvas.

2 Type the new canvas dimensions.

This example uses relative mode to expand the canvas with a three-inch border.

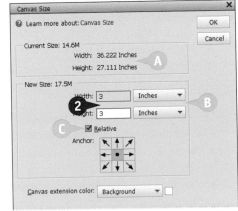

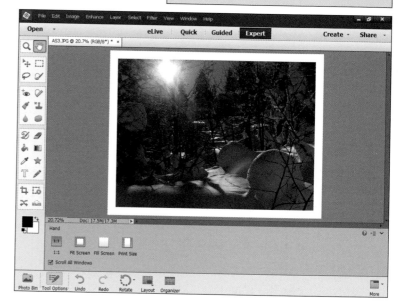

D You can click the arrows in these boxes to move the image after resizing the canvas.

Note: For example, the top-left arrow moves the image to the top left of the canvas: if cropping, this removes the content at the bottom and right of the photo.

Note: If you do not change the default, Photoshop Elements leaves the image in the center of the canvas.

E You can click this color picker to open a color selector and choose a new border color.

Note: This option works only when you increase the canvas size. It does nothing when cropping.

Note: For more about using a color selector, see Chapter 11.

3 Click **OK**.

Note: If you decrease a dimension, Photoshop Elements displays a dialog box asking whether you want to proceed. Click **Proceed**.

Photoshop Elements changes the image's canvas size.

In this example, the canvas is resized to add a symmetrical three-inch border around the image.

TIP

When should I use percentages and dimensions, and relative or absolute changes?
Use absolute dimensions for even borders and percentages to crop without changing the height/width ratio. Use the relative option unless you have a good reason not to, because you can specify an exact offset without working out the exact new size. Note that generally, resizing may not be simple. For example, it can take some math to work out how to fit a photo taken with one aspect ratio onto printer paper with another aspect ratio and leave an even border. Sometimes you need to crop and resize in two steps.

Resize an Image by Resampling

You can *resample* an image to make it bigger or smaller — for example, to save a version of a large photo optimized for a web page or to make a large high-quality print.

Resampling squeezes or stretches the image like a rubber sheet. It also changes the canvas size. Because the image is "pinned" to the corners of the sheet, resampling does not crop the image or add a border. Resampling always loses detail. If you expand or shrink an image by more than a factor of two, sharp features become soft.

Resize an Image by Resampling

1 In the Editor, click **Image** ⇨ **Resize** ⇨ **Image Size**.

Note: For more on opening the Editor, see Chapter 1.

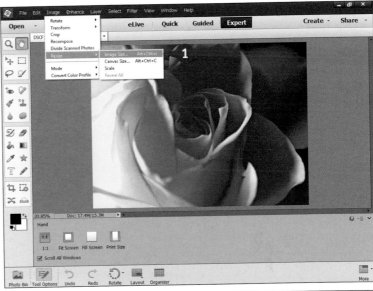

The Image Size dialog box opens.

Ⓐ You can see the current image dimensions here.

Ⓑ You can click these menus to change the width and height units.

2 To resize by a certain percentage, click the menu and select **Percent**.

3 Make sure **Resample Image** is checked (☑).

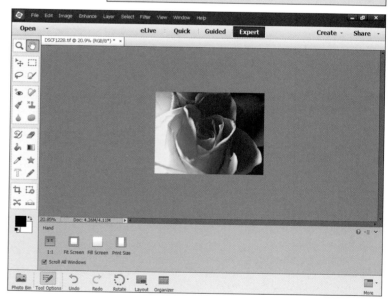

C You can uncheck **Constrain Proportions** (☑ changes to ☐) if you want to stretch the width and height by different amounts.

Note: You can do this, but you do not usually need to.

4 Type a percentage here.

Note: A setting of 50% halves the width and height, and a setting of 200% doubles the width and height.

Note: When **Constrain Proportions** is checked (☑), typing a number into the width box copies it to the height box, and vice versa.

D Photoshop Elements calculates the new dimensions and shows them here.

5 Click **OK**.

Photoshop Elements resizes the image.

In this example, the image is resampled to half its original size.

Note: If you zoom in to magnify the image, you will see that it is less sharp than the original.

TIP

What does the menu at the bottom of the dialog box do?

The menu selects how Photoshop Elements resamples the image. In spite of the text in the menu, the Bicubic Sharper option works well for both enlargement and reduction. The best option depends on photo content. For the best possible results, try all the options and see which looks best — except for Bilinear, which you can usually ignore. Nearest Neighbor works well for whole number ratios such as 25%, 50%, 200%, 300%, and so on, and it is good for text and graphics.

Crop an Image

You can use the Crop tool to remove unwanted content around the edges of an image. Cropping can help you remove clutter. You can also use it to reposition a subject in the photo frame. Note that cropping a photo cuts off content around the sides of the image and shrinks the canvas size.

When use the Crop tool, it suggests possible cropping options. You can accept these suggestions or set up a crop manually.

Crop an Image

1 In the Editor, click **Expert**.

Note: For more on opening the Editor, see Chapter 1.

2 Click the **Crop** tool (🔲).

Crop by Hand

Ⓐ You can click and drag to select a crop area.

Ⓑ Photoshop Elements shows the selected area as you drag.

Ⓒ Photoshop Elements shows the dimensions of the area.

When you release the mouse, the crop preview appears.

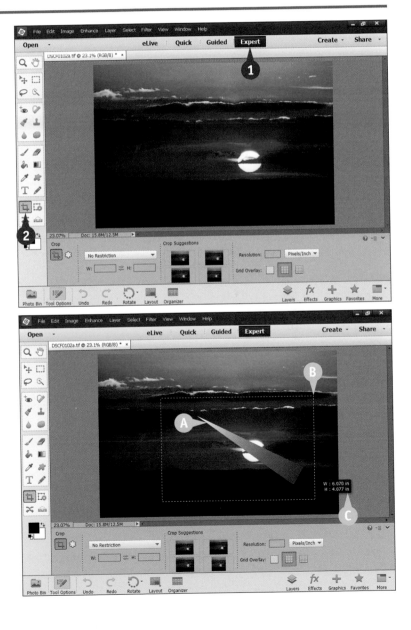

Select a Crop Suggestion

Ⓓ You can click the menu to select an aspect (height/width) ratio for the crop suggestions.

Note: The ratios match popular photo formats and standard print sizes.

Note: You can set a different aspect ratio by typing numbers into the W (Width) and H (Height) boxes.

Ⓔ Click one of the Crop Suggestions to show it in the preview area.

Fine Tune the Crop

Ⓕ You can click and drag the corners of the preview to fine-tune the crop. You can also hover over a corner to rotate the crop.

Ⓖ You can drag the crop area to reposition it on the photo.

Ⓗ You can type a number here to resample the image at the same time as you crop it.

Note: Use the Resample dialog box for better results. See the "Resize an Image by Resampling" section for details.

Ⓘ You can click these buttons to select a different preview grid to help you position and resize the crop.

❸ Click the ✓ to crop the photo.

Photoshop Elements crops the image, shrinking the photo to the boundary you select.

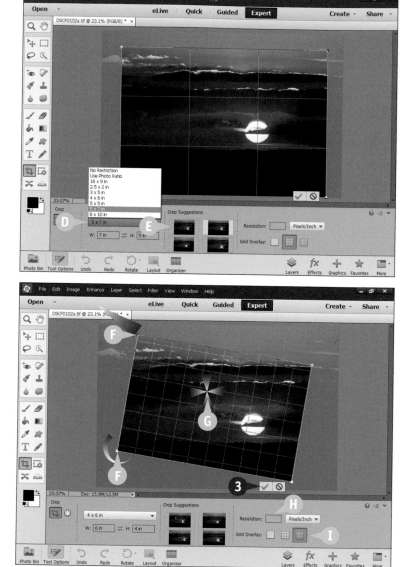

TIP

What does the Cookie Cutter tool do?

Select the Cookie Cutter tool (Ⓐ), and click the menu (Ⓑ) to select a shape. You can now crop your photo to the shape, instead of to a rectangle. You can drag the shape to position it over the photo before you confirm the crop.

Straighten an Image

Y ou can use the Straighten tool to fix a slanted horizon. The Crop tool includes a similar feature, but the Straighten tool is easier to work with. Typically, you straighten an image and then crop it to match an aspect ratio.

To use the tool, select it and draw a line along the horizon or some other horizontal feature in a photo. Note that some photos need extra editing to correct for curves introduced by the lens or perspective distortions such as keystoning, which is described in Chapter 8.

Straighten an Image

1 In the Editor, click **Expert**.

Note: For more on opening the Editor, see Chapter 1.

2 Click the **Straighten** tool (📷).

3 Click the **Remove Background** option.

Note: You can also select **Crop to Original Size** and click the **AutoFill Edges** check box (☐ changes to ☑).

4 Click and drag along a horizon line or other horizontal feature.

Photoshop Elements rotates the image and crops the corners.

If you selected **AutoFill Edges**, Photoshop Elements fills in extra content at the edges to avoid white space.

Note: Some photos have multiple conflicting horizontals and verticals. You may need to try different versions to see which works best.

Rotate an Image

Y ou can use a selection of tools and options to rotate an image. The simplest option rotates your photo by 90 degrees left or right. You can use this tool to correct the orientation of phone camera shots.

You can also use the **Image** ➪ **Rotate** menu to select a range of options. You can rotate an image by 180 degrees, flip it horizontally or vertically, or display a dialog box to rotate an image by any number of degrees.

Rotate an Image

To Rotate or Flip

1 In the Editor, click **Expert**.

Note: For more on opening the Editor, see Chapter 1.

A You can click the Rotate button to rotate an image 90 degrees to the left.

B You can click the menu triangle (▾) next to the Rotate button and select the Rotate Right option to rotate the image 90 degrees to the right.

C You can select **Image** ➪ **Rotate** to select a range of other options.

To Rotate by an Arbitrary Amount

1 Select **Image** ➪ **Rotate** ➪ **Custom.**

2 Type a rotation angle into the dialog box.

3 Use the radio buttons to select left or right rotation.

4 Click **OK.**

Photoshop Elements rotates the image.

Note: Photoshop Elements creates a rectangle in the background color around the rotated image. To remove the corner wedges, use the Crop tool (🔲.)

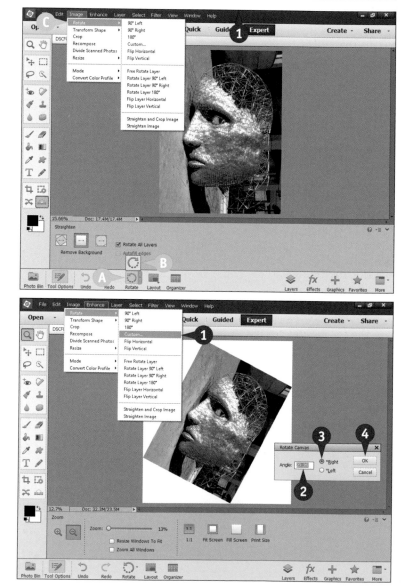

Work in Quick Mode

In Quick mode, you can enhance your photos using a simple interface that includes all the most useful tools. Use the Zoom and Hand tools to see details in your photo, and use the Quick Selection tool to select an area for editing. For more about these and the other tools in the Quick mode toolbar, see Chapters 8, 9, and 11.

Quick Mode includes a selection of quick editing tools in the panel at the right, with one-click presets and useful settings. For finer control, use Expert mode, which is described throughout the rest of this book.

Work in Quick Mode

Pan and Zoom a Photo

1 In the Editor, click **Quick.**

Note: For more on opening the Editor, see Chapter 1.

2 Click the **Zoom** tool (![zoom]).

Note: For more about the Zoom tool, see the section "Magnify with the Zoom Tool."

3 Click and drag a box around an object or detail.

Photoshop Elements zooms the image and enlarges the detail.

A After zooming, you can click the **Hand** tool (![hand]) to move your image within the image window.

Select an Area for Editing

1 Click the **Quick Selection** tool (![quick selection]).

B You can set the brush size by dragging with the Size slider.

2 Click and drag over an object in your image.

For good results, select an object with strong edges and contrasting color against the background.

3 Repeat Step **2** until the entire object is selected.

C Photoshop Elements selects the object.

Note: For more about making selections, see Chapter 6.

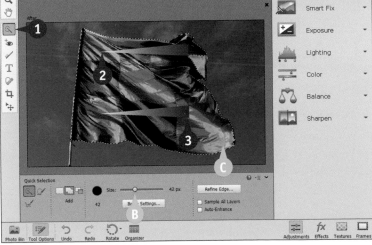

Make an Adjustment

1 Click a tool in the Adjustments panel.

The tool displays settings for adjusting a photo.

A Some tools include a number of tabs. You can click the tabs to select further adjustments.

B You can hover the mouse over a preset preview to see how it changes the image and click the preview to apply the change.

C You can click and drag the slider to make more precise changes.

If you have selected an object, the adjustments change only the object, not the background.

Photoshop Elements applies the changes.

This example uses the Hue slider to shift colors in the selected object.

D You can reset all adjustments and undo the change by clicking the **Reset** button (⬛).

Note: To save your changes, see Chapter 2.

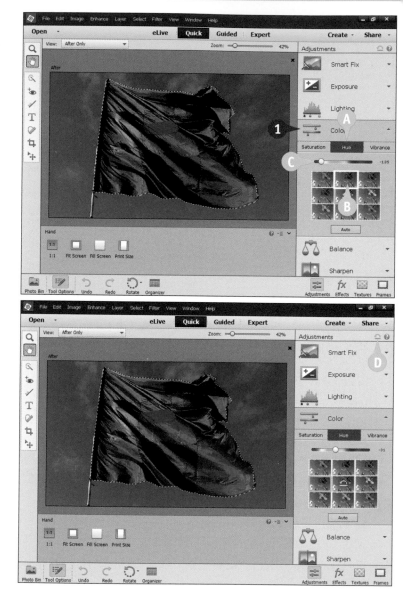

TIP

What do the adjustments do?

Use **Smart Fix** to apply combined one-click edits that improve color, tone, and contrast. **Exposure** makes the image brighter or darker. **Lighting** works like three different **Exposure** adjustments with separate control over shadows, midtones, and highlights. **Color** can shift colors, make them stronger or weaker, or add color punch (vibrance). **Balance** adjusts blue/red and pink/green balance for improving flesh tones and warming the color in portraits. **Sharpen** sharpens details and adds bite to textures.

Apply an Effect in Quick Mode

Y ou can apply a selection of preset effects in Quick mode. The effects change the tone and color of a photo to add atmosphere and character. Similar effects are very popular on social networking sites.

To use the effects, click the Effects panel to see a list of effects. Click an effect to see previews of possible variations. Click a variation to apply it to your photo.

Apply an Effect in Quick Mode

1 In the Editor, click **Quick** to enter Quick mode.

Note: For more on opening the Editor, see Chapter 1.

2 Click **Effects**.

A The Effects panel opens, listing example effects.

3 Click an effect.

B Preset variations appear.

4 Click the variations to see which works best.

Photoshop Elements applies the effect to your image.

C You can remove the effect by clicking the **Reset** button (▣).

Add a Frame in Quick Mode

You can add surrounding decoration to a photo by adding a frame. Quick mode offers a variety of frame styles to add elegance or whimsy to your project.

The frame effects are applied to the image as layers. If you switch to Expert mode and view the Layers panel after adding a frame, you can temporarily turn off the frame by hiding the frame layers. For more about layers, see Chapter 13.

Add a Frame in Quick Mode

1 In the Editor, click **Quick** to enter Quick mode.

Note: For more on opening the Editor, see Chapter 1.

2 Click **Frames**.

The Frames panel opens with a collection of border graphics.

3 Click a frame.

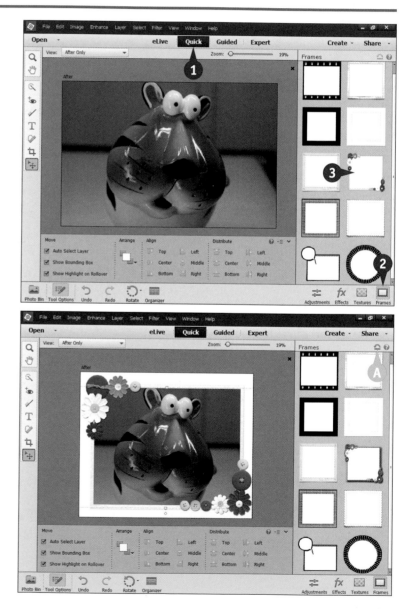

Photoshop Elements applies the frame to your image.

Note: You can drag the photo within the frame to position it. You can also drag the edges to stretch it or shrink it.

 To remove the frame, click the **Reset** button ().

Apply Automatic Enhancements

All of the standard Photoshop Elements enhancement tools are available in Quick mode. The tools have **Auto** versions that can apply easy one-click fixes.

To use the enhancements, click the **Enhance** item in the main menu and select one of the options. This section introduces a couple of the more useful enhancements. The more complex adjustable enhancements are described in later chapters.

Apply Automatic Enhancements

Auto Smart Fix

1. In the Editor, click **Quick.**

Note: For more on opening the Editor, see Chapter 1.

2. Click **Enhance ⇨ Auto Smart Fix.**

Photoshop Elements automatically fixes exposure and color.

Note: To adjust the effect, select **Enhance ⇨ Smart Fix** and drag the slider in the dialog box to modify the result. Click **OK** to apply the enhancement.

Auto Levels

 In the Editor, click **Quick.**

Note: For more on opening the Editor, see Chapter 1.

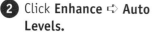 Click **Enhance ⇨ Auto Levels.**

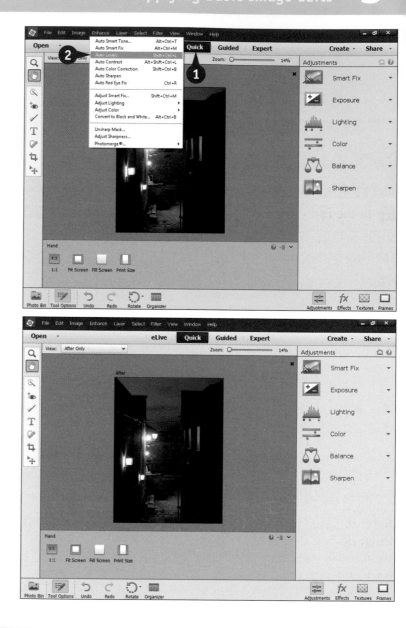

Photoshop Elements adjusts the exposure to make dark areas as dark as possible and bright areas as bright as possible.

Note: Try this tool when Smart Fix makes the midtones too bright and washes out the photo. In this example, the enhancement subtly lifts some of the colors.

Note: To adjust the effect, select **Enhance ⇨ Adjust Lighting ⇨ Levels.** For details, see Chapter 9.

Note: To save your changes, see Chapter 2.

TIP

What do the other enhancements do?

Use **Auto Smart Tone** to adjust brightness and contrast in two dimensions. **Auto Contrast** tries to fix contrast issues. Auto Smart Fix and Auto Levels are more complex effects and better at fixing problems with exposure. **Auto Color Correction** can remove color casts. For details, see Chapter 9. **Auto Sharpen** subtly sharpens the image to bring out the textures. **Auto Red Eye Fix** attempts to fix red eye — the effect that sometimes appears when you take a face-on photo of a model using a flash. It is not as effective as the Red Eye Removal tool in the tool bar (🔲).

Add a Texture

You can use the Quick mode textures to add character to a photo. Photoshop Elements blends the textures with your photos to add depth and atmosphere. Use textures for creative effects. They are not intended for corrective adjustments.

To add a texture, click the Textures button in the toolbar and click a texture to apply it. Different textures work well with different photos. You may need to try them all to find the one that creates the best result.

Add a Texture

1 In the Editor, click **Quick.**

Note: For more on opening the Editor, see Chapter 1.

2 Click **Textures.**

The Textures panel appears.

3 Click a texture to apply it.

Ⓐ Photoshop Elements blends the texture with the photo, changing the color, tone, and mood.

Note: This example warms the original photo, adding more orange and toning down the blue.

4 Click a different texture.

B Photoshop Elements removes the old texture and applies the new one.

TIP

Can I use my own textures?

You cannot add textures to the Textures panel. However, you can use the Layers tools described in Chapter 13 to create your own version of the Texture effect. When you use layers, you can apply any photo as a texture. But you must turn down a setting called *opacity* — which sets transparency — to blend two layers to create the effect. For details, see Chapter 13. Texture and layer blending can create an almost infinite range of creative effects that enhance atmosphere and impact.

Undo Edits

You can undo edits in Photoshop Elements in two ways. The simple option is to type `Ctrl`+`Z` (`⌘`+`Z` on the Mac), click the Undo button in the toolbar, or select **Edit** ⇨ **Undo** in the main menu. This option reverses the last edit. You can repeat it to step back through the last 50 edits.

You can also use **History Window** to see the last 50 edits, displayed as a list. Click any item in the list to return your photo to that edit. You can use this option to skip back over mistakes or to experiment with new edits.

Undo Edits

1 In the Editor, click **Expert**.

Note: For more on opening the Editor, see Chapter 1.

Note: You can use the History window only in Expert mode.

2 Apply a series of edits.

3 Click **Window** ⇨ **History**, or press `F10`.

Ⓐ The History window opens, showing your edits.

4 Click any item in the edit list.

Ⓑ Photoshop Elements restores the photo to that edit state.

Ⓒ Later edits are grayed out to show they are not active.

Ⓓ You can click a later edit to move forward to that state.

Note: If you make a new edit, Photoshop Elements updates the list and deletes any grayed out items because they are no longer available.

Note: You can change the maximum number of edits stored in the list in the Preferences. For details, see Chapter 1.

Revert an Image

I f you do not like your edits, you can **Revert** a photo. This option reloads the file from disk. If you have not saved the file, it restores the original unedited content. If you have already saved the file, it reloads the last saved version.

Revert an Image

1 Open a file in the Editor, and make some changes to it.

Note: For more on opening the Editor, see Chapter 1.

2 Click **Edit** ➪ **Revert**.

Note: You do need to have the History window open to use the revert option. This example includes the History window so you can see its contents.

Note: Revert counts as an edit operation. You can undo it.

Photoshop Elements reloads the image from disk.

A You can click Undo to un-revert the image.

B You can also click an earlier item in the History list.

Note: The History list is available until you close a photo. You can even use it to restore a photo to an edit state before your last save.

Import a RAW Image

I f your camera creates RAW files, you can open them in Photoshop Elements. Loading the file into the Editor displays a special RAW dialog box that you can use to "develop" your photos digitally. Use the dialog box to fine-tune the color and exposure. You can then use the Editor tools to apply more creative effects and to select/copy/paste objects in the image.

The RAW dialog box includes its own version of the Quick mode toolbar and a set of sliders for adjusting color, exposure, and balance. The RAW dialog box works like the Quick mode adjustment pane, with a few differences: There are no one-click previews, there is no hue adjustment, and you can see all the sliders at once.

Import a RAW Image

Explore the RAW Dialog Box

1 In the Organizer, click a RAW file to select it.

Note: If you set up your camera to create RAW files, the Organizer loads them in the usual way and creates a thumbnail when you import files from the camera or a memory card.

2 Click **Editor** to load the RAW dialog box.

Photoshop Elements loads the RAW dialog box instead of the Editor.

A You can click these icons to zoom and pan the image.

Note: The RAW dialog box toolbar is almost identical to the Quick mode toolbar and has similar icons.

B You can click this icon to apply a crop tool to the image.

C You can click this icon to apply a straighten/rotate tool to the image.

D You can click this icon to fix red-eye.

E You can click these icons to rotate the image left or right.

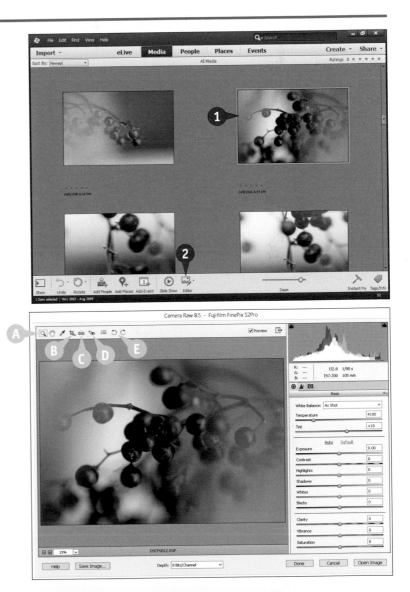

Adjust the White Balance

1 Click the menu, and select **Custom.**

F The color balance of the image changes.

2 Adjust the Temperature slider to set the Blue/Yellow color balance.

3 Adjust the Tint slider to set the Green/Pink color balance.

Note: If you move the Temperature and Tint sliders after selecting a preset, the menu automatically selects **Custom.**

Note: If the **Custom** option does not improve for your image, try the other menu items in order until you find a preset that does.

Adjust the Color

1 Move the **Clarity** slider to the left to blur colors and to the right to bring out color detail.

2 Move the **Saturation** slider to the left to remove color and to the right to make it more intense.

Note: This slider does not create grainy and noisy over-saturated colors produced by saturation adjustments in the Editor.

3 Adjust the **Vibrance** slider to adjust color contrast.

Note: You may want to fine-tune the Temperature and Tint sliders slightly after these steps to further correct the color.

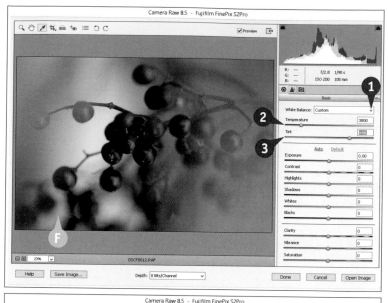

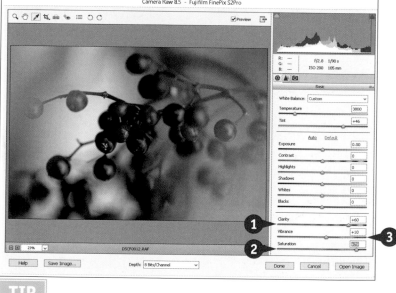

TIP

How should I set all the color sliders?

Start by using the White Balance menu and the Temperature and Tint sliders to find a color combination you like. Then use the Clarity, Saturation, and Vibrance sliders, in that order, to fine-tune the colors. You can work with the RAW dialog box to create different versions of the same photo. Use trial and error to explore the many different effects and styles that are possible.

continued ▶

The RAW dialog box includes comprehensive control over exposure, tone, and contrast. Use the Exposure and Contrast sliders to make changes across the image. Use the Highlights and Whites sliders to set the exposure of brighter areas, and use the Shadows and Blacks to do the same for darker areas.

When you use the RAW dialog box, it automatically saves the dialog box settings with the RAW file. Click **Done** to save the settings, and click **Open Image** to save settings and open the image in the Editor. Click **Save Image** to save settings to a new file. You can create as many versions as you want.

Import a RAW Image (continued)

Adjust Exposure and Contrast

1 Adjust the **Exposure** slider to make the photo brighter or darker.

2 Adjust **Contrast** to add or remove contrast.

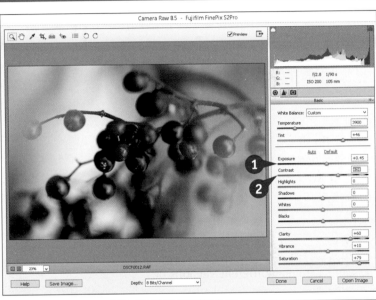

Adjust Highlights and Shadows

1 Adjust the **Highlights** slider to bring out brighter areas.

2 Adjust the **Shadows** slider to add light to darker areas.

Note: Drag **Shadows** to the right to lighten darker areas and to the left to darken them.

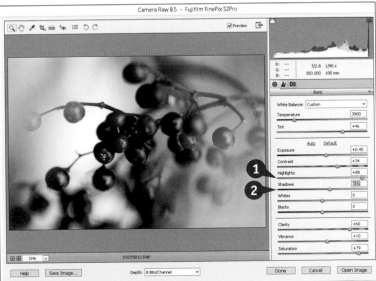

Adjust Whites and Blacks

 1 Adjust the **Whites** slider to bring out brighter areas.

2 Adjust the **Blacks** slider to add light to darker areas.

Note: As a guideline, Highlights brightens whiter areas, while Whites expands the contrast in brighter areas. Similarly, **Shadows** darkens dark areas, and **Blacks** expands the contrast.

Note: This explanation is a rough guideline. The details are complex and outside the scope of this book. For an intuitive understanding, experiment on a selection of photos.

Save and/or Open the Image

A Click **Save Image. . .** to copy the file and save it with the current RAW settings.

Note: Photoshop Elements saves the file with a DNG (Digital Negative) extension and adds a thumbnail to the Organizer. You can save many different versions of the same file.

B Click **Done** to write the dialog box settings to the RAW file and close the dialog box.

Note: This option updates the RAW file and the thumbnail, but it does not save a new version.

C Click **Open Image** to save the settings and also open the image in the Editor.

Photoshop Elements "develops" the RAW file using your settings, with improved color, exposure, contrast, and overall impact.

TIP

When should I use RAW files?

RAW files are useful for creative, professional, and artistic photography. They include more detail, but they take up more space on disk and memory card. As a guide, if you are taking snaps, you can use standard TIFF, PNG, and JPEG files. If you want to experiment with creative effects and do not mind taking extra time to "develop" every image you shoot, use RAW files.

Making Selections

Do you want to edit some parts of an image but leave other parts unchanged? You need to make a selection. This chapter explains how you can use the selection tools in Photoshop Elements to select objects, areas, shapes, colors, and other useful photo features. You can even save selections and reload them later.

Select an Area with the Marquee

You can select parts of an image for editing by using the *marquee* — a tool that creates selections using simple shapes. After selecting an area, you can edit it with the editing tools built into Photoshop Elements.

Two marquee shapes are available. Use the Rectangular Marquee to select rectangular areas, including squares. Use the Elliptical Marquee to select elliptical areas, including circles. To use either tool, select Expert Mode, select the tool, and click and drag diagonally in the image to define the area. You can use the Tool Options panel to set the dimensions or width/height ratio.

Select an Area with the Marquee

Select with the Rectangular Marquee

1 In the Editor, click **Expert**.

Note: For more on opening the Editor, see Chapter 1.

2 Click the **Rectangular Marquee** tool (▣).

Note: This tool shares a space with the Elliptical Marquee tool (▣.) If the wrong tool is visible, press Ⓜ.

3 Click and drag diagonally inside the image window.

You can press and hold Shift while you click and drag to create a square selection.

A Photoshop Elements shows the dimensions of the area as you drag.

B Photoshop Elements selects a rectangular portion of your image.

You can reposition the selection by pressing the arrow keys: ⬇, ⬅, ⬆, ➡. You can also click and drag inside the selection while a marquee tool is active.

You can deselect a selection by clicking **Select** ⇨ **Deselect**, pressing Ctrl+D (⌘+D on a Mac), or by clicking outside the selection area.

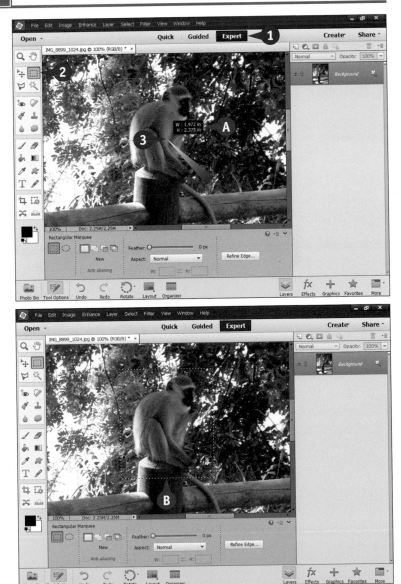

Select with the Elliptical Marquee

1 Click the **Elliptical Marquee** tool ().

Note: Pressing **M** toggles between the Elliptical and Rectangular Marquee tools when either is selected.

2 If the Tool Options panel is not open, click here to open it.

3 Click and drag diagonally inside the image window.

You can press and hold **Shift** while you click and drag to create a circular selection, or you can press and hold **Shift** + **Alt** (**Shift** + **Option** on a Mac) to expand the circle from the center.

4 You can reposition the selection by pressing the arrow keys: **⬇**, **⬅**, **⬆**, **➡**. You can also click and drag inside the selection while a marquee tool is active.

Note: You often need to reposition circular/elliptical selections.

Photoshop Elements selects an elliptical portion of your image.

You can deselect a selection by clicking **Select ➪ Deselect**, pressing **Ctrl** + **D** (**⌘** + **D** on a Mac), or by clicking outside the selection area.

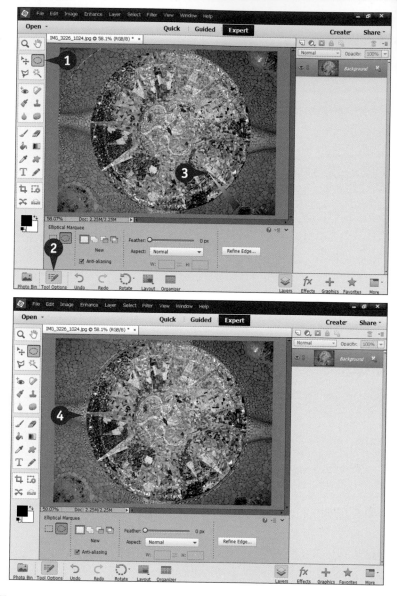

TIP

How do I customize the marquee tools?

You can customize the marquee tools by using the boxes and menus in the Tool Options panel.

- **Feather:** Moving the slider softens the edges of the selection when you apply an edit.
- **Aspect:** Selecting an option from the Mode list defines the operation of the marquee tool as Normal (no restrictions), Fixed Ratio, or a Fixed Size.
- **Width and Height:** Select **Fixed** Size in the Aspect menu, then type values into the W (width) and H (weight) boxes to set the height and width of your selection in pixels or other dimensions.

Select an Area with the Lasso

You can use the Lasso tools to select areas with irregular outlines. Use the Regular Lasso to draw a selection area with the mouse. Use the Polygonal Lasso to select an area using line segments. Both Lasso types require a steady hand and plenty of concentration.

You can use the Magnetic Lasso to select edges automatically. It includes some simple intelligence that guesses where the selection should go, based on the colors and textures near the mouse cursor. This makes it easier to use than the other Lasso tools. But it is not as useful for challenging irregular selections.

Select an Area with the Lasso

Select with the Regular Lasso

1 In the Editor, click **Expert**.

Note: For more on opening the Editor, see Chapter 1.

2 Click the **Lasso** tool ().

Note: This tool shares space with the Polygonal Lasso () and the Magnetic Lasso (). If the wrong tool is visible, press L until it appears.

3 Click and drag with your mouse pointer to make a selection.

Note: You may need to make a number of attempts before you get a clean selection.

Note: To accurately trace a complicated edge, you can zoom in to the image with the Zoom tool (). See Chapter 5 for more on the Zoom tool.

4 Drag to the beginning point, and then release the mouse button.

Photoshop Elements completes the selection.

Note: If you release the mouse button before completing the selection, Photoshop Elements completes the selection for you with a straight line.

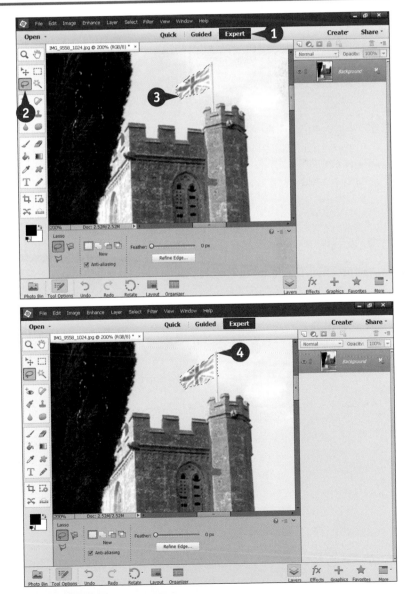

Select with the Polygonal Lasso

1 Click the **Polygonal Lasso** tool (🔲).

Note: This tool shares space with the Lasso (🔲) and the Magnetic Lasso (🔲). If the wrong tool is visible, press **L** until it appears.

2 Click multiple times along the border of the area you want to select.

Note: This example creates a selection inside the edges of a wall panel so you can see the tool working. Typically, you click around the visible edges of an object.

3 To complete the selection, click the starting point.

You can also double-click anywhere in the image.

Photoshop Elements adds a final straight line that connects to the starting point.

Photoshop Elements completes the selection.

TIPS

How do I select all the pixels in my image?
For a single-layer image, you can use the Select All command to select everything in your image. Click **Select** ⇨ **All**. You can also press **Ctrl**+**A** (**⌘**+**A** on a Mac). Note that you must select all pixels before you can copy an image. You do not need to select all pixels before adjusting or editing the image.

What if my selection is not as precise as I want it to be?
Drawing selections with a mouse is difficult. You can try again by clicking **Select** and then **Deselect**. Or you can switch to the Magnetic Lasso tool (🔲). You can also add to a selection or subtract an area from it. For details, see Chapter 7. Professional artists often use a *graphics tablet* — a device with a virtual pen that is easier to draw with than a mouse.

continued ▶

You can quickly and easily select elements of your image that have well-defined edges by using the Magnetic Lasso tool. The Magnetic Lasso looks for contrast to find edges. A building set against a clear sky works well. A gray building against a gray sky of similar brightness does not.

As you drag the Magnetic Lasso along an edge, Photoshop Elements places *anchor points* along the edge that fix the selection outline. The selection is made of the lines that join the anchor points. You can press Backspace (Delete on a Mac) to remove unwanted anchor points as you draw the selection.

Select an Area with the Lasso (continued)

Select with the Magnetic Lasso

1 Click the **Magnetic Lasso** tool ( ).

Note: This tool shares a space with the Lasso ( ) and the Polygonal Lasso ( ). If the wrong tool is visible, press L until it appears.

2 If the Tool Options panel is not open, click here to open it.

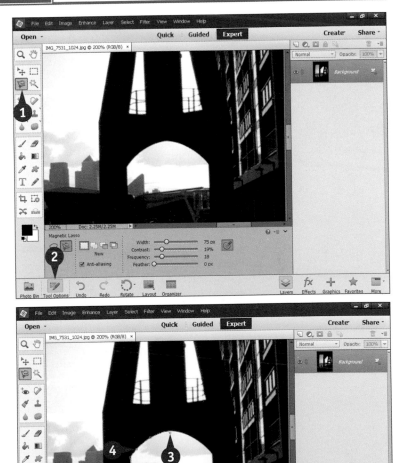

3 Click the edge of the object you want to select.

This creates the first anchor point on the lasso path.

4 Drag your mouse pointer along the edge of the object.

The Magnetic Lasso's path snaps to the edge of the object as you drag.

5 To help guide the lasso, you can click to add anchor points as you go along the path.

Note: For good results, add a point at every corner.

130

6 Keep following the edge of the object or area, adding points until you get close to the first anchor point.

7 Double-click to complete the selection with a straight line to the first anchor point.

Note: You can also click the first anchor point.

The path is complete, and the object is selected.

Note: Even though the Magnetic Lasso is easier to use than the other lasso tools, you usually still need to fine-tune the selection. For details see Chapter 7.

Adjust the Precision of the Magnetic Lasso Tool

You can adjust the Magnetic Lasso tool's precision with different settings.

Note: Adjust the settings before using the tool.

A Width sets the width of the area the tool looks at when finding edges.

B Contrast sets the minimum contrast needed to find an edge.

C Frequency determines how often anchor points appear.

D The Feather setting softens the selection edges.

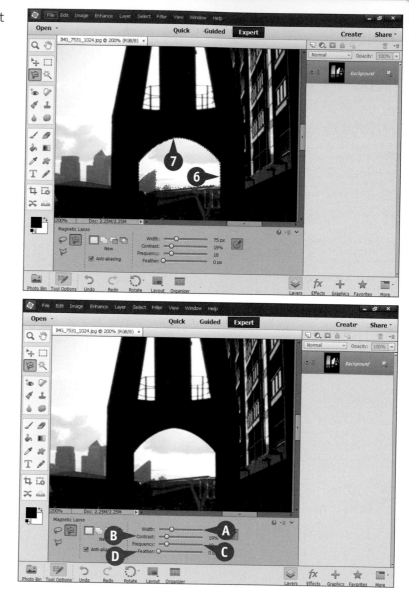

TIP

How can I get a more accurate selection?

When using the Magnetic Lasso, adjust the precision carefully. The contrast and width settings are critical, and small changes can have a big effect. However, you can also add and remove areas from an existing selection. If you "sculpt" the selection in stages, you do not have to worry about getting it right first time, and you can make extremely precise selections that do not rely on luck and a steady mouse. For details see Chapter 7.

Select an Area with the Magic Wand

You can use the Magic Wand tool to automatically select areas with a similar color. You may find this useful if you want to remove an object from a background. This tool is especially good at making selections in photos that feature the sky, the sea, a lawn, or sand on a beach.

You can control the accuracy of the selection by setting a *tolerance* value, from 0 to 255. Smaller numbers force Photoshop Elements to select a smaller range colors. Larger numbers select an area with a wider range of colors. You need to experiment with the tolerance to get the area you want. Different photos and selection areas often need different values.

Select an Area with the Magic Wand

1 Click the **Magic Wand** tool (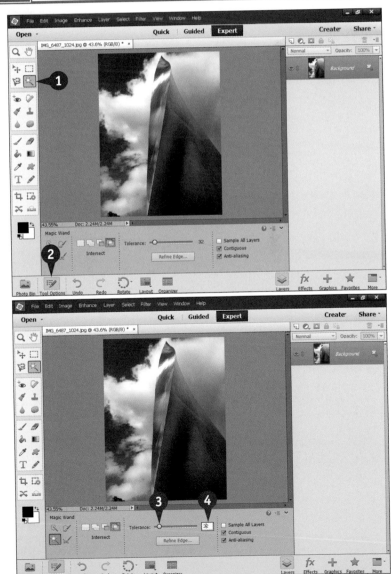).

Note: This tool shares a space with three other tools. (, , .) If the wrong tool is visible, press **A**.

2 If the Tool Options panel is not open, click here to open it.

3 Optionally, click and drag the **Tolerance** slider to select a value from 0 to 255.

4 You can also click the value and type a number. The default value of 32 often produces good results.

To select a narrow range of colors, select or enter a small number; for less precision, select or enter a large number.

5 Click the area you want to select inside the image.

Ⓐ Photoshop Elements selects the pixel you clicked and all the pixels with similar colors around it.

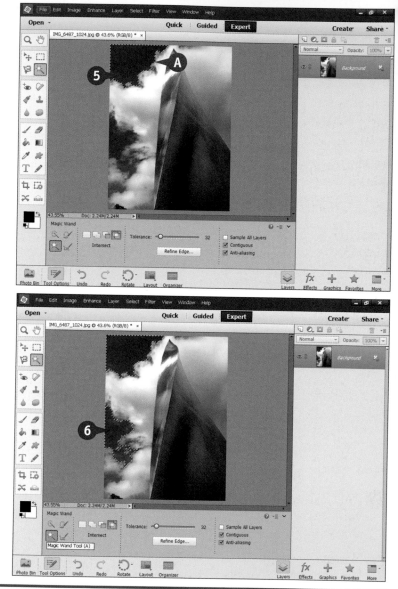

6 To add to your selection, press **Shift** and click elsewhere in the image.

Photoshop Elements adds to your selection. The new selection does not have to connect with the previous area.

Note: You do not have to select the same colors every time you click. For example, you can build up a selection from similar colors at different brightness levels.

Note: For more details on editing selections, see Chapter 7.

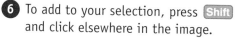

TIPS

How can I select the same color across an image?

You can deselect **Contiguous** (☑ changes to ☐) in the Tool Options panel to make the Magic Wand tool find all similar colors in the image, even if they are not close to each other or part of a linked area. This can be useful when objects are in front of the area you are trying to select.

What is anti-aliasing?

If you leave the anti-aliasing option selected, Photoshop Elements applies some subtle smoothing to the edges of the selection. This helps avoid jagged edges when the selection edge changes by whole pixels. For most applications, leave anti-aliasing on. If you want to make the edges of a selection look crisp or rough as a special effect, deselect it.

Select an Area with the Quick Selection Tool

Y ou can paint selections onto your images with the Quick Selection tool. The tool is "smart." It looks for areas of similar color and expands the selection to the edges around them. If your image has areas of contrasting color with clean edges, the Quick Selection tool can make accurate selections with very little effort.

You can control the size of the tool and the softness of the selection edges. Start by using a large brush to "paint" an area. You can then use a "subtract" mode to remove unwanted areas with a smaller brush. You can also select an "add" mode to add further new areas.

Select an Area with the Quick Selection Tool

1 Click the **Quick Selection** tool (🖊).

Note: This tool shares a space with three other tools. (🖊, 🖊, 🖊.) If the wrong tool is visible, press Ⓐ.

2 If the Tool Options panel is not open, click here to open it.

3 Drag the slider to set the brush size. Start with a brush around a quarter to half the size of your object.

4 Click and drag inside the object you want to select.

Ⓐ Photoshop Elements selects parts of the object based on its coloring and the contrast of its edges.

Ⓑ After you make a selection, you can select the Add to Selection button (▣) or the Subtract from Selection button (▣) to fine-tune the selection.

❺ Select a smaller brush size for finer control.

❻ Click and drag to "sculpt" your selection, adding and removing further areas as needed.

Photoshop Elements modifies the selection.

Note: This example removes the green foliage from the poppy.

Note: The Quick Selection tool is also available in Quick mode.

TIP

What do the Brush Settings do?

To work with the brush settings, click the **Brush Settings** button. Decrease the **Hardness** slider setting to blur the edges of the selection. When you apply an edit to a selection, the effect or filter fades in at the edges of the selection. Increase **Spacing** when selecting an object with jagged edges. Decrease **Roundness** to make the brush more elliptical. You can set the angle by dragging in the **Angle** box. If you have a graphics tablet or a wheel/touch mouse, you can use the **Pen Pressure** menu to set up your device so you can change the size of the brush with stylus pressure or with the mouse wheel.

Select an Area with the Selection Brush

With the Selection Brush, you can select areas by painting them with the mouse. This brush is not "smart." It follows your mouse movements but does not look for edges or colors. Use this brush when you need to select an area that has similar color and contrast to the areas around it.

Like the Quick Selection tool, you can modify a selection by selecting add or subtract modes and painting again. You can also set the size and hardness of the brush. Typically, you paint with a large brush to sketch the selection and then fine-tune it with smaller brushes, adding or subtracting smaller areas.

Select an Area with the Selection Brush

Select with the Selection Brush

1 Click the **Selection Brush** tool (⬚).

Note: This tool shares a space with three other tools. (⬚, ⬚, ⬚.) If the wrong tool is visible press Ⓐ.

2 If the Tool Options panel is not open, click here to open it.

Note: You can use the zoom tool (🔍) to zoom in to the image to make it easier to make a clean selection.

3 Drag the slider to set the brush size. Start with a size about a quarter the size of your object.

4 Drag the slider to set the hardness. Use 75% to 100% unless you need soft borders around an edit.

5 Click and drag inside the object you want to select.

Ⓐ Photoshop Elements selects the areas you paint.

Note: This example selects the thumb area in the image; it has no contrast or color differences with the palm it is attached to.

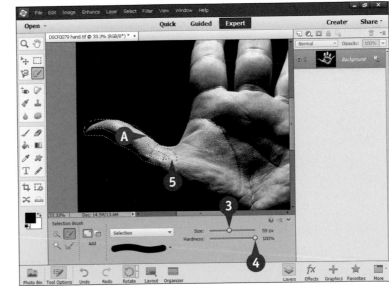

136

B After you make a selection, you can select the Add to Selection button (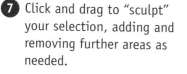) or the Subtract from Selection button (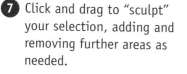) to fine-tune the selection.

6 Select a smaller brush size for finer control.

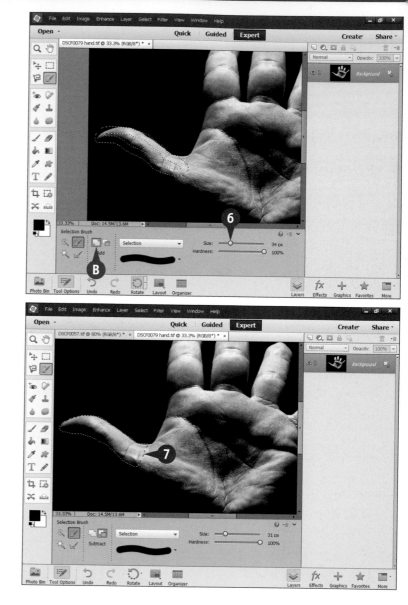

7 Click and drag to "sculpt" your selection, adding and removing further areas as needed.

Note: Typically you outline the area you want to select by drawing around its edges, then fill in the center, and then fix the edges.

Photoshop Elements modifies the selection.

TIP

What does the "wavy line" menu do?

You can use this menu to select various brush presets, with a range of ready-made sizes and hardness values. You can also paint a selection with textures, including stars and grainy paint-like lines. The textures are included because this brush tool uses the standard brushes bundled with Photoshop Elements. Textured selections are a special effect, but can be useful in photo-edited art. For more about painting and drawing with the standard brushes, see Chapter 11.

Save and Load a Selection

You can save a selected area in your image to reuse later. If you make a selection and save the file as a Photoshop file, the selection is stored with the file and is available when you reopen the file. See Chapter 16 for more about saving image files.

You can save more than one selection and give each one a different name. The selections are tied to a single image. You cannot use this option to copy selections between images. However, you can reload any saved selection for any one image with **Select** ➪ **Load Selection.**

Save and Load a Selection

Save a Selection

1 Make a selection by using one or more of the selection tools.

2 Click **Select** ➪ **Save Selection**.

The Save Selection dialog box opens.

3 Make sure New is chosen in the Selection field.

4 Type a name for the selection.

Note: You can reuse the same names in different images. Photoshop Elements does not get them confused.

5 Click **OK**.

Photoshop Elements saves the selection.

Load a Selection

1 Click **Select** ➪ **Load Selection**.

The Load Selection dialog box opens.

2 Click the Selection menu.

3 Choose the saved selection you want to load.

4 Click **OK**.

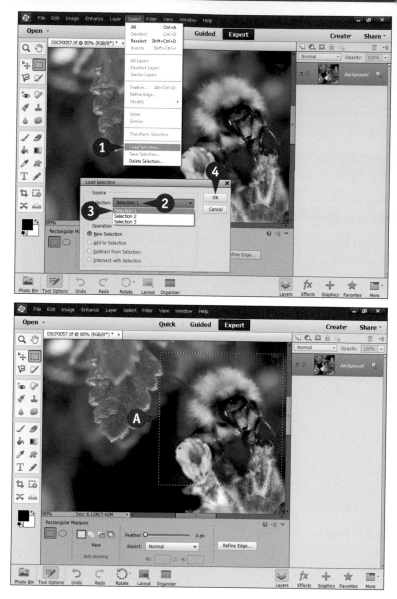

A The selection appears in the image.

TIPS

What do the Operation radio buttons do?

Instead of reloading a selection, you can use it to modify a selection you have already made in your image. Use the **Add to Selection** option to combine the current and saved selections. Use the **Subtract from Selection** option to remove the saved selection from the current selection. Use the Intersect with Selection to select only the overlapping areas between the current and saved selection.

Why do I lose all my saved selections when I close the image?

You must save the file as a PSD (Photoshop file) to save and load selections. If you save a file in any other format, Photoshop Elements forgets your selections.

Invert a Selection

You can use the Invert Selection option to select the background around an object instead of the object itself. Inverting a selection deselects the area inside it and selects the area around it — all the way to the edges of the photo. You can now edit the background selectively.

The inverted selection has the same properties as your initial selection, but it's a "negative" of it. For example, if you have *feathered* a selection to soften its edges, the inverted selection also has soft edges. For more information about feathering and modifying selections, see Chapter 7.

Invert a Selection

1 Make a selection by using one of the selection tools.

Note: For more on the various selection tools, see the previous sections in this chapter. For more on opening the Editor, see Chapter 1.

2 Click **Select** ➪ **Inverse**.

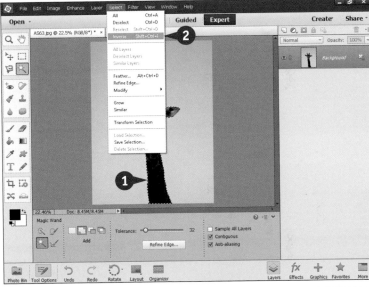

A Photoshop Elements inverts the selection.

Note: You can also press Shift + Ctrl + I (Shift + ⌘ + I on a Mac) to invert a selection.

Note: If you have an object against a plain background such as the sky, you can use the Magic Wand tool (⬚) to select the background and then invert the selection to select the object.

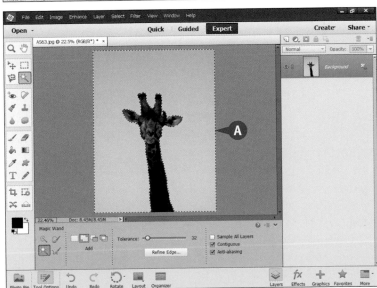

Deselect a Selection

You can deselect a selection when you have finished editing your image or if you decide that a selection is not necessary. When you deselect an image, the "marching ants" outline around the selection disappears. If you make further edits, Photoshop Elements applies them to the entire image.

If you deselect an area by accident, select **Edit** ➪ **Undo.** Photoshop Elements restores your selection.

Deselect a Selection

1 Make a selection using any of the selection tools.

2 Click **Select** ➪ **Deselect**.

Photoshop Elements deselects the selection.

Note: You can also press Shift + Ctrl + D (Shift + ⌘ + D on a Mac) to invert a selection.

Manipulating Selections

Making a selection in Photoshop Elements isolates a specific area of your image. This chapter shows you how to move, stretch, erase, and work with a selection. You can use these selection techniques to rearrange people and objects in your image, enlarge elements to make them stand out, or delete them altogether.

Add to or Subtract from a Selection

You can make your selection bigger or smaller without having to reselect it from scratch. You can add to a selection to combine more than one selected area. You can subtract from a selection to remove an area. If you zoom in, use a small selection brush, and take your time, you can create a very accurate selection area.

Most of the selection tools in Photoshop Elements have add and subtract settings in the Tool Options panel. You can also create a selection using one tool, and add or subtract an area selected by another. See Chapter 6 for an introduction to the different selection tools you can use.

Add to or Subtract from a Selection

Add to Your Selection

① In the Editor, click **Expert**.

Note: For more on opening the Editor, see Chapter 1.

② Make a selection with any selection tool.

This example uses the Magic Wand tool ().

③ Either continue with the same selection tool, or click a different tool to select it.

④ Click the **Add to Selection** button (▣).

⑤ Select the area you want to add.

This example uses the Selection Edit Brush (▣) to expand the selection area.

Photoshop Elements adds to the selection.

You can enlarge the selection further by repeating steps **3** to **5**.

You can also add to a selection by pressing **Shift** as you select an area.

Subtract from Your Selection

1 Make a selection with a selection tool.

This example uses the Magic Wand tool ().

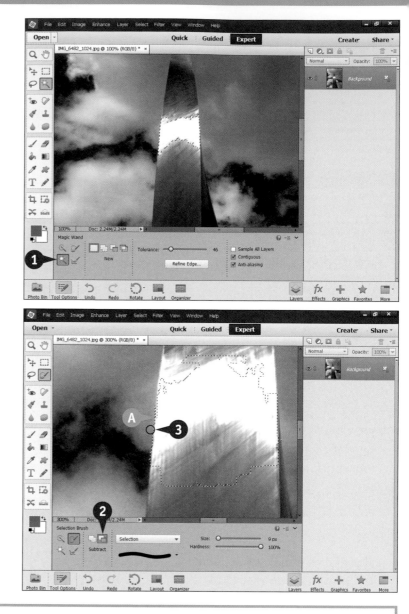

2 Click the **Subtract from Selection** button (⊟).

3 Select the area you want to subtract.

This example uses the Selection Brush (⬚) to paint a small selection area.

A Photoshop Elements deselects (subtracts) the selected area.

You can subtract other parts of the selection by repeating steps **2** and **3**.

You can also subtract from a selection by pressing **Alt** (**Option** on a Mac) as you select an area.

TIPS

What is an intersection?
An intersection is the area where two selections overlap, excluding the original areas. For example, when two rectangles overlap, the intersection creates a smaller rectangle. You can create an intersection by clicking the **Intersect with Selection** button (⊡) in the Tool Options panel before selecting a new area. This selects the overlap between the old and new areas.

Can I move the selection marquee without moving the item selected?
Yes. Use any of the selection tools to select an area and then press an arrow key — ⬅, ➡, ⬆, ⬇ — to move the selection in 1-pixel increments. Press and hold **Shift** while pressing an arrow key to move the selection in 10-pixel increments.

145

Move a Selection

You can move a selection to a different part of your photo. If you select areas carefully, you can use the Move tool to recompose your photo, putting features into different — better — places.

By default, Photoshop Elements keeps pixels in a *background layer* — the original photo. If you use the Move tool on the background layer, the tool leaves a gap and Photoshop Elements fills the gap with the background color. If you move an area to some another layer, Photoshop Elements fills the gap with transparent pixels. For more about making and using layers, see Chapter 13.

Move a Selection

1 In the Editor, click **Expert**.

2 Make a selection.

This example uses the Rectangular Marquee tool ().

Note: For more on selecting elements, see Chapter 6.

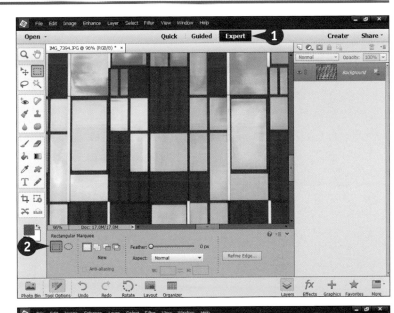

3 Click the **Move** tool (⊕).

A Photoshop Elements adds handles to the selection to show you can move or edit the selection.

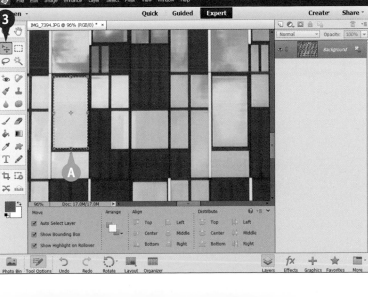

④ Click inside the selection, and then drag.

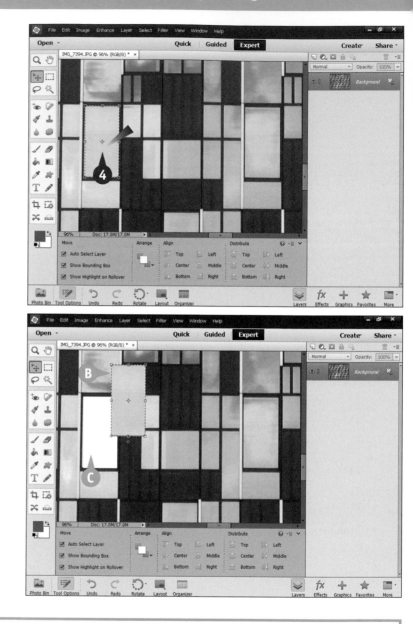

Ⓑ Photoshop Elements moves the selection and fills the original location with the current background color (Ⓒ).

If you press **Alt** (**Option** on a Mac) while you drag, Photoshop Elements creates a copy of the selection and moves it instead of the original area.

TIPS

How do I move a selection in a straight line?

Press and hold **Shift** while you drag with the Move tool (⊕). This fixes the movement to one dimension. You can now move the selection horizontally, vertically, or diagonally, depending on the direction you drag.

Why would I copy an area to a layer?

You can use layers to keep different elements in a photo separate and make them visible/invisible with a single click. You can also move layers without changing the background. So layers are ideal for assembling a photo composition out of different elements. If you save and load a file with layers, you can continue working with them in a later session.

Apply the Content-Aware Move Tool

You can use the Content-Aware Move Tool to move a selected area. Unlike other move tools, the Content-Aware Tool is smart. Instead of leaving a gap or filling the original location of the object with a solid color, it fills it automatically with surrounding colors and textures.

Although the tool is smart, it is not miraculous. For good results, use it with objects surrounded by simple colors and textures.

Apply the Content-Aware Move Tool

1 In the Editor, click **Expert**.

Note: For more on opening the Editor, see Chapter 1.

2 Click the **Content-Aware Move** tool (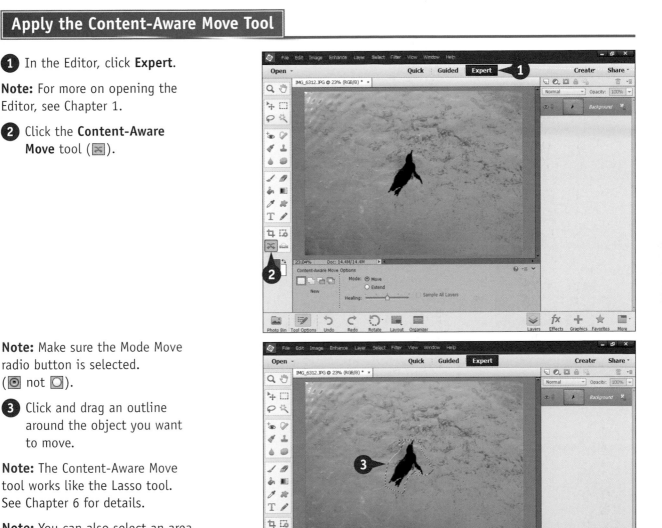).

Note: Make sure the Mode Move radio button is selected. (◉ not ○).

3 Click and drag an outline around the object you want to move.

Note: The Content-Aware Move tool works like the Lasso tool. See Chapter 6 for details.

Note: You can also select an area with any other selection tool and then click the Content-Aware Move tool to move it.

④ Click inside the selection, and drag it to another location in your image.

Ⓐ Photoshop Elements displays the distance moved in the current selected units.

⑤ Release the mouse button.

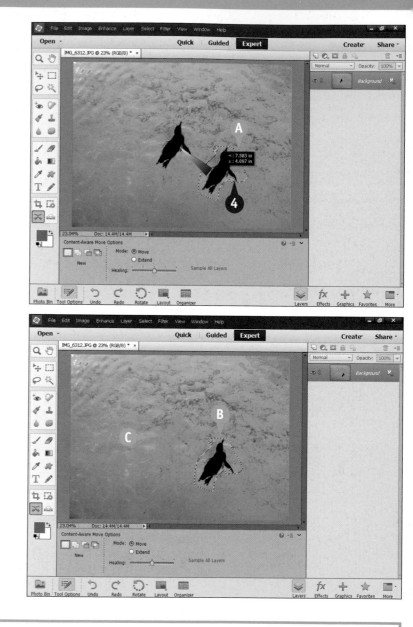

Ⓑ Photoshop Elements copies the object to the new location.

Ⓒ The original location is filled with surrounding content.

Note: The object stays selected, so you can copy it again.

TIPS

How can I extend an object in my image?
You can use the Content-Aware Move tool to extend objects such as buildings and fences. With the Content-Aware Move tool (⊠) selected, click the Extend radio button. Select an object, click and drag the selection, and then release the mouse button. Photoshop Elements extends the object. It adjusts colors and textures automatically, based on the content near the selection.

How can I get better results?
For good results, try to move your object to an area with very similar colors and textures. The tool cannot fix large differences. Smaller objects give better results than large objects.

Hide Flaws by Duplicating Selections

Y ou can copy a selection and paste a selection to cover flaws and blemishes. For good results, duplicate the source to an area with matching colors and textures. Use many small areas instead of one big area. If you use the Move tool without copying a selection, Photoshop Elements automatically pastes the area back into the background layer.

You can also use the Copy and Paste commands to create new layers. If you select a layer, you can experiment with different positions without changing the background. You can also filter it, edit it, or use of any other editing tool, without changing the original background layer. For more about layers, see Chapter 13.

Hide Flaws by Duplicating Selections

1 In the Editor, click **Expert**.

2 Make a selection with a selection tool.

Note: For more on opening the Editor, see Chapter 1. For more on using selection tools, see Chapter 6.

3 Select **Copy** in the Edit menu.

4 Select **Paste** to paste the selection to a new layer (Ⓐ).

Note: You can also press Ctrl+J (⌘+J on a Mac).

5 Click the **Move** tool (⊞).

6 Drag the layer to a location that hides a blemish. (The layer is not highlighted, but you can see it as you move it.)

Note: You can repeat steps **2** to **6** with another area. Select the Background layer from the list at the right before starting from Step **2**.

Note: This example creates two duplicates to hide an unwanted feature on the rear wall.

Note: Optionally, choose Select Layer ⇨ Flatten Image to merge the layers back into the background.

Delete a Selection

You can delete a selection to remove unwanted features from an image. By default, Photoshop Elements fills the deleted area with the background color. This is rarely useful, except for very obvious special effects or for editing scanned text. For more about setting the background color, see Chapter 11.

If you delete a selection in any other layer, Photoshop Elements removes the pixels and leaves a transparent hole. Layers under the hole show through. This is more useful. You can "sculpt" the layer until it is the right size and shape, without changing the background. For more about working with layers, see Chapter 13.

Delete a Selection

1 In the Editor, click **Expert**.

2 Make a selection with a selection tool.

Note: This example uses the Rectangular Marquee tool. (.)

Note: For more on opening the Editor, see Chapter 1. For more on using selection tools, see Chapter 6.

3 Press **Delete**.

Ⓐ Photoshop Elements deletes the contents of the selection.

Ⓑ If you are working in the Background layer, the original location fills with the background color — in this example, white.

If you are working in a layer other than the Background layer, deleting a selection turns the selected pixels transparent, and layers below it show through.

Rotate a Selection

You can use the Free Rotate Selection command to *rotate* — spin — a selection. You can drag the selection to rotate it by hand, or you can specify an exact number of degrees; for example, rotating by 180 degrees turns the selection upside down. You can use rotation to make corrections — for example, to fix a horizon — or for creative effects.

When you rotate a selection in the Background layer, Photoshop Elements replaces the exposed areas that the rotation creates with the current background color. If you rotate a selection in another layer, the underlying layers appear in the exposed areas. See Chapter 13 for more details.

Rotate a Selection

① In the Editor, click **Expert**.

② Make a selection with any selection tool.

③ Click **Image** ➡ **Rotate** ➡ **Free Rotate**.

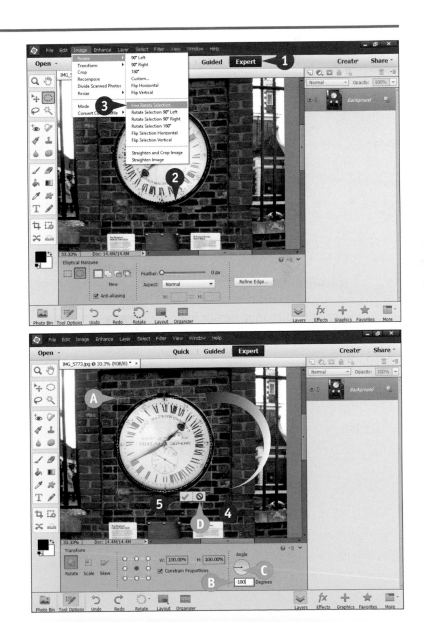

Ⓐ A box with handles on the sides and corners surrounds the selection.

The mouse cursor changes into a special rotation cursor.

④ Click and drag anywhere outside the selection.

Ⓑ You can set an exact rotation by typing a degree value into the Degrees field in the Tool Options panel. You can also drag the line in the Angle control (Ⓒ).

⑤ Click ☑ or press Enter to complete the rotation.

Ⓓ You can click ⊘ or press Esc to cancel.

Scale a Selection

You can *scale* a selection to make it larger or to shrink it. Scaling is useful when you want to change how obvious a feature is or to make it seem it closer to or farther from the camera. Photoshop Elements fills in blank areas around a shrunken selection with the background color. If you shrink part of a layer, the tool leaves a transparent gap.

Scaling an image to make it much larger often makes it blurry. You can partially correct this by applying the Sharpen filter. See Chapter 8 for details. But as a guide, you cannot scale by more than about 200% (2×) without losing sharpness.

Scale a Selection

1 In the Editor, click **Expert**.

2 Make a selection with a selection tool.

This example reuses the circular selection from the previous example.

Note: See Chapter 6 for more on using selection tools. See Chapter 8 for more on layers.

3 Click **Image** ➪ **Resize** ➪ **Scale**.

A box with handles on the sides and corners surrounds the selection.

4 Click and drag a side handle to change height or width, or click a corner handle to change height and width.

Ⓐ You can set the new size accurately by typing percentages into your selection by typing percentage values in the W and H fields in the Tool Options panel.

Ⓑ With Constrain Proportions selected, the ratio of height and width is locked.

5 Click ☑ or press Enter to complete the rotation.

Ⓒ You can click ⊘ or press Esc to cancel.

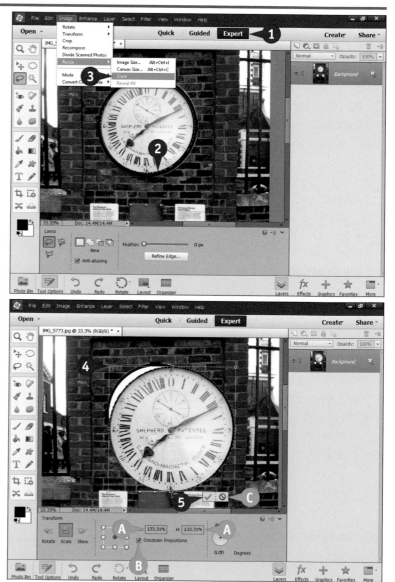

153

Skew or Distort a Selection

You can *transform* a selection with the Skew and Distort commands. These commands pin the selection to a piece of virtual rubber. You can pull the corners and sides of the rubber to stretch or shrink the selection by different amounts in different directions. You can also pin the corners or sides to limit the effect and make it easier to work with.

Use these tools to correct leaning perspective in photos with strong verticals, such as columns. You can also use them for creative experiments. Note that you can distort a selection created by any tool including the Magic Wand. You do not have to start with a rectangular area.

Skew or Distort a Selection

Skew a Selection

1 In the Editor, click **Expert**.

2 Make a selection with any selection tool.

Note: This example uses the lasso tool to draw straight lines around the window frame.

Note: For more on opening the Editor, see Chapter 1. See Chapter 6 for more on using selection tools.

3 Click **Image** ⇨ **Transform** ⇨ **Skew**.

A rectangular box with handles on the sides and corners surrounds the selection.

4 Click and drag a handle.

Photoshop Elements skews the selection.

Because the Skew command works along a single axis, you can drag either horizontally or vertically.

5 Click ☑ or press Enter to complete the edit.

Ⓐ You can click Ⓝ or press Esc to cancel.

Distort a Selection

1 Make a selection with a selection tool.

Note: See Chapter 6 for more on using selection tools.

2 Click **Image** ➪ **Transform** ➪ **Distort**.

A rectangular box with handles on the sides and corners surrounds the selection.

3 Click and drag a handle.

Photoshop Elements distorts the selection. The Distort command works independently of the selection's axes; you can drag a handle both vertically and horizontally.

Note: You can repeat Step **3** any number of times.

Note: You can scale your selection and rotate it by typing values into the W, H, and Degrees boxes.

4 Click ✓ or press **Enter** to complete the edit.

Ⓐ You can click ◎ or press **Esc** to cancel.

TIPS

What do the Free Transform and Perspective transforms do?

Free Transform does not allow you to move the corners independently. It forces you to scale the selection when you drag any corner or side. Perspective applies mirror symmetry when you drag corners. When you move a corner in one direction, the matching corner on the other side moves in the opposite direction.

Can I transform a selection without modifying my photo?

Make a selection, right-click it, and select any of the items from the menu that appears. You can scale, distort, and rotate your selection without editing the photo. Click the green check mark to apply the selection to the photo. You can right-click and change the selection as many times as you need to.

Refine the Edge of a Selection

You can use the Refine Edge dialog box to improve any selection by softening it, smoothing sharp edges, and widening it or shrinking it. Use this option to improve and correct edits made with any selection tool. It is a good way to smooth rough selections drawn with a mouse.

You can also use this dialog to *feather* — soften the edges of — a selection. Feathered selections look more natural than the "hard torn paper" edges created by an unfeathered selection. For more on feathering, see the next section, "Feather the Border of a Selection."

Refine the Edge of a Selection

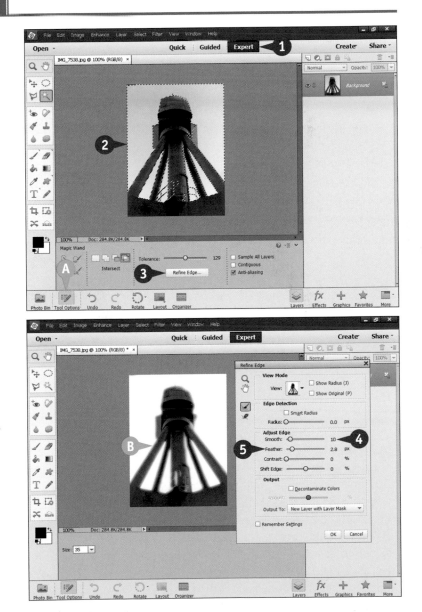

1. In the Editor, click **Expert**.

2. Make a selection with a selection tool.

Note: For more on opening the Editor, see Chapter 1. For more on using selection tools, see Chapter 6.

Note: This example uses the Magic Wand tool to select the sky.

Note: Remember to invert the selection if you want to edit or remove the background.

Ⓐ If the Tool Options panel is not open, click here to open it.

3. Click **Refine Edge**.

   The Refine Edge dialog box opens.

Note: If the dialog box covers your photo, drag it to one side.

4. Click and drag the **Smooth** slider to determine the smoothness of the edge.

5. Click and drag the **Feather** slider to determine the softness of the edge.

Note: The Smooth slider makes selection edges more curved. The Feather slider blurs selection edges.

Ⓑ Photoshop Elements previews the changes.

6 Click and drag the **Contrast** slider to sharpen a selection that is now too soft.

7 Click and drag the **Shift Edge** slider to move the selection edge in or out from the selected object.

Note: Explore these settings until you get as much of the object as you can, with as little of the background. Be careful around fine edges such as fences and hair.

8 Click **OK**.

C Photoshop Elements adjusts the selection.

Note: Refine Edge does not change the photo. It improves the selection so you can make more precise and professional edits.

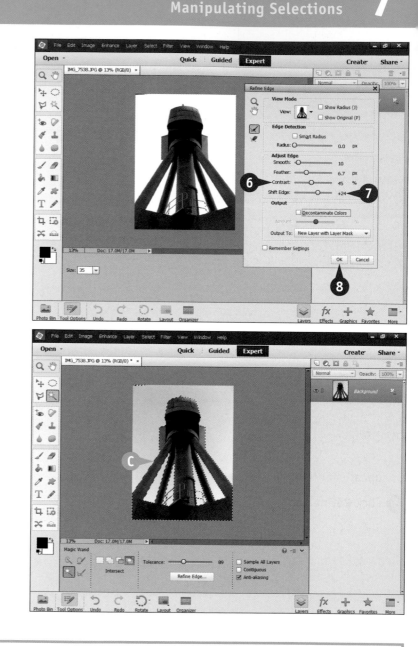

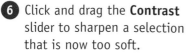

TIPS

Can I copy my selection to a new layer?
Yes. Open the Refine Edge dialog box and make your adjustments. In the Output To menu, select **New Layer**. Photoshop Elements creates a new layer containing your selection. Other output options include sending the selection to a layer mask or a new document. For more on layers, see Chapter 13.

Does Photoshop Elements remember my settings?
Not unless you tell it to. In the Refine Edge dialog box, click **Remember Settings** (☐ changes to ☑). The next time you open the Refine Edge dialog box, the previous settings appear. Click **OK** to apply them.

Use Feathering to Create a Soft Border

You can feather a selection's border to create soft edges. You can create feathering with the Refine Edge tool introduced in the previous section. You can also create it directly from a menu option. Wide soft edges can create a sentimental or romantic feel. Thinner soft edges create subtle blending and help make edits look more natural.

To create a soft border around an object, select the object, feather the selection border, and then delete the part of the image that surrounds your selection. Optionally, you can vary the mood by changing the background color.

Use Feathering to Create a Soft Border

Feather a Selection

1. In the Editor, click **Expert**.

2. Make a selection with a selection tool.

Note: Smooth selections look better than rough ones. This example uses the Elliptical Marquee Tool () to create a circle.

3. Select **Select** ⇨ **Inverse.**

   Photoshop Elements inverts the selection.

4. Select **Select** ⇨ **Feather.**

Note: You can also right-click the image and click **Feather** from the pop-up menu.

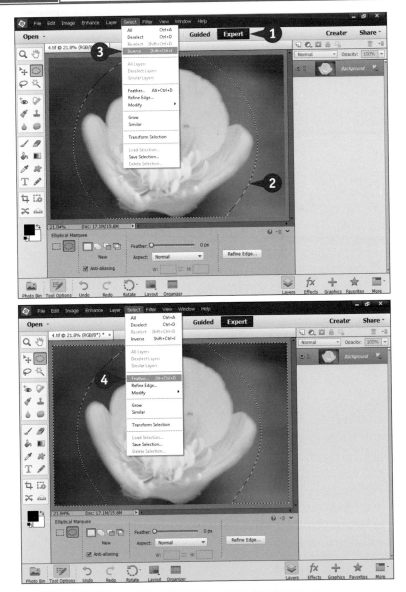

The Feather dialog box opens.

5 Type a number into the Feather Radius box.

Note: This sets the width of the feather in absolute pixels. Use larger numbers on larger images.

6 Click OK.

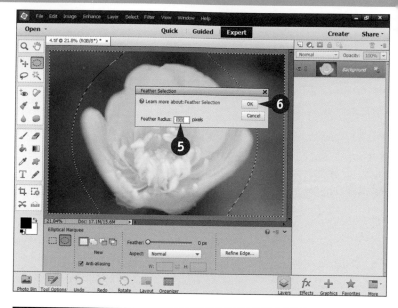

 Photoshop Elements feathers the edge of the selection.

Note: It may not look different.

7 Press Delete or Ctrl+X (Alt+X on a Mac.)

B If you are working with the Background layer, the deleted area fills with the current background color (**C**).

Note: If you are working with a layer other than the Background layer, the deleted area becomes transparent, and the layers below show through.

You can now see the effect of the feathering.

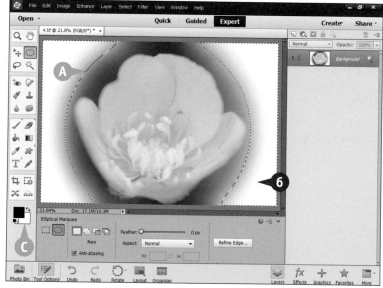

TIPS

How do I feather my selection into a colored background?

Select a different background color before you begin. If you are working with layers, you can paste your selection to a new layer and try out different background colors behind it. For more about selecting colors and blending layers, see Chapter 13.

What happens if I feather a selection and then apply an edit command to it?

The strength of the effect fades out toward the feathered edge of your selection. For example, if you remove color from a selection with the Hue/Saturation command, the center of the selection becomes black and white, but color fades again in toward the edge of the selection. This can create a more professional look. For more on Hue/Saturation, see Chapter 10.

Enhancing and Retouching Photos

Do you need to fix a photo fast? This chapter offers quick-fix techniques for retouching digital photos. You can correct color problems, remove flaws, fix problems with perspective, and combine elements from different photos.

Quickly Fix a Photo

You can use the Quick mode in Photoshop Elements to make instant corrections. You can adjust lighting, contrast, color, and focus. You can also see Before and After views of your edits.

The Quick mode pane includes a selection of tools designed for ease of use. The Smart Fix tool automatically corrects lighting, color, and contrast; the Exposure and Levels tools fix lighting problems; the Color and Balance tools fix color problems; and the Sharpen tool sharpens photos.

Quickly Fix a Photo

1 In the Editor, click **Quick**.

Note: For more on opening the Editor, see Chapter 1.

A Quick mode opens, and the Quick mode pane shows a selection of quick-fix retouching tools.

B You can use the items in the toolbar to zoom/drag the image and perform basic edits such as cropping, adding text, and removing red-eye. For details, see Chapter 5.

2 Click the menu to see a selection of view modes, and select **Before & After - Horizontal**.

The After Only view shows your photo after editing.

The Before Only view shows your photo before editing.

The Before and After views show both. Horizontal mode places the images side by side; Vertical mode places them on top of each other.

③ Click **Smart Fix**.

The Smart Fix tool opens.

④ Click and drag the slider to improve the image.

ⓒ You can also click a thumbnail.

ⓓ Photoshop Elements makes immediate adjustments to the lighting, contrast, and colors in the image.

ⓔ You can click the reset thumbnail to return to the original settings.

ⓕ You can click Auto, and Photoshop Elements applies a "best guess" setting.

⑤ Click the Color tool.

⑥ Click Vibrance.

Note: The Vibrance tool always boosts colors in a more natural way than the Saturation tool.

ⓖ You can use the thumbnails, slider, auto, and reset buttons to enhance the color in the image.

Photoshop Elements enhances the image.

You can follow similar steps to use the other Adjustments to improve exposure, lighting, sharpness, and overall balance.

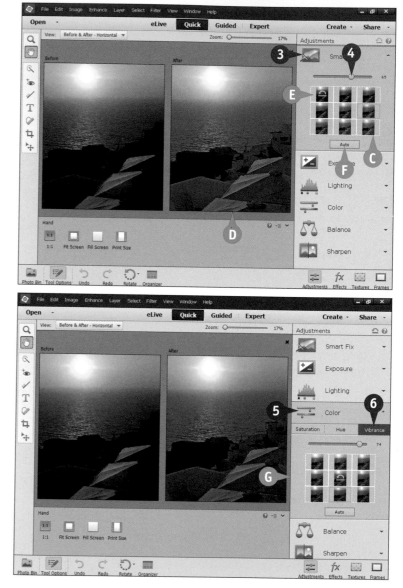

TIPS

Why does Photoshop Elements duplicate the same edit options elsewhere?

Quick mode is designed for quick edits. It gives you simple tools that apply useful edits. The items in the Enhance menu and in Expert mode offer more control over similar edits, but they give you more options and finer control.

How can I improve the look of teeth in Quick mode?

You can use the Whiten Teeth tool (▨). Click and drag the tool over a smile; it selects the teeth and whitens them all at once. The result is similar to using the Quick Selection tool (see Chapter 6) to select the teeth and then applying the Dodge tool (see Chapter 9) to lighten them and the Sponge tool (see Chapter 9) to remove any colorcast.

Remove Red Eye

You can use the Red Eye Removal tool to remove *red eye* — a common problem in photos taken with a flash. The red color appears because light bounces off the blood vessels at the back of the eye. Animal eyes can show a similar effect, but the color may be yellow, blue, or green.

With the Red Eye Removal tool, you can fix eye color without changing the shape of the eyes. The tool paints a dark circle over red areas and adds a small highlight. It includes an option for fixing the eyes of pets and other animals.

Remove Red Eye

1 In the Editor, click **Quick**.

Quick mode opens.

Note: For more on opening the Editor, see Chapter 1.

2 Click the **Red Eye Removal** tool (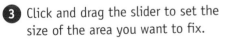).

Note: This tool is also available in Expert mode.

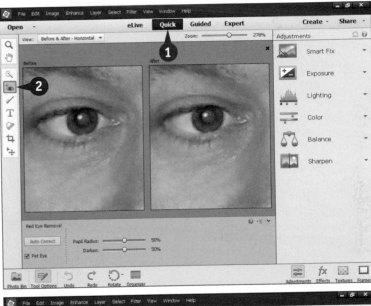

3 Click and drag the slider to set the size of the area you want to fix.

4 Click and drag the slider to the adjust how much the tool replaces red areas with black areas.

Note: You often need to experiment with these values until you get a good result.

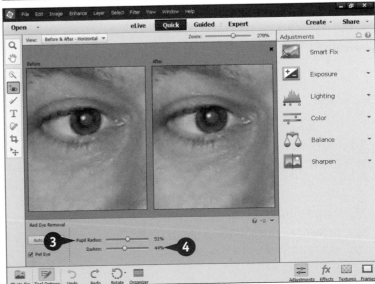

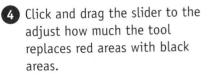

⑤ Click the pupil of the eye you want to fix.

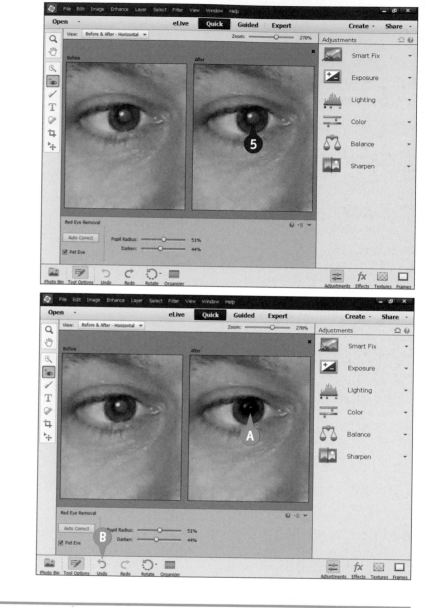

Ⓐ Photoshop Elements repairs the color.

Ⓑ If you need to try again with different settings, you can click **Undo** to undo the color change.

TIPS

My pet photos have a yellow, blue, or green eye problem. How do I fix this?
Click the **Red Eye Removal** tool (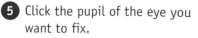), and then click **Pet Eye** in the Tool Options panel (☐ changes to ☑). You can then use the tool to remove the colors that can sometimes appear in non-human eyes.

How can I get a more natural result?
For a better effect, select Expert mode, create a selection for the red area, and select **Enhance ⇨ Adjust Color ⇨ Remove Color**. Then use **Enhance ⇨ Adjust Lighting ⇨ Levels** to darken the pupil while leaving any highlights. Manual fixes take much longer but often look more realistic.

Retouch with the Clone Stamp Tool

You can clean up flaws or erase elements in your image with the Clone Stamp tool. The tool copies — "clones" — part of an image. You can then paste — "stamp" — the detail to a different area. To remove blemishes, you often clone the area around the blemish to cover it.

You can adjust the opacity of the tool to let some of the original detail show through. Copying from multiple areas in an image is often a good way to remove an unwanted object. For good results, clone areas with matching textures, and try not to break or distort lines and edges.

Retouch with the Clone Stamp Tool

1 In the Editor, click **Expert**.

Note: For more on opening the Editor, see Chapter 1.

2 Click the **Clone Stamp** tool (🔲).

A You can click the menu to choose a brush size and type.

B You can also click and drag the slider to change the brush size.

You can change the brush size by pressing [and].

C You can click and drag the slider to set the opacity (transparency) of the cloned copy.

A setting of 100% opacity is completely opaque and does not allow any of the original content to show through.

Note: Experiment with the default settings before changing them.

3 Press and hold **Alt** (**Option** on a Mac), and then click the image to set the content to be cloned.

In this example, the Clone Stamp removes a sign by cloning the grass around it.

4 Click and drag the area of the photo that you want to correct.

Photoshop Elements copies the cloned area to where you click and drag.

5 Continue clicking new areas to clone and dragging over the area as many times as needed to achieve the desired effect.

Photoshop Elements replaces old content with cloned content.

Note: Long strokes can copy content from areas you do not want. Short strokes can create repeating textures. Try to avoid obvious artifacts. You may have to make a few attempts before you get a good result.

C You can click **Undo** to undo the tool's effects.

TIPS

How can I make the Clone Stamp's effects look seamless?

To erase elements from your image with the Clone Stamp without leaving a trace, try the following:

- Clone between areas of similar color and texture.
- To apply the stamp more subtly, lower its opacity.
- Use a soft-edged brush shape.

What can I do with the Pattern Stamp?

You can use the Pattern Stamp tool (▦), which shares space in the Tool Options panel with the Clone Stamp tool (▦), to paint repeating patterns on your images. You can select a pattern, brush style, and brush size, and then stamp the pattern on your photo by clicking and dragging.

Remove a Spot

You can use the Spot Healing Brush to quickly repair flaws or remove small objects in a photo. The tool works well on small spots or blemishes on both solid and textured backgrounds. For good results, adjust the brush size to cover the feature you want to remove.

The tool's Proximity Match analyzes pixels surrounding the selected area and replaces the area with a patch of similar pixels. The Create Texture setting replaces the area with a blend of surrounding pixels. The Content Aware setting, which is often the most useful, is similar to Proximity Match but recognizes and keeps patterns in the surrounding pixels.

Remove a Spot

1 In the Editor, click **Expert**.

Note: For more on opening the Editor, see Chapter 1.

2 Click the **Spot Healing Brush** tool (🖌️).

Ⓐ You can click the menu to choose a brush size and type that will cover the spot.

Ⓑ You can also set a brush size by clicking and dragging the slider.

Ⓒ You can use the radio buttons to select the type of healing effect.

The Content Aware option is often a good choice.

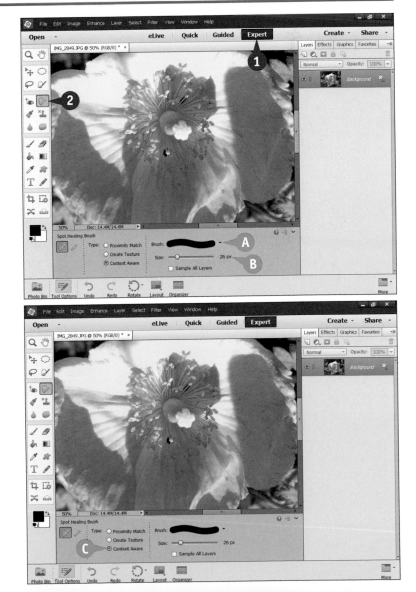

③ Click and paint the spot you want to correct.

Photoshop Elements covers the spot with black as you draw.

Note: The black is a temporary marker. It is not painted permanently onto the image.

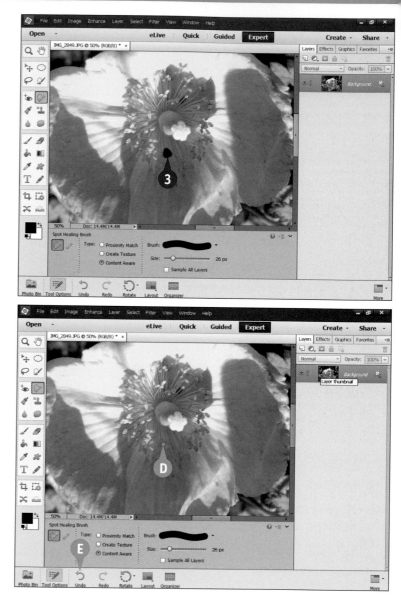

④ Release the mouse.

Ⓓ Photoshop Elements selects nearby pixels and replaces the area you painted on.

Ⓔ You can click **Undo** to undo the change.

TIP

What is the difference between the Spot Healing Brush and the Healing Brush?
The **Spot Healing Brush** tool () works on small areas. The **Healing Brush** tool (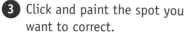) works like a version of the **Clone Stamp** tool (🔲). Instead of copying from a source area, it uses the pixels as guide and copies related content. To use the Healing Brush tool, press and hold **Alt** (**Option** on a Mac) and click the area you want to use as a source. Click and drag over the problem area to blend the cloned pixels into the new area.

Sharpen an Image

You can use the Adjust Sharpness dialog box to sharpen an image. This tool can improve soft images, but it is not a complete cure for focus problems. It cannot transform a badly blurred image into a sharp one.

Sharpening can bring out grain and noise in image. You often need to adjust the amount of sharpening to get a good balance between noise and sharpness.

Sharpen an Image

1 In the Editor, click **Expert**.

Note: For more on opening the Editor, see Chapter 1.

2 Click **Enhance** ⇨ **Adjust Sharpness**.

The Adjust Sharpness dialog box opens.

A You can click **Preview** to preview the effect in the main window (☐ changes to ☑.)

B You can click plus or minus (⊞ or ⊟) to zoom in and out.

C You can set the Amount slider to control the intensity of the effect.

D You can set the Radius slider to make the effect bigger or smaller.

Note: If you set a large radius and a high intensity, the effect creates haloes and blobs of color.

E You can click the menu to fix different types of blur. The Gaussian Blur option applies sharpening across the image. Lens Blur sharpens details. Motion Blur removes blur caused by camera or subject motion and includes a control to set the direction.

170

3 If you have applied a large amount and a high radius and the image looks unrealistic, click **Shadows/Highlights**.

The dialog box expands and shows further options for Shadows and Highlights.

F You can increase the **Tonal Width** slider to make the effect look more natural around dark areas.

G You can increase the **Tonal Width** slider to make the effect look more natural around bright areas and to minimize "salt and pepper" noise.

4 Click **OK**.

Photoshop Elements applies the enhancement.

Note: For good results, avoid adding artifacts and noise.

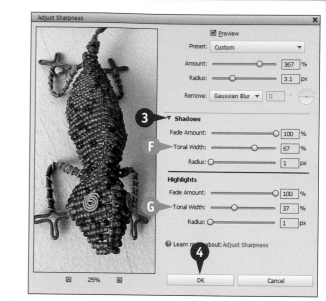

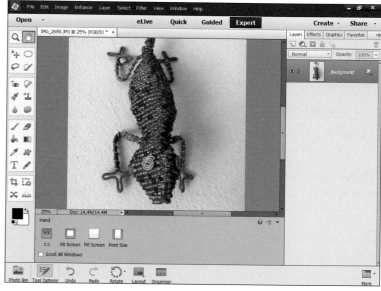

TIPS

When should I apply sharpening?
Apply sharpening after you have finished improving the photo. You can also sharpen after resizing. Making an image bigger or smaller loses detail. Sharpening can bring some of the detail back.

How can I sharpen an image in Quick mode?
You can quickly sharpen an image in Quick mode by opening the Sharpen tool in the right panel and then clicking and dragging the slider or clicking a thumbnail image. The Quick mode Sharpen tool is less sophisticated than the Sharpen dialog box, but is often good for quick enhancements.

Remove a Color Cast

You can use the Balance tool to fix a *color cast*. Photos can have a color cast when a camera is set up incorrectly — for example, when it is set to take photos in daylight but you are shooting indoors.

The Balance tool applies two color shifts — red to blue, and green to pink. Use a red-to-blue shift to correct for indoor/outdoor colors, and use the green-to-pink shift to fix skin tones.

Remove a Color Cast

1 In the Editor, select **Quick** mode.

Note: For more on opening the Editor, see Chapter 1.

2 Use the menu to select simultaneous Before & After previews.

For details, see the Quickly Fix a Photo section in this chapter.

3 Click **Balance**.

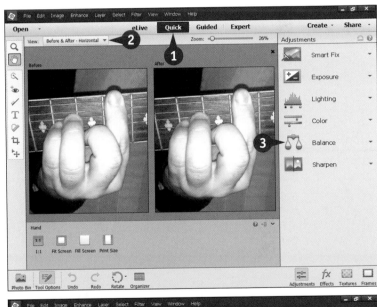

The Balance Adjustment panel opens.

4 Click **Temperature**.

5 Use the slider to correct the red/blue balance.

Note: This example looks orange, so it needs more blue and less red.

Note: If skin tones look pale after this step, you can correct them in the next step.

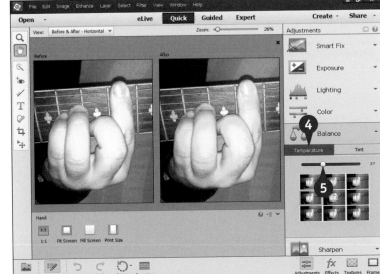

6 Click **Tint**.

7 Use the slider to correct the green/pink balance.

Note: This example looks green and unhealthy after the previous correction, so it needs more pink.

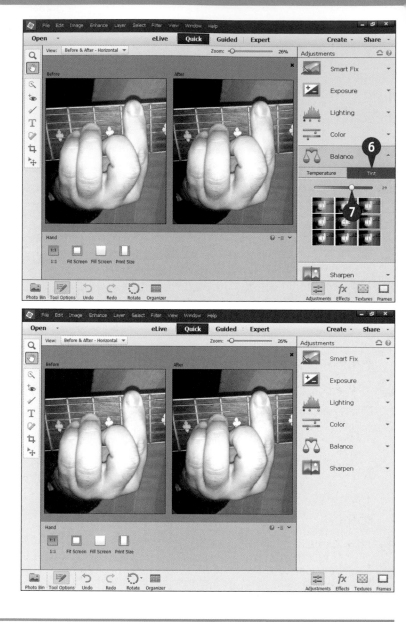

Photoshop Elements applies the correction.

TIPS

Why do the colors still look wrong after using this tool?
The Balance tool has limited power. Color balance is also a choice; it depends on the look you want to achieve. It can also be limited by the original lighting. So a technically accurate correction can still look wrong. Skin tones look healthier with extra red/pink, even though a neutral gray balance is more technically correct.

Can I use this tool creatively?
Yes. You can often improve a portrait by applying a slightly warm red cast and perhaps adding a further hint of pink. Skies often look cooler with extra blue. You can also use this tool to create strikingly unnatural but atmospheric color distortions.

Fix Keystone Distortion

You can use the camera distortion tools in Photoshop Elements to fix perspective problems. *Keystoning* appears when you take a photo by tilting your camera and can make buildings look like they're leaning.

You can use the Correct Camera Distortion tool to stretch and squeeze an image to remove this distortion. The tool includes a *vignette* — lens shadow — option that can fix the darker areas at the edges of an image introduced by cameras or lenses.

Fix Keystone Distortion

1 In the Editor, open a photo that has keystone distortion.

Note: For more on opening the Editor, see Chapter 1.

2 Click **Filter** ⇨ **Correct Camera Distortion**.

The Correct Camera Distortion window opens.

3 Click the menu, and select **Fit in View**.

Note: For good results, view the complete image while correcting perspective.

Ⓐ You can click and drag the slider to correct vertical distortion.

Photoshop Elements tilts the image up and down around a horizontal centerline.

Note: Use this feature to fix vertical lines.

Ⓑ You can click and drag the slider to correct horizontal distortion.

Photoshop Elements tilts the image left and right around a vertical centerline.

Note: Use this feature to balance left and right perspective.

Ⓒ You can click and drag the **Angle** tool to rotate the image.

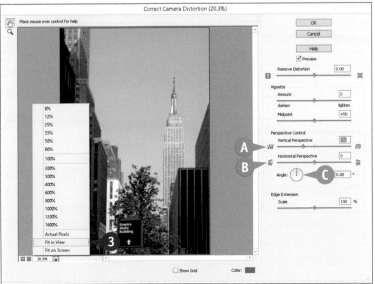

Ⓓ You can click and drag the slider to lighten or darken the corners of the image.

Ⓔ You can click and drag the slider to adjust the overall lightness.

④ Click **OK**.

Note: This example fixes some very subtle darkening introduced by the camera lens.

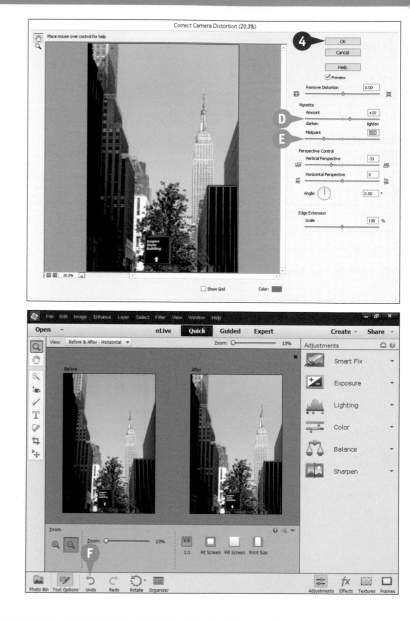

Photoshop Elements corrects the perspective in the photo.

Ⓕ You can click **Undo** to undo the correction.

TIPS

How can I use the Perspective command to correct buildings with keystone distortion?

In some cases, you may want to have more control over how you correct an image. Click **Image** ▷ **Transform** ▷ **Perspective**. Handles appear on the edges and corners of the image. Drag the top corner handles outward and the lower corner handles inward to fix the distortion. Click ☑ or press Enter to confirm your changes.

Why does the perspective still look wrong?

If you have many different vertical elements in an image, it can be impossible to get them all pointing in the same direction. Some images cannot be fixed.

Recompose a Photo

You can recompose a photo to change its size while keeping important objects within it intact. Recomposition is an alternative to cropping for when you want to reduce an image's size without trimming or deleting some of the content. For more on using the Crop tool, see Chapter 5.

Before you apply the Recomposition tool, you select areas of your photo that you want to keep by painting over them. You also paint over areas that you would prefer to eliminate. Photoshop Elements intelligently rearranges your selections as you resize the photo.

Recompose a Photo

1 In the Editor, click **Expert**.

Note: For more on opening the Editor, see Chapter 1.

2 Click the **Recompose** tool (⊡).

3 Click the **Mark for Protection** button (⊿).

4 Click and drag the slider to specify a brush size.

Note: The best size depends on the resolution of your image and the size of the objects you are keeping. Make the brush slightly wider than the objects.

5 Click and drag to paint a green protection mask over the objects and areas you want to keep.

Note: You do not need to paint accurately.

6 Click the **Mark for Removal** button (⊿).

7 Click and drag the slider to specify a brush size.

8 Click and drag to paint a red mask over areas and objects you do not want to keep.

Note: You can paint multiple areas. They can be in different parts of the photo.

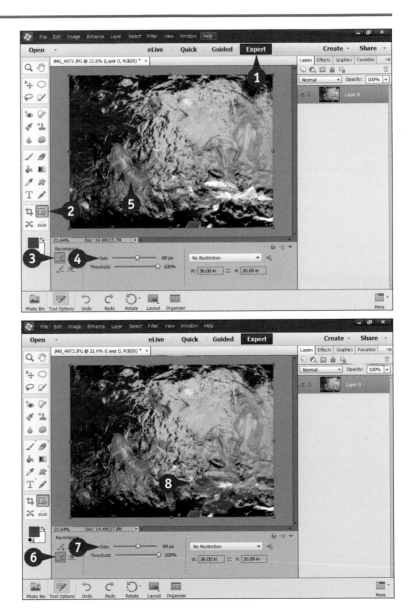

9 Click and drag the side and corner handles to resize the image.

10 Click ☑ or press **Enter** to confirm your changes.

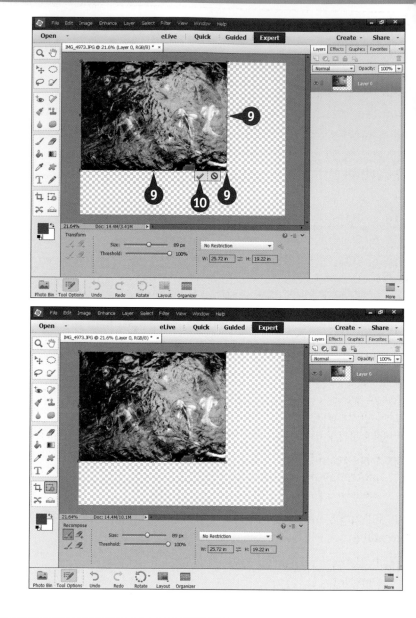

Photoshop Elements rearranges the objects and backgrounds in the image, keeping the objects you protected.

Note: You can now crop the image to remove the empty areas. See Chapter 5 for details.

TIPS

Can I edit the selection areas?

You can click **Erase Highlights Marked for Protection** (🖍) and drag the mouse to remove part of the area you protected in steps **3** to **5**. You can also click **Erase Highlights Marked for Removal** (🖍) to remove some of the area you selected for deletion in steps **6** to **8**.

Why do I get a distorted result?

This tool works best when you use it with objects placed on an unvarying background, such as a beach, an area of water, or the sky. If the background changes — for example, if it is shaded or if the texture changes across it — the tool may not give a seamless result. You can sometimes fix this with the clone and healing tools introduced earlier in this chapter.

Create a Photo Panorama

You can use the Photomerge Panorama feature to stitch several images together into a single panoramic image. Photoshop Elements can find the common features in the photos, arrange them in order, and paste them into a single wide image. Use this feature to create wide landscapes or unusually detailed location shots.

You can specify how the images are merged, or you can leave Photoshop Elements to guess the best option for you. Optionally, you can fill any space left at the sides of the panorama with computer-generated content.

Create a Photo Panorama

1 Before starting, copy the images you want to use into a separate folder on your hard drive.

Note: This step avoids a bug in the software. Do not try to load the images from the Organizer or the Editor Photo Bin.

2 In the Editor, click **Enhance** ⇨ **Photomerge©** ⇨ **Photomerge© Panorama**.

The Photomerge dialog box opens.

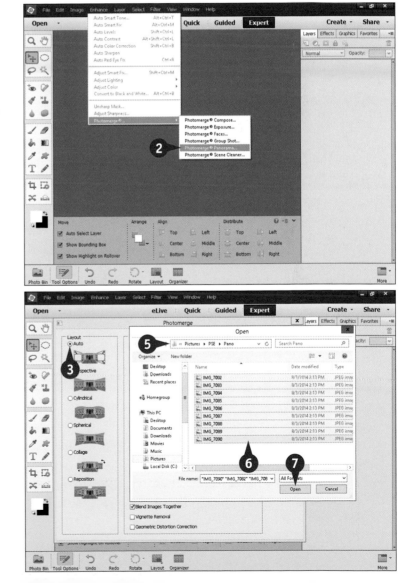

3 Select one of the **Layout** options.

Note: Auto is a good first choice. You can experiment with the other options if Auto does not give a good result.

4 Click **Browse** (not shown).

The Open dialog box opens.

5 Navigate to the folder that contains your images and open it.

6 Select all the files in it.

7 Click **Open**.

Ⓐ The filenames of the images appear in the Source Files list.

8 Click **OK** to build the panoramic image.

Photoshop Elements merges the images into a panorama.

Note: The process goes through various stages and can take a few minutes.

Ⓑ The images are combined into layers and masks.

Note: For more about layers and masks, see Chapter 13.

Ⓒ The stitching process can leave empty areas around the panorama.

Ⓓ In the Clean Edges dialog box that appears, you can click **Yes** to automatically fill in the edges.

Note: Alternatively, you can crop the panorama to a rectangle if you have enough space around it.

Photoshop Elements combines the photos into a panorama.

TIP

How can I create photos that merge successfully?

To merge photos successfully, you need to align and overlap the photos as you shoot them. Some hints:

* You do not need to use a tripod, but try to take all your photos at roughly the same height. Shoot photos with 15 to 30 percent overlap.
* Do not use lenses that distort your photos, such as fisheye, and do not change zoom settings.
* Use the same exposure settings for all the photos. Avoiding shooting into light or shadow, or in varying light (such as passing clouds).
* Experiment with the different layout modes in the Photomerge dialog box.

CHAPTER 9

Enhancing Lighting and Color

Does your photo suffer from shadows that are too dark? Are the colors in your photo faded? Photoshop Elements has an impressive selection of tools for fixing lighting and color.

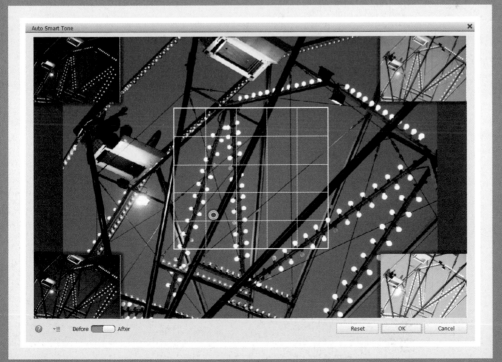

Adjust Levels

You can use the Levels dialog box to fine-tune the balance between shadows, highlights, and the areas in between, known as *midtones*. You can use the Levels tool to bring detail out of shadows and to set the overall brightness and contrast.

The Levels dialog box displays a *histogram* — a graph that counts the number of pixels at every possible brightness level, with darker pixels to the left and brighter pixels to the right. Adjusting the settings stretches and squeezes the graph to change the lighting in the image.

Adjust Levels

1 In the Editor, click **Expert**.

Note: For more on opening the Editor, see Chapter 1.

2 Click **Enhance** ⇨ **Adjust Lighting** ⇨ **Levels**.

Note: Alternatively, you can press Ctrl + L (⌘ + L on a Mac).

The Levels dialog box opens.

3 Make sure **Preview** is selected (☐ changes to ☑).

When Preview is selected, Photoshop Elements updates the photo as you make changes.

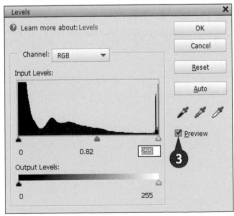

Ⓐ You can click and drag the black slider to control the shadows.

Ⓑ You can click and drag the gray slider to control mid-tones.

Ⓒ You can click and drag the white slider to control highlights and bright areas.

Note: Drag the sliders to the right to make the image darker, and to the left to make it brighter.

Ⓓ You can also click a box under each slider and type in a number to set the value.

Photoshop Elements displays a preview of the adjustments.

Ⓔ You can click and drag the black output slider to the right to lighten the image.

Ⓕ You can click and drag the white output slider to the left to darken the image.

Note: You do not usually need to move these sliders. Bringing them closer shrinks the contrast in the image.

④ Click **OK**.

Photoshop Elements applies the adjustments.

Note: You can make a selection to change the levels in part of an image. See Chapter 6 for more about selections.

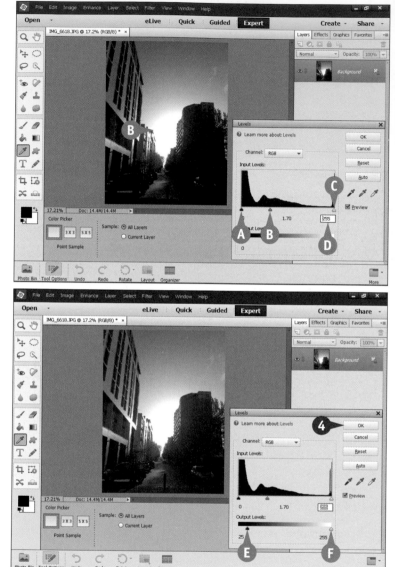

TIPS

How do I adjust the brightness levels of an image automatically?

Click **Enhance** and then **Auto Levels**. Photoshop Elements sets the lightest pixels to white and the darkest pixels to black. The other brightness levels are stretched or squeezed to fit between these extremes. This improves most photos, but some front-lit or back-lit photos may need manual adjustment.

Can I set the darkest, mid-gray, and brightest light levels directly from the image?

Yes. The Levels dialog box includes three Eyedropper tools, one for the darkest (🖊), midtone (🖊), and lightest tones (🖊). Select an Eyedropper tool, and click the image to set the dark/midtone/bright levels. Note that if you click colored pixels instead of black/gray/white pixels, this changes the color balance in your image. Click **Reset** to restore the original balance and try again.

Adjust Shadows and Highlights

You can use the Shadows and Highlights feature to make quick adjustments to the dark and light areas of your image. The feature is less complicated than the Levels tool but also less flexible.

You can use it to fix poor exposure. Use Lighten Shadows to improve underexposed areas, and use Darken Highlights to tone down overexposed highlights. You can also adjust the midtones to show further detail.

Adjust Shadows and Highlights

1 In the Editor, click **Expert**.

Note: For more on opening the Editor, see Chapter 1.

2 Click **Enhance** ⇨ **Adjust Lighting** ⇨ **Shadows/Highlights**.

The Shadows/Highlights dialog box opens.

3 Make sure **Preview** is selected (☐ changes to ☑).

When Preview is selected, Photoshop Elements updates the photo as you make changes.

4 Click and drag the Lighten Shadows slider to the right to make dark areas lighter.

5 Click and drag the Darken Shadows slider to the right to make bright areas darker.

Note: This slider does not darken burned-out white areas. It darkens the slightly darker areas with a little less brightness.

6 Click and drag the slider to increase or decrease the midtone contrast.

Note: Decreasing contrast brings detail out of darker areas but can also make the image look washed out.

A You can also click any of the boxes and type values for the slider settings.

7 Click **OK**.

Photoshop Elements makes the adjustment permanent.

TIPS

Why does the image look noisy after using this enhancement?

The less light a camera receives, the noisier the image. Usually, the noise remains dark, so you cannot see it. If you brighten a dark area, the noise becomes obvious. The **Lighten Shadows** feature is not a magic fix for underexposure. It corrects the lighting, but the corrected areas can look noisy. On a budget camera, they can be very noisy indeed.

When I open the Shadows/Highlights dialog box, Photoshop Elements immediately adjusts my image. What is happening?

The Shadows/Highlights filter automatically lightens shadows by 35 percent. You cannot change this. It is built into the effect. If you do not want this adjustment, move the **Lighten Shadows** slider all the way to the left before making other changes.

Change Brightness and Contrast

You can use the Brightness/Contrast dialog box to make simple adjustments to the light/dark balance in your image. **Brightness** makes the image lighter, and **contrast** increases the difference between light and dark areas.

The Brightness/Contrast settings are easy to use but not as powerful as the Levels tool. For good results, use this tool for very quick fixes, but take the time to learn how to use the Levels tool so you can rely on it for more complex changes. See the section "Adjust Levels" for more information.

Change Brightness and Contrast

1 In the Editor, click **Expert**.

Note: For more on opening the Editor, see Chapter 1.

2 Click **Enhance ➪ Adjust Lighting ➪ Brightness/ Contrast**.

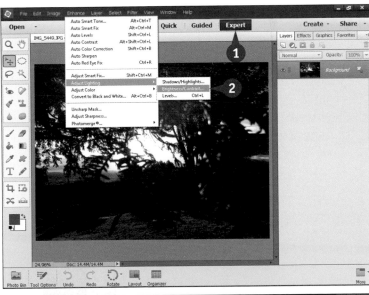

The Brightness/Contrast dialog box opens.

Ⓐ The Preview check box is selected by default.

3 Click and drag the **Brightness** slider to adjust brightness.

Drag the slider to the right to lighten the image.

Drag the slider to the left to darken the image.

Ⓑ You can also type a number from 1 to 150 to lighten the image or from −1 to −150 to darken the image.

④ Click and drag the **Contrast** slider to adjust contrast.

Drag the slider to the right to increase contrast.

Drag the slider to the left to decrease contrast.

Ⓒ You can also type a number from 1 to 100 to increase contrast or from −1 to −50 to decrease contrast.

Note: You often need to repeat steps **3** and **4** until you get the overall balance right.

⑤ Click **OK**.

Photoshop Elements applies the adjustment.

TIPS

How can I automatically adjust the contrast of an image?

Click **Enhance** and then **Auto Contrast** to automatically convert light and dark pixels. The Auto Contrast feature converts the very lightest pixels in the image to white and the very darkest pixels to black. This is a one-click tool, and you cannot fine-tune it.

Is there a tool that makes it easier to check contrast and lighting?

Yes. Click **Window** ⇨ **Histogram** to open the *Histogram* — a brightness graph. The 256 possible dark/bright levels appear along a line, left to right. The curve shows how many pixels there are at each level. Blown-out highlights appear as a spike at the far right. Poor contrast appears as a gap in the curve at the left or the right.

Use the Dodge and Burn Tools

You can use the **Dodge** and **Burn** tools to "paint" on an image to lighten or darken areas. The Dodge tool lightens, and the Burn tool darkens — which may be the opposite of what you expect. The unusual names come from old darkroom processes.

You can change the brush size for these effects, and select whether they work on shadows, midtones, or highlights. These are creative effects, so you can use them to reinterpret an image, adding and removing light from the original scene.

Use the Dodge and Burn Tools

Use the Dodge Tool

1 In the Editor, click **Expert**.

Note: For more on opening the Editor, see Chapter 1.

2 Click the **Sponge** tool (🔲).

A If the Tool Options panel is not open, click here to open it.

The Dodge tool shares space with the Sponge and Burn tools in the Tool Options panel.

3 Click the **Dodge** tool (🔍).

B You can click the menu and choose the brush you want to use.

C You can click this menu to select whether the tool works on shadows, midtones, or highlights.

D You can move the Size slider to change the brush size.

4 Click and drag over the area that you want to lighten. The brush appears as a circle.

This example lightens the area around the plant pots.

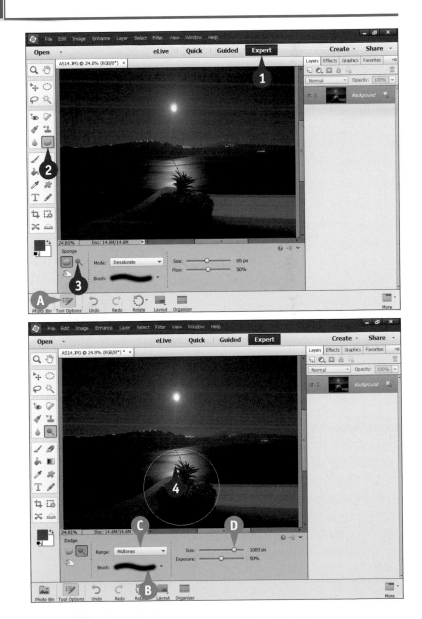

188

Use the Burn Tool

1 In the Editor, click **Expert**.

2 Click the **Sponge** tool ( ).

A If the Tool Options panel is not open, click here to open it.

The Burn tool shares space with the Sponge and Dodge tools in the Tool Options panel.

3 Click the **Burn** tool ( ).

B The Burn tool has the same settings as the Dodge tool.

4 Click and drag over the area that you want to darken.

This example paints over the cliffs on the horizon to make them stand out more from the sky and the sea.

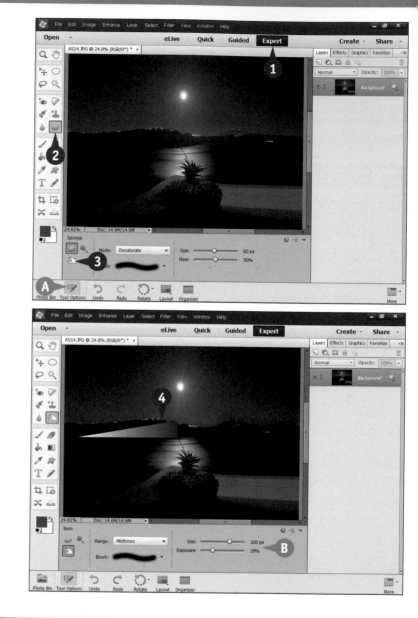

TIPS

Is there a way to make small changes?
If you set Exposure to a low value, both tools make small changes. You can paint over an area repeatedly to make more obvious changes. Use this option when you want very fine control over these effects.

Why does my image still look wrong?
Dodge and Burn are artistic effects, not corrections. You can use them to add and remove light from a scene — for example, to simulate adding a light source, or a light baffle. Getting a good result takes practice and a good eye. A good result makes a photo look stronger and more dramatic, but also natural and not obviously processed.

Fix Exposure

You can use the Photomerge Exposure tool to combine photos of the same scene taken with different exposures. Many cameras have a *bracketing* feature that takes multiple exposures automatically. You can use the Exposure tool to merge these images and produce a composite with a good mix of visible detail in the shadows and highlights.

You can also use a manual option to select areas from each photo by painting them. This option can be less effective, because the selection tools have hard edges and it is often easy to see the joins.

Fix Exposure

1 In the Editor, click **Expert**.

Note: For more on opening the Editor, see Chapter 1.

2 **Ctrl**+click (⌘+click on a Mac) to select the photos in the Photo Bin.

3 Click **Enhance** ⇨ **Photomerge©** ⇨ **Photomerge© Exposure**.

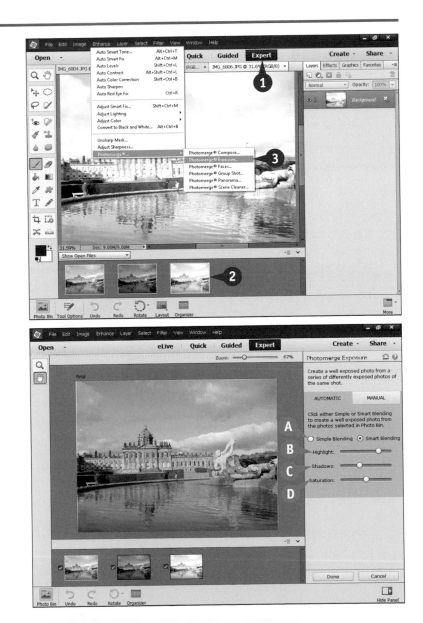

A The Photomerge Exposure panel opens and produces a composite preview.

B You can click and drag this slider to change the highlights.

C You can click and drag this slider to change the darker areas.

Note: When Smart Blending is selected, the sliders may not do what you expect. For example, moving the Highlight slider to the left may brighten the image.

D You can click and drag this slider to adjust the overall color intensity.

Photoshop Elements applies the adjustments.

Ⓔ You can click any photo to remove it from the composite.

④ Click **Done** to save the changes and to close the Photomerge Exposure panel.

Photoshop Elements merges the photos.

Ⓕ The merged image appears in the Photo Bin.

Ⓖ It also appears in the Layer list.

For more about layers, see Chapter 13.

Note: If you bracket without a tripod and do not keep the camera steady, the composite may have white borders. You can crop the image to fix this. See Chapter 5 for details.

TIP

How can I manually combine the elements in my photos?
Repeat steps **1** to **5** to open the Photomerge Exposure panel. Click **Manual**. Click and drag a photo to the Final window. Click to select a photo with objects to combine with the Final photo. This photo appears in the Source window. Click the **Pencil** tool. Click and drag over an area to select it. Use the Eraser tool to remove areas. You can adjust the opacity of your selection to refine the Photomerge effect. Photoshop Elements merges the selected objects with the background photo.

Use the Blur and Sharpen Tools

You can use blurring and sharpening to draw attention to parts of your photo. Typically, you blur a background to make it less eye-catching and sharpen a subject to draw the eye toward it.

The Blur and Sharpen tools in this section are very subtle. You may not be able to see the difference they make unless you look closely. For less subtle effects that you can apply to the entire image, see Chapters 8 and 12.

Use the Blur and Sharpen Tools

Use the Blur Tool

1 In the Editor, click **Expert**.

Note: For more on opening the Editor, see Chapter 1.

2 Click the **Blur** tool (▣).

A If the Tool Options panel is not open, click here to open it.

The Blur tool shares space in the Tool Options panel with the Sharpen and Smudge tools.

B You can click the menu and choose a different brush.

C You can use these sliders to change the size and strength of the effect.

3 Click and drag the mouse pointer to blur an area of the image.

Photoshop Elements blurs the area.

The blur is very subtle, even at 100 percent strength. You can only see it if you look closely.

Use the Sharpen Tool

1 Click the **Sharpen** tool (🔺).

The Sharpen tool shares space in the Tool Options panel with the Blur and Smudge tools.

D You can click the menu and choose a different brush.

E You can use these sliders to change the size and strength of the effect.

2 Click and drag the mouse pointer to sharpen an area of the image.

Photoshop Elements sharpens the area.

The effect is more obvious than the blur, and it is easier to see it working, but it is still a subtle effect.

TIPS

What is the Smudge tool?
The Smudge tool (👆) is another tool you can use to create interesting blur effects in your photos. It simulates dragging a finger through wet paint, shifting and smearing colors in your image. The Smudge tool shares space in the Tool Options panel with the Blur and Sharpen tools.

What does the Mode menu do?
In Normal mode, the tools change the image. In the other modes, they change texture of the image and also adjust color and/or contrast. The best way to understand the modes is to experiment with them. But because these are subtle tools, you can usually ignore these options.

Adjust Skin Color

You can improve skin colors that appear tinted or washed out or that were distorted by poor light. The **Skin Tone Adjustment** dialog box includes an eyedropper color sampler. Use it to select an area of skin as a color reference.

The adjustment tool uses the reference to guess a better skin tone and to correct other colors in the image. You often need to fine-tune the effect by adding or removing tan (orange) or blush (pink.) You can also shift the color between cool blue and a warmer red/orange.

Adjust Skin Color

1 In the Editor, click **Expert**.

Note: For more on opening the Editor, see Chapter 1.

2 Click **Enhance** ⇨ **Adjust Color** ⇨ **Adjust Color for Skin Tone**.

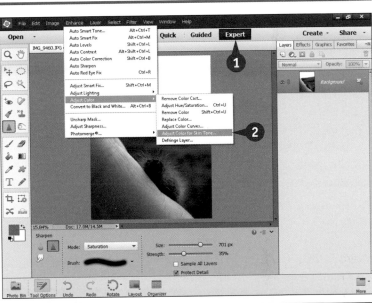

The Adjust Color for Skin Tone dialog box opens.

A The mouse pointer changes into an eyedropper.

3 Click an area of skin to use it as a color reference.

Note: This unusual example shows a close-up of a caterpillar on a model's hand.

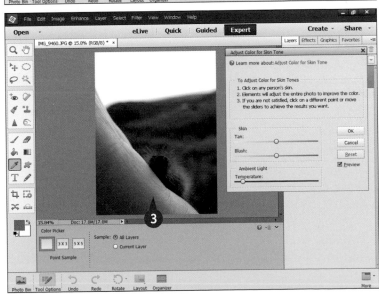

4 Click and drag the **Tan** slider to adjust the level of brown.

5 Click and drag the **Blush** slider to adjust the level of red/pink.

6 Click and drag the **Temperature** slider to adjust the overall coloring of the image.

Dragging to the left creates a cooler, bluish tint; dragging to the right casts a warmer, reddish tint.

7 Click **OK**.

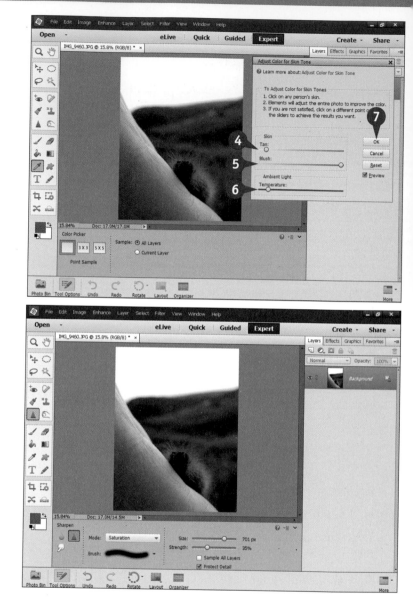

Photoshop Elements adjusts the colors in the image. In this example, the result is slightly warmer and more orange than the original.

Note: Skin tone varies depending on ethnicity, location, and even whether or not a subject is feeling too hot or cold. Often, many interpretations are possible. The "right" adjustment is the one that works best for your photo.

TIP

Can Photoshop Elements correct the colors in my image automatically?
Yes. Follow these steps to apply the command. Click **Enhance** ➪ **Auto Color Correction**. Photoshop Elements corrects the colors. The result is often "close enough," but may not be what exactly what you want. For better results, you can adjust the colors manually using other tools — including the **Sponge** tool, described in the next section.

Adjust Color with the Sponge Tool

You can use the Sponge tool to "paint" color adjustments onto your image. For example, you can make a person's clothing more colorful, tone down the color in some objects but not others, or even remove the color from most — but not all — of the image.

You can adjust the size and softness of the brush to customize it. You can also "paint" multiple times to increase the effect.

Adjust Color with the Sponge Tool

Decrease Saturation

1 In the Editor, click **Expert**.

Note: For more on opening the Editor, see Chapter 1.

2 Click the **Sponge** tool (□).

A If the Tool Options panel is not open, click here to open it.

The Sponge tool shares space with the Dodge and Burn tools.

B You can click this menu to select a different brush.

C You can click and drag the slider to change the brush size and flow.

3 Click the menu, and select **Desaturate**.

4 Click and drag the mouse pointer to tone down or remove color from the image.

Note: Even with 100% flow, you need to paint over an area a few times before the color disappears.

In this example, all the limes but one lose their color.

To confine the effect to a particular area, you can make a selection prior to applying the tool. See Chapter 6 for more on making selections.

Increase Saturation

1 Perform steps **1** to **3** in the subsection "Decrease Saturation."

2 Click the menu, and select **Saturate**.

3 Click and drag the mouse pointer to increase the saturation of an area of the image.

Note: You can also click areas instead of painting them.

In this example, the colors in the fish become more saturated.

TIPS

What does the Flow setting do?
The Flow slider in the Tool Options panel controls the intensity of the effect. You can set the Flow between 1% and 100%. Because the effect is subtle, you may want to start with Flow set to 100%.

How do I find the right brush style and size?
The Brush menu displays a variety of brush styles with soft, hard, and shaped edges. To blend your sponging effect into the surrounding pixels, select a soft-edged brush style. To make your sponging effect appear more distinct, use a hard-edged brush style. To change your brush size, click the **Size** slider in the Tool Options panel.

Replace a Color

You can use the **Replace Color** feature to alter a color range in your image. First, click the image to select a color. Next, use a **Fuzziness** slider to include a range of similar colors. You can also use eyedroppers to add or remove colors. Finally, modify the colors with hue, saturation, and lightness sliders.

Colored objects often have fringes and shadows, and colors can also spill across objects. It is not always easy to get a good result with this tool. It can take several attempts to create an effect that looks natural.

Replace a Color

1 In the Editor, click **Expert**.

Note: For more on opening the Editor, see Chapter 1.

2 Click **Enhance** ➪ **Adjust Color** ➪ **Replace Color**.

The Replace Color dialog box opens. The mouse pointer changes to an eyedropper.

3 Click in the image to select the color you want to change.

Ⓐ The preview area shows where that color appears in the image.

4 Click and drag the **Fuzziness** slider to add or remove similar colors.

You can also type a value for the fuzziness.

The white areas in the preview expand or shrink to show the selected color range in the image.

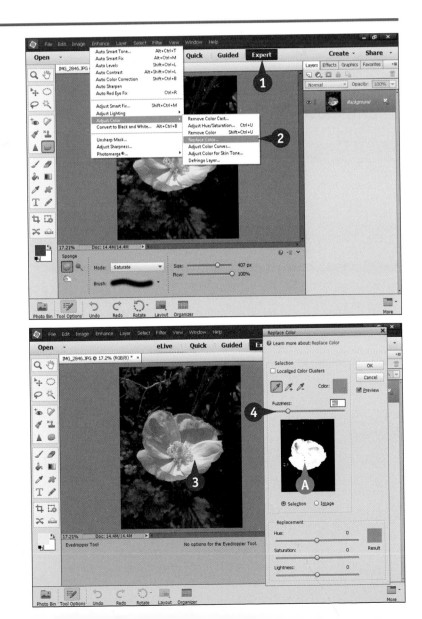

5 Click and drag the **Hue** slider to change the color.

6 Click and drag the **Saturation** slider to change the intensity of the color.

B You can click and drag the **Lightness** slider to change the lightness/darkness of the color, but you do not often need to do this.

You can also type values for the hue, saturation, and lightness.

7 Click **OK**.

Photoshop Elements replaces the selected color range.

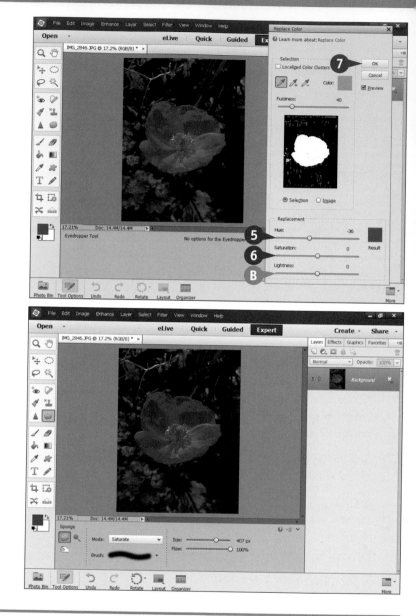

TIPS

How can I replace more than one area of color?

You can press **Shift** and then click inside your image to add other colors to your selection. The white area inside the preview box expands as you click. To deselect a color, press **Alt** (**Option** on a Mac) and click the color inside the image.

How can I avoid color spill?

Colors often spill across objects. Selecting colors in a foreground object sometimes selects the same colors in background areas you do not want to change. To avoid this, paint a selection around your object before using this tool. See Chapter 7 for more about selections.

Turn a Color Photo into Black and White

You can remove the colors from an image to create a black and white photo. The **Convert to Black and White** tool includes a range of creative options. You can use them to add drama or to change the light/dark balance for other creative reasons.

You may want to save the original color image and various versions of the black and white image as you work. See Chapters 2 and 3 for more about saving and viewing versions.

Turn a Color Photo into Black and White

1 In the Editor, click **Expert**.

Note: For more on opening the Editor, see Chapter 1.

2 Click **Enhance** ➪ **Convert to Black and White**.

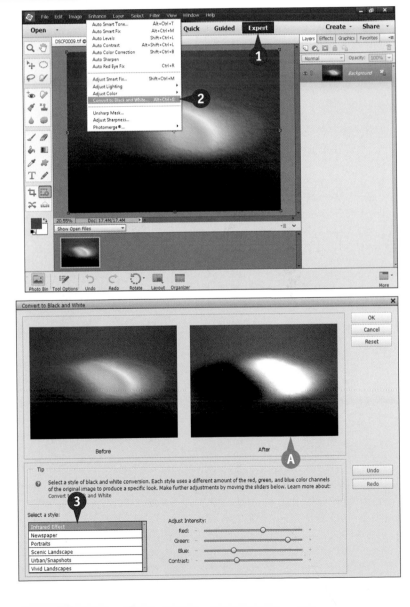

The Convert to Black and White dialog box opens.

3 Click any style in the list to select it.

A Photoshop Elements displays a preview of the black and white version.

Note: Each style creates a different effect by varying the brightness of red, green, and blue separately and setting the overall contrast.

Ⓑ You can click and drag the sliders to set the lightness/darkness of red, green, and blue manually.

Ⓒ You can also click this slider to increase or decrease the contrast.

❹ Click **OK**.

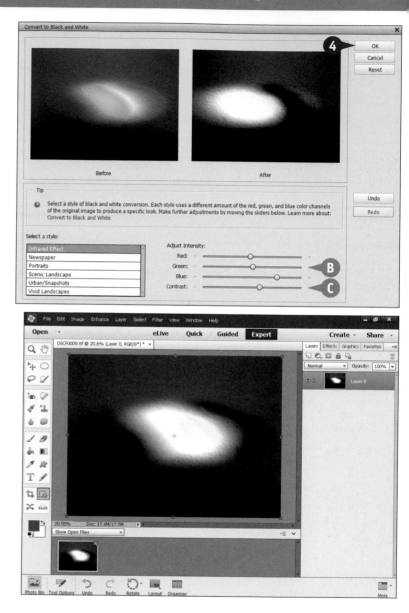

Photoshop Elements converts the image to black and white.

This example shows the result with the green slider set to maximum and the other sliders moved toward the left.

TIP

How do I know how to set the color sliders?
If you move the red slider to the right, red areas in the photo become brighter. This brightens skin in portraits and is one of the techniques used by professional photographers to improve the look of black and white portraits. You can use the blue slider to control sky brightness and the green slider to control the brightness of grass and foliage. Color balance is a creative choice, so the "right" answer depends on the mood you want to create and the content of the image. Simply desaturating an image often creates an uninteresting photo. The Convert to Black and White tool gives you more choices.

Add Color to a Black and White Photo

You can enhance a black and white photo by adding color with the painting tools in Photoshop Elements. For example, you can add color to a baby's cheeks or to articles of clothing. You can also simulate the hand-tinted color effects used in vintage photos.

Hand-tinting is an artistic process, so you may need to try different colors and opacities before you create a good result. For many photos, an opacity of less than 30 percent works colors with less than 50 percent saturation can work well. Brighter saturated colors can look garish and unconvincing.

Add Color to a Black and White Photo

1 In the Editor, click **Expert**.

Note: For more on opening the Editor, see Chapter 1.

2 Click the **Brush** tool (![brush icon]).

A You can click this menu to select a different brush preset.

3 Click the foreground color box, and select a color using the color picker dialog box that appears.

For more about setting the foreground color with the color picker, see Chapter 11.

4 Click the blending mode menu, and select **Color**.

This sets up the brush tool so it paints colors over the black and white content.

5 Click and drag the slider to set the brush size.

Use a large brush to cover a large area with a few strokes and a small brush to fill in details.

6 Click and drag the slider to set the opacity of the color.

7 Click and drag to paint a color onto the image.

B You can repeat steps **2** to **7** to paint more colors onto the image.

Photoshop Elements creates a tinted image.

TIP

Can I add color without changing the original image?
Yes. You can use *layers* to create colored effects. Instead of painting on the image, you paint on a layer. You can then adjust the hue of each layer to change the color and the opacity to change the color intensity. Layers float above the original image, so you can try different layer combinations until you get an effect you like without changing the original black and white file. For more about layers, see Chapter 13.

Adjust Colors by Using Color Curves

You can make your images look less muddy and more punchy by using the **Color Curves** dialog box. The tool graphs the relationship between shadows, midtones, and highlights. You can change the shape of the graph to improve your image.

The dialog box includes a small selection of presets. Click a preset to select it. For the best results, use the sliders to adjust the graph manually. Note that you cannot click and drag points on the graph directly. You must use the sliders to change the shape.

Adjust Colors by Using Color Curves

1 In the Editor, click **Expert**.

Note: For more on opening the Editor, see Chapter 1.

2 Click **Enhance ⇨ Adjust Color ⇨ Adjust Color Curves**.

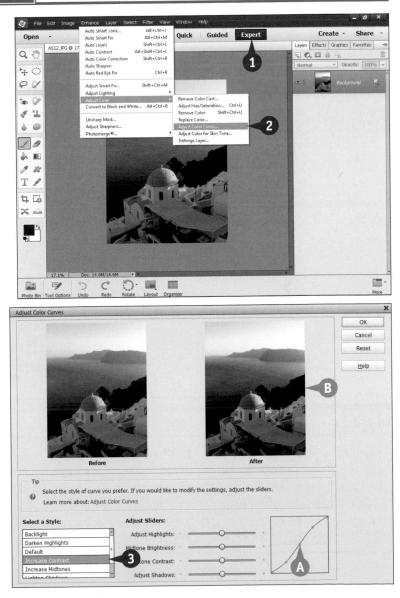

The Adjust Color Curves dialog box opens.

3 Click a style preset.

A The curve changes to match the new setting.

B The window previews the result.

In this example, choosing the Increase Contrast style gives the graph a slight S shape.

C You can click and drag the four sliders to fine-tune the result.

4 Click **OK**.

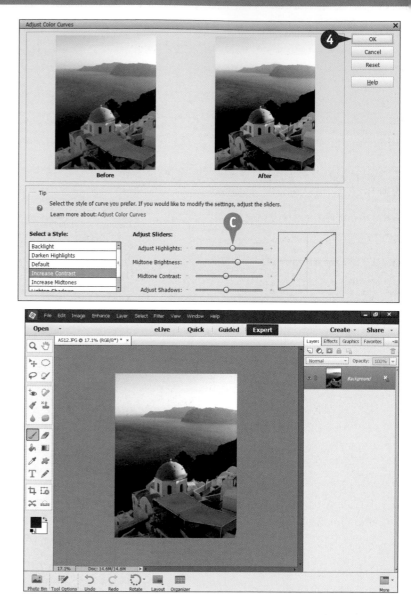

Photoshop Elements applies the adjustment to the image.

TIPS

How do I know how to set the sliders?

The right setting depends on the image. You can start by trying the different style presets and seeing which one — if any — improves the image. If you see an obvious improvement, try moving the sliders to make the curve even bigger. You often need trial and error to get a good result.

Why can I not adjust curves for each color?

This feature is available only in the full version of Adobe Photoshop. The settings in Photoshop Elements offer a simplified version of the effect. The full version is more powerful, but much harder to use.

Apply the Auto Smart Tone Tool

You can use the **Auto Smart Tone** tool to improve lighting and contrast. Auto Smart Tone combines Levels, Shadows/Highlights, Brightness/Contrast, and Curves corrections introduced earlier in this chapter, and hides the details behind a simple and intuitive interface.

To use the tool, click the grid and drag the mouse in any direction. Each corner of the grid has a preview to show how each direction changes the image. A bigger active preview appears behind the grid.

Apply the Auto Smart Tone Tool

1 In the Editor, click **Expert**.

Note: For more on opening the Editor, see Chapter 1.

2 Click **Enhance** ⇨ **Auto Smart Tone**.

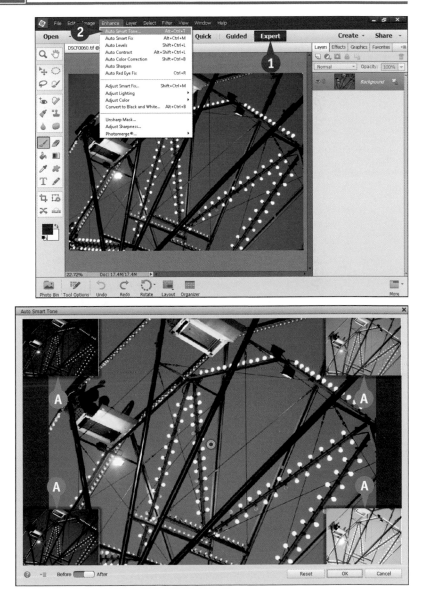

The Auto Smart Tone interface appears.

A Thumbnails in each corner show how the photo changes as you drag the cursor toward them.

Click and drag the cursor.

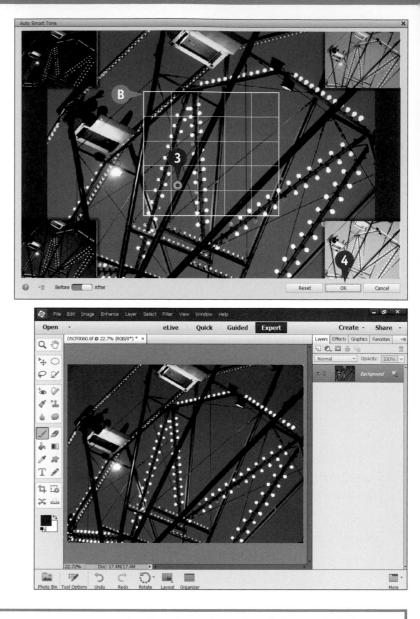

B A grid appears to help you gauge dragging distances.

Dragging from upper left to the lower right changes the lightness.

Dragging from the upper right to the lower left changes the contrast.

4 Click **OK**.

Photoshop Elements corrects the image.

TIPS

What does the dialog menu do?
You can click the dialog menu (🖹) and select **Learn from this correction** to tell Photoshop Elements to remember your edit. If you load another photo and use the tool again, Photoshop Elements remembers the previous cursor position. You can also deselect **Show corner Thumbnails** to hide the thumbnails.

What does the Before/After switch do?
If you set this switch to Before, you can see the unedited image. This is not usually useful while editing, but you can use it to compare edited and unedited versions of the image when you find a setting you like.

Apply Guided Edits

Photoshop Elements' Guided mode gives you step-by-step instructions for fixing photos and adding special effects. You can retouch old photos, apply creative effects, or even turn a photo into a virtual jigsaw puzzle. Guided mode uses the tools and commands available in the other modes but presents them in a structured way that helps you create professional edits.

Restore an Old Photo

You can use the Restore Old Photo steps in the Touchups section of Guided mode to fix common problems in scans of old photos — creases, tears, fading, dust specks, and color shifts.

This Touchup includes a selection of tools that can help you fix these problems. Note that you do not always have to apply guided edits in order. For example, you may want to use the Dust Remover before Spot Healing, because it gets rid of many small flaws automatically.

Restore an Old Photo

1 In the Editor, click **Guided**.

Note: For more on opening the Editor, see Chapter 1.

Guided mode opens.

A If the Touchups list is not open, click the down arrow (⌄ changes to ⌃ as shown in the figure).

2 Click **Restore Old Photo**.

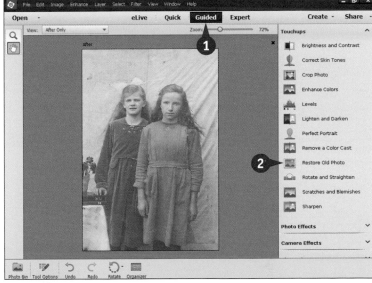

A The Restore Old Photo panel appears.

3 Scroll down, and click **Dust Remover**.

B The Dust Remover (Dust & Scratches) dialog box opens.

Note: This is another name for the Blur tool.

4 Drag the slider left or right until you remove dust without losing detail.

Note: On smaller scans, the correct setting is 1 or 2 pixels.

5 Click **OK**.

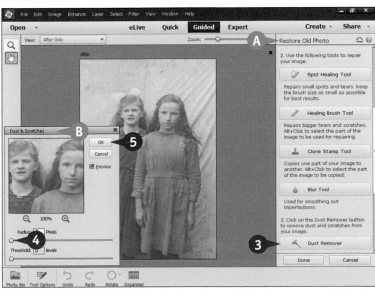

6 Scroll up, and select the **Spot Healing Tool**.

7 Click the image to remove small blemishes.

Note: You can also use the **Healing Brush Tool** and the **Clone Stamp Tool** to repair larger tears.

Note: If the tool brush size is too big or small, click Expert, select the tool, set the brush size, and return to Guide mode. For details see Chapter 8.

Note: Be careful not to make the photo too perfect. It may lose its character.

8 Scroll down, and click **Auto Levels**.

9 Scroll down, and click **Auto Contrast**.

10 Scroll down, and click **Sharpen**.

11 Click **Done**.

Photoshop Elements creates a retouched old photo.

TIPS

How can I fix a color photo?
Click the **Auto Color** button. It guesses the best color balance. Old photos often lose blue and then green, and if the photo is very yellow Auto Color may not work. If all else fails, click **Convert to B&W** to remove all color.

When should I crop?
You can click the **Crop** button to remove unwanted areas before you start editing. However, you may get better results if you crop before you click **Done.** Other steps may reveal details and features you want to keep.

Improve a Portrait

You can use the Perfect Portrait panel to improve portraits of all kinds, including head-and-shoulders shots, face-only views, and full body shots. The panel includes tools for removing wrinkles and blemishes, adding subtle enhancements, and even for making a subject look slightly slimmer.

Professional digital artists use similar techniques to create the flawless portraits seen on magazine covers. You can use them to make friends and family look younger and more attractive.

Improve a Portrait

1 In the Editor, click **Guided**.

Note: For more on opening the Editor, see Chapter 1.

Guided mode opens.

2 If the Touchup list is not open, click the arrow to open it (▽ changes to ▲).

Click **Perfect Portrait**.

Ⓐ The Perfect Portrait panel opens.

Ⓑ You can use the Zoom tool (🔍) to magnify areas as you work on them.

3 Click **Apply Smart Blur**.

Ⓑ The Smart Blur dialog box opens.

4 Click and drag the Radius slider to blur the image.

Note: Set the radius to remove fine details such as wrinkles but to leave larger details.

5 Click **OK**.

Photoshop Elements applies the blur to the entire photo.

6 Click **Reveal Original** to remove the blur.

7 Click the **Blur Brush** tool.

8 Click and drag the brush around areas you want to fix.

Note: Typically you fix wrinkles around the eyes, neck, and mouth.

Note: This example exaggerates the edits so you can see them.

Photoshop Elements paints the areas you select with blurred pixels, smoothing away wrinkles and other flaws.

TIPS

How can I whiten the teeth of a subject?
In the Create a Perfect Portrait panel, click **Whiten Teeth**. Click and drag the cursor across teeth to remove any mild colorcast. Be careful not to overuse this effect. When combined with other improvements, it can make a model look unrealistically shiny.

How do I slim a model?
Click the **Slim Down** button at the bottom of the panel. This is not a complex effect; it simply makes the photo less wide. If you overuse this effect, it makes faces too narrow.

continued ▶

You can use Smart Blur and Spot Healing to remove wrinkles and other blemishes. You can also make your models look better by brightening their eyes and darkening their eyebrows.

Be careful not to overuse these effects. A model who looks too perfect moves into a waxy-looking "uncanny valley" and no longer appears human. Portraits of friends and family are more realistic if you tone down blemishes and wrinkles without removing them altogether.

Improve a Portrait (continued)

9 Click **Increase Contrast.**

Photoshop Elements increases the contrast of the image.

10 Click the **Spot Healing Tool.**

11 Click around the image to remove spots, lumps, bumps, and other minor blemishes.

⑫ Click the **Brighten Eyes** tool.

⑬ Click the pupils of both eyes to make them brighter.

⑭ Click the **Darken Eyebrows** tool.

⑮ Click and drag the eyebrows to darken them.

⑯ Click **Done**.

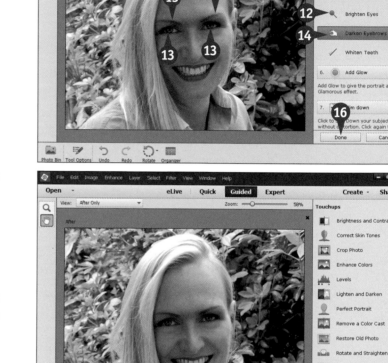

Photoshop Elements applies all the changes.

Ⓒ You can click **Undo** to undo the changes one by one.

Note: When you use Undo, the commands use the standard Photoshop Element command names, which do not always match the names of the buttons you see in Guided mode.

TIP

What does the Add Glow button do?

The Add Glow button applies a glow effect, adding an unearthly nimbus of glowing highlights around the subject. Used very subtly, it can improve lighting and exposure and make a portrait look brighter. Visually, this makes the subject appear friendlier. Used less subtly, it creates a misty and unrealistically romantic effect. For realistic results, set the **Graininess** slider to 0. For more about filters, see Chapter 12.

Apply a Lomo Camera Effect

You can make your image look as if it was shot with a Lomo film camera. Lomo cameras are famous for creating warm, vivid images. The Lomo look was a big influence on various popular camphone sharing services. You can learn more at www.lomography.com.

The Guided steps shift the color balance, increase saturation, and add the characteristic vignette (dark corners) to the image.

Apply a Lomo Camera Effect

1 In the Editor, click **Guided**.

Note: For more on opening the Editor, see Chapter 1.

Guided mode opens.

2 If the Camera Effects list is not open, click the arrow to open it (☑ changes to ☒).

3 Click **Lomo Camera Effect**.

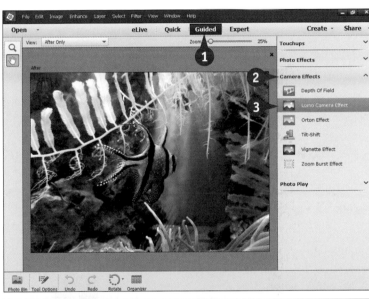

4 Click **Lomo Camera Effect**.

Photoshop Elements makes the colors more intense and increases the contrast.

You can click the button multiple times to increase the effect.

216

5 Click **Apply Vignette**.

Ⓐ Photoshop Elements darkens the corners of the image.

You can click the button multiple times to increase the effect.

6 Click **Done**.

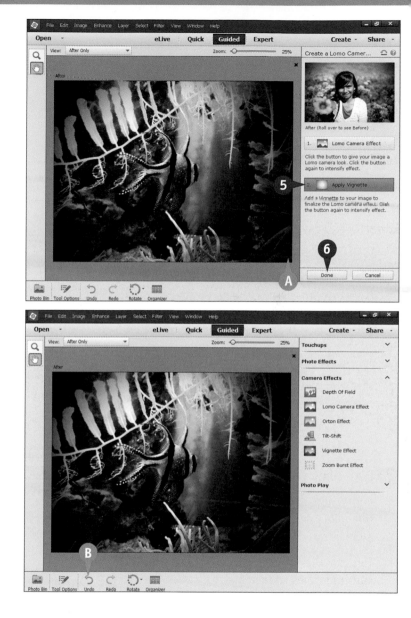

Photoshop Elements applies the effect.

Ⓑ You can click **Undo** to undo the changes.

TIPS

How do I enhance the colors in an image?
The Saturated Film Effect feature in Guided mode adds punch and intensity to the colors in your image, making them look more like traditional film. You can click the button more than once to increase the intensity.

How do I just add vignetting to an image?
The Vignette Effect in Guided mode enables you to add shadowing to the periphery of your image. You control the opacity, shape, and color of your vignette. You can also select a black or white vignette.

Add Motion with Zoom Burst

You can use Zoom Burst to simulate motion, add drama, and make a photo look more dynamic. The effect recreates the look you can produce by leaving the shutter open on a professional camera and zooming the lens. For good results, crop the image first to put the main subject in the center.

After you add the zoom effect, you can add a Focus Area to remove unwanted blurring. You can also add a vignette (corner shadow) to pull attention toward your subject.

Add Motion with Zoom Burst

1 In the Editor, click **Guided**.

Note: For more on opening the Editor, see Chapter 1.

Guided mode opens.

2 If the Camera Effects list is not open, click the arrow to open it (⌄ changes to ⌃).

3 Click **Zoom Burst Effect**.

A Optionally, you can use the crop tool to cut away the sides of the image and place the subject in the center.

4 Click **Add Zoom Burst**.

Photoshop Elements adds radial blur to the image. You can click the button multiple times to intensify the effect.

5 Click **Add Focus Area**.

6 Click and drag a line to remove some of the blur. You can repeat this step to bring the main subject back into focus.

Photoshop Elements removes the blur from the area you select.

B Optionally, you can click **Apply Vignette** to add shadowing to the edges of the image.

You can click the button multiple times to darken the shadowing.

Note: This is a strong effect, and it can make a photo look dark, so you may want to skip this step.

7 Click **Done**.

Photoshop Elements applies the effect.

TIP

How else can I add the appearance of motion to my image?
Different blur filters are available that make objects in your image look like they are moving. Click **Expert** to switch to Expert mode. Click **Filter** and then **Blur** to access the Blur filter menu. Click **Radial Blur** to apply the effects seen in the Zoom Burst feature, or click **Motion Blur** to add blurring along a straight line.

Miniaturize Scenes with Tilt Shift

Y ou can use the Tilt Shift effect to make scenes look like miniatures. The effect applies a strong blur while keeping a horizontal area in focus. This makes the image look like a close-up, which appears to shrink it. The effect works well on scenes with buildings, but not on portraits.

The default blur often works well, but you can modify the focus area to customize the effect. You can also refine the effect with sliders that set the amount of blur, and add contrast and color saturation.

Miniaturize Scenes with Tilt Shift

1 In the Editor, click **Guided**.

Note: For more on opening the Editor, see Chapter 1.

Guided mode opens.

2 If the Camera Effects list is not open, click the arrow to open it (∨ changes to ∧).

3 Click **Tilt-Shift**.

4 Click **Add Tilt-Shift**.

Photoshop Elements blurs the image but leaves a horizontal band in focus.

Note: This one-click version of the effect often produces good results.

Click **Modify Focus Area**.

 Click and drag a line to customize the in-focus area.

Note: A vertical line creates a horizontal in-focus area, and vice versa.

Note: The relationship between the line you draw and the in-focus area is rather loose. You can keep redrawing the line until you get an effect that looks good.

Photoshop Elements modifies the focus area.

7 Click **Refine Effect**.

8 Click and drag the sliders to adjust the blur, contrast, and saturation.

Note: You can usually leave Blur unchanged. For a good result, increase Contrast and Saturation slightly.

Note: The sliders affect only the area that is blurred.

9 Click **Done**.

The scene now looks like a miniature.

 TIP

Why is the effect called Tilt Shift?

Tilt shift was invented to fix keystoning — leaning perspective distortion — in architectural photography. It uses special lenses that can be tilted and shifted manually to eliminate distortion. Photographers discovered that using a small depth of field created scenes that looked like miniatures. The blur tools in Photoshop Elements make it easy to simulate the effect digitally without special equipment.

Create Soft Focus with the Orton Effect

You can use the Orton Effect to add a misty soft focus look to an image. The effect works well on portraits and on nature scenes.

To create the effect manually, you make a copy of your image, blur it, and make it partially transparent so sharp details from the original image show through. The Guided edit in Photoshop Elements creates the effect with a single click. However, you can customize the amount of blur, add noise to simulate film grain, and adjust the brightness.

Create Soft Focus with the Orton Effect

1 In the Editor, click **Guided**.

Note: For more on opening the Editor, see Chapter 1.

    Guided mode opens.

2 If the Camera Effects list is not open, click the arrow to open it (☑ changes to ☒).

3 Click **Orton Effect**.

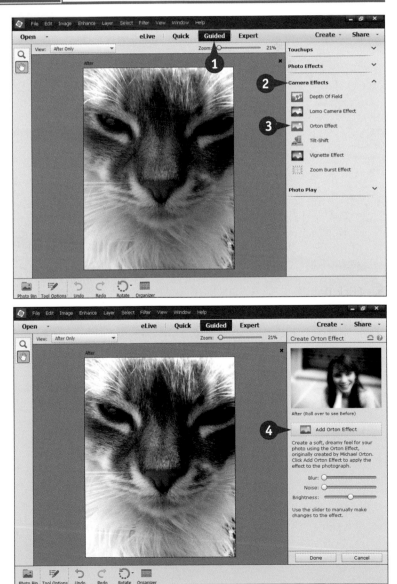

4 Click **Add Orton Effect**.

    Photoshop Elements blurs the image but lets some of the original sharpness show through.

Note: This one-click version of the effect often produces good results.

5 Click and drag the Blur slider to modify the blur radius.

Note: The extreme positions of the slider create two very different looks. Both can be equally successful.

Photoshop Elements modifies the blur.

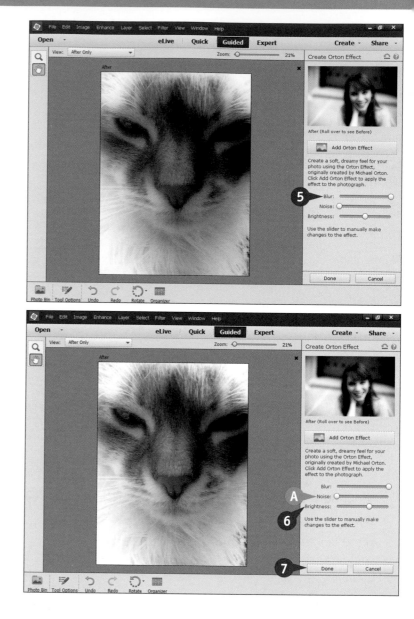

6 Click and drag the Brightness slider to make the blurred layer brighter.

A You can add grainy noise with the Noise slider. Use noise as an occasional refinement, not as an essential part of the effect.

7 Click **Done**.

Photoshop creates a bright soft focus look.

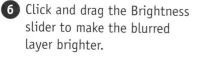

TIP

Why is this edit called the Orton Effect?
The effect was originally created by photographer Michael Orton in the 1980s. His version combined two shots of the same scene — one shot normally, one deliberately over-exposed and blurred. He then combined the two shots optically to create a dreamy "painted" look. You can find out more at www.michaelortonphotography.com.

Apply a Reflection

In Guided mode, you can complete steps to create a realistic reflection of the content in your image. The result makes it appear that your content is over water or a shiny surface. The plain mirror effect works better than the water simulation.

To produce the effect, Photoshop Elements duplicates your content and places it below the original image. Then you add color fill, blur, and a gradient to make the reflection more convincing.

Apply a Reflection

1 In the Editor, click **Guided**.

Note: For more on opening the Editor, see Chapter 1.

   Guided mode opens.

2 If the Photo Play list is not open, click the arrow to open it (☑ changes to ☒).

3 Click **Reflection**.

4 Click **Add Reflection**.

Ⓐ Photoshop Elements copies and inverts the photo to create a reflection effect.

5 Click the **Eyedropper tool**.

6 Click inside the image to select a background color. A neutral or light gray is often a good choice.

7 Click **Fill Background** to fill the reflection with the selected color.

8 Click an effect button to add texture to the reflection.

The Floor button adds blur, the Glass button distorts the image, and the Water button adds distortion and blur in two separate steps.

9 In the dialog box that appears, adjust the effect settings and click **OK** to apply the effect.

Note: This example shows the Glass effect with a large distortion setting.

B You can use the Intensity slider to make the effect more or less obvious.

C You can click **Add Distortion** to simulate perspective and shrink the reflection vertically.

D If you add distortion, you can use the **Crop** tool to remove the colored background that appears under the image.

10 Click the **Gradient Tool**.

11 Click and drag from the bottom of the reflection up to fade the reflection.

12 Click **Done**.

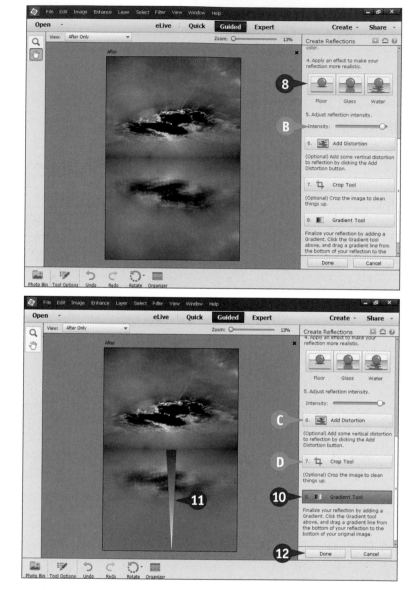

TIP

How can I improve the look of the reflection?
The Guided edit works well with plain mirror reflections, but the water reflection effect is not completely convincing. For a better result, create a plain mirror reflection using this tool. Switch to Expert mode. Use the Marquee tool (▦) to select the reflected area. Then use the **Filter ➪ Distort** menu to experiment with various other distortion effects. **Ocean Ripple, Wave, Glass**, and **ZigZag** can all add more detail, especially if you apply a combination of effects and add more horizontal motion blur afterwards.

Put an Object Out of Bounds

In Guided mode, you can edit your image so that part of an object in it extends outside the bounds of the main image frame. For example, you can make a treetop stick out of the top of a picture of a park or a swinging bat extend out of the side of a baseball scene.

You create the effect by cropping to define the main content frame and then selecting the part of the object that should extend outside the cropped area. You can enhance the 3D effect by adding a background gradient and drop shadow.

Put an Object Out of Bounds

1 In the Editor, click **Guided**.

Note: For more on opening the Editor, see Chapter 1.

Guided mode opens.

2 If the Photo Play list is not open, click the arrow to open it (☑ changes to ⊡).

3 Click **Out of Bounds**.

4 Click **Add Frame**.

5 Click and drag the crop handles to define a frame.

You can click Ctrl + Alt + Shift (⌘ + Option + Shift on a Mac) and drag the corner handles to skew the frame to give it depth.

6 Click ☑ or press Enter to accept the crop.

Photoshop Elements crops the image to the frame.

7 Click ☑ or press Enter a second time to complete the frame.

Photoshop Elements restore the area outside the frame with reduced transparency.

8 Click the **Selection Tool**.

9 Click and drag the selection tool to define the out-of-bounds part of the image.

10 Click **Out of Bounds Effect**.

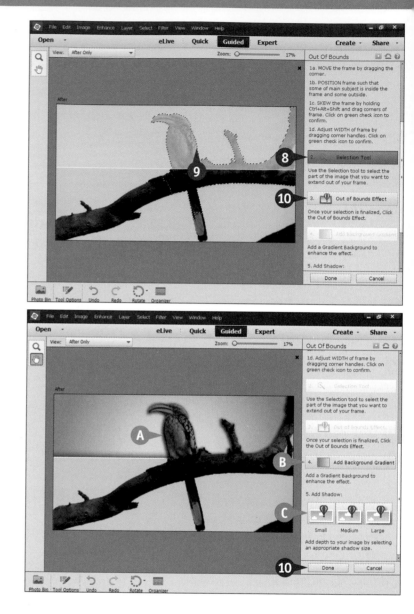

A Photoshop Elements extends the selected content outside the main frame.

B Optionally, you can click **Add Background Gradient** to enhance the background.

C Optionally, click a Shadow button to apply a drop shadow and emphasize the out-of-bounds content.

11 Click **Done**.

Photoshop Elements applies the Out of Bounds effect.

TIP

When would I add a gradient and a shadow?
You can use the gradient effect creatively. The default light gray radial gradient subtly enhances the out of bounds area. You can select any other gradient or shape in the associated dialog box. Some options are more obvious and eye-catching. The shadow effect is unsubtle and does not always enhance a photo. But you can use the effect on marketing and promotional photography to make an image stand out from the page.

Create a Vintage Look

You can use the new Old Fashioned Photo Guided Edit to give a photo a vintage look. The edit converts the photo to black and white, changes the brightness and contrast, and applies an overall tint. You can also add some subtle noise to bring out textures.

The edit does not fade the photo or add tears, spots, stains and other blemishes. You can add these effects by hand later in Expert mode. However, it does create a "good enough" vintage look for casual applications.

Create a Vintage Look

1 In the Editor, click **Guided**.

Note: For more on opening the Editor, see Chapter 1.

Guided mode opens.

2 If the Touchups list is not open, click the arrow to open it (☑ changes to ☒).

3 Click **Old Fashioned Photo**.

4 Click one of the three Black and White presets to remove all color.

The three presets are slightly different. You can select **Edit ⇨ Undo** after each preset to try a different one.

Photoshop Elements converts the image.

5 Click **Adjust Tone**.

Photoshop Elements makes a small change to the contrast, brightness, and lighting balance.

6 Click **Add Texture**.

Photoshop Elements adds a hint of noise to bring out the textures in the image.

7 Click **Add Hue/Saturation**.

8 Click and drag the **Hue** slider to change the color.

Note: The default sepia color looks good on many images.

9 Click and drag the **Saturation** slider to change the color intensity.

Note: A subtle tint often looks more convincingly vintage than a more intense color.

A You can click and drag the **Lightness** slider to change the brightness of the image, but you do not usually need to.

10 Click **OK**.

11 Click **Done**.

Photoshop Elements applies the effect.

B You can click **Undo** to undo all the changes and start again.

TIP

Why would I use a different color for a vintage photo?

The sepia effect, created with light orange and low saturation, is the definitive vintage look. But you can use other colors. Deep blue creates a colder and more stark effect. Light blue creates a cooler, more abstract look. You can use any tint creatively. The effect often works best with just a hint of color. Professional photographers tint black and white images so subtly that you often cannot see any obvious color at all — but the tint still creates a mood.

Using Selective Color

You can use the new B&W Selection Guided Edit to combined areas of color and black and white in the same image. To use the tool, paint over the areas you want to convert to black and white. The B&W Selection Brush does not always make perfect selections, so you can correct it with a B&W Selection Detail Brush.

The effect is simple but can be very striking. It works well with flowers, pets, other animals, and human portraits. You can use the alternative B&W Color Pop edit to "pop" a color automatically.

Using Selective Color

1. In the Editor, click **Guided**.

2. If the Touchups list is not open, click the arrow to open it (☑ changes to ☒).

3. Click **B&W Selection**.

4. Click **B&W Selection Brush**, and drag the slider to select a brush size.

5. Paint on the image to remove color.

Note: Ignore areas where the selection spills over. You can fix them in the next step.

6. Scroll down, and click the **B&W Detail Brush**.

7. Click add or subtract to expand or shrink the area without color.

8. Drag the slider to select a brush size.

9. Paint on the photo to fix any errors added in step **5**.

10. Click **Done**.

    Photoshop Elements creates a selective black and white effect.

Note: You can click the **Invert Effect** check box to swap the areas of color and black and white.

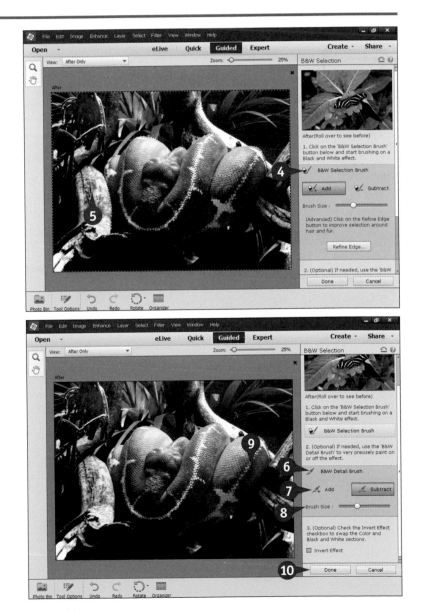

230

Create Black and White Noir

You can use the new Black and White Guided Edit to add drama and intensity to photos. In black-and-white photos contrast, tone, and texture stand in for color. You can use this Guided Edit to enhance all three elements in any black-and-white image. You can emphasize highlights (bright areas) or shadows to change the tone. You can also add a grainy glow, and increase the overall contrast even further.

Create Black and White Noir

1 In the Editor, click **Guided**.

2 If the Touchups list is not open, click the arrow to open it (changes to).

3 Click **Black and White**.

4 Click one of the four **Black & White** presets.

Note: Select the Darker preset for a noir effect.

5 Click **Diffuse Glow**.

6 Use the **Size** and **Opacity** sliders to add a hint of glow to the image.

Note: The effect is subtle.

7 Click **Increase Contrast** to add contrast and make the image more dramatic.

Note: You can repeat this step more than once. Try to avoid blowing out the highlights.

8 Click **Done**.

Photoshop Elements creates a darker and moodier version of your photo.

Painting and Drawing on Photos

Photoshop Elements offers a comprehensive set of tools for painting and drawing on images, adding shapes and text, and using single colors or gradients.

Set the Foreground and Background Colors

The painting and drawing tools in Photoshop Elements work with foreground and background colors. The Brush, Pencil, and Text tools apply the foreground color. The Eraser tool applies the background color.

You can set the colors by clicking the color selection boxes in the toolbar to set these colors. You can also swap the colors, reset them to white and black, and access a selection of popular and/or useful colors called swatches.

Set the Foreground and Background Colors

1 In the Editor, click **Expert**.

Note: For more on opening the Editor, see Chapter 1.

2 Click the foreground color box.

The Color Picker dialog box opens.

3 Click and drag the slider to select a hue.

4 Click and drag in the box to set the saturation and lightness for the hue.

Note: You can "pick up" a color from a preview image by clicking in the Editor preview window. The hue slider and saturation/lightness box and cursor change to match the color.

5 Click **OK**.

(A) The color appears in the foreground color box.

You can now paint and draw with this color. Repeat steps **2** to **5** to select a different color.

(6) Click the background color box.

(7) Repeat Steps **3** to **5** to set the color.

(B) The color appears in the background color box.

(C) You can reset the colors by clicking the Default icon (◼).

(D) You can swap the foreground and background colors by clicking the switch icon (↰).

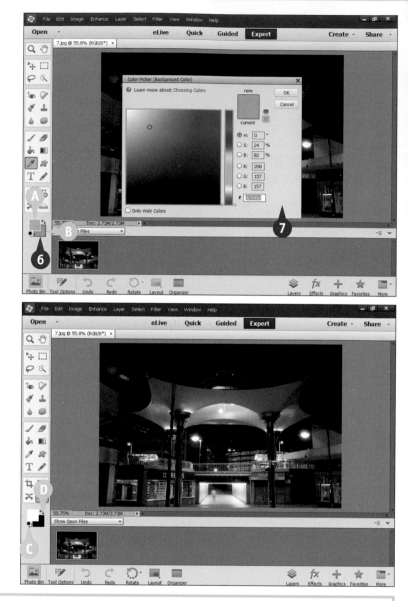

TIPS

What do the numbers in the dialog box mean?
Colors are defined as a mix of red, green, and blue (RGB) values, or as Hue, Saturation, and Brightness (HSB) values. RGB values are between 0 and 255. The numbers after the hash (#) are the RGB values in hexadecimal (base 16), as used by web designers. Hue is a value between 0 and 360 degrees, and selects a base color. Saturation defines the color intensity between 0% (no color) and 100%. Brightness sets the light/dark balance between 0% and 100%.

Where can I find preset colors?
Click **Window ⇨ Color Swatches**. To set the foreground color, click one of the swatches. To set the background color, `Ctrl`+click (`⌘`+click on a Mac).

Add Color with the Brush Tool

You can use the Brush tool to paint color onto your image. By default, the color has no texture, so it does not look very realistic. But you can use the brush tool as a virtual paintbox: You can change the size and softness of the brush, or you can select a virtual airbrush.

To paint color onto the shading and texture in a photo, select the Hue or the Color option in the brush Mode menu. These modes keep the black-and-white detail in the image but paint new colors onto it. Use the Opacity slider to set the color intensity.

Add Color with the Brush Tool

1 In the Editor, click **Expert**.

Note: For more on opening the Editor, see Chapter 1.

2 Click the foreground color selector, and set the foreground color.

Note: See the previous section for details.

3 Click the **Brush** tool ().

Ⓐ You can click the **Brush** menu and select a brush preset to create different effects.

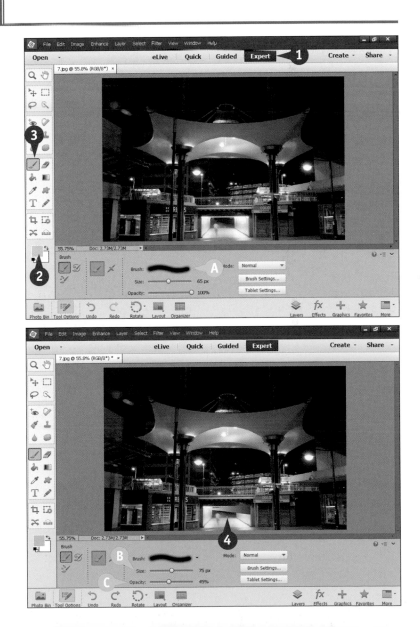

Ⓑ You can click and drag the **Size** slider to set the brush size.

Ⓒ You can click and drag the **Opacity** slider to set the color intensity.

Note: The lower you set the opacity, the more transparent and less intense the color.

4 Drag the mouse to paint on the image.

The mouse paints solid color onto the photo. Even with lowered opacity, the effect does not look realistic.

5 Click the Mode menu, and select **Color.**

6 Drag the mouse to paint on the image.

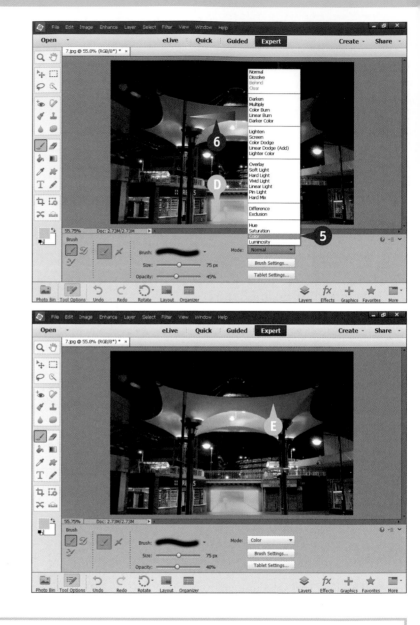

 In this mode, the black-and-white detail blends with the color to create a more realistic look.

Note: The color in this example is exaggerated for effect.

Note: You can select **Hue** and/or drag the opacity slider to the left to paint with more subtle color.

TIPS

How do I paint hard-edged lines?
Use the Pencil tool (). It works like the Brush tool () and applies the foreground color, but paints lines with hard edges.

What can I do with the Impressionist Brush tool?
The Impressionist Brush () blends colors from the image to create blob-like Impressionistic effects. It does not use the foreground or background colors. You can select the tool from the menu that appears when you right-click the Brush tool (). Click the Advanced menu to open further options. You can create different effects by changing the drawing mode.

Change Brush Styles

You can vary your edits by selecting various preset brush styles. The selection includes plain brushes with varying sizes and hard or soft edges, textured brushes, and special effect brushes that paint recognizable shapes and objects.

You can customize any brush to set the spacing of each "stroke," the fade, the amount of color variation, the hardness, and the roundness.

Change Brush Styles

Select from a Predefined Set

1 In the Editor, click **Expert**.

Note: For more on opening the Editor, see Chapter 1.

2 Click the **Brush** tool (▱).

3 Click the **Brush** menu in the Tool Options panel.

4 Click the **Brush menu** within the menu to select a set of brushes.

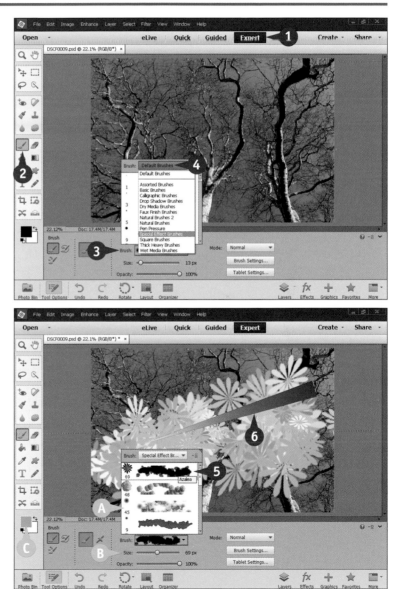

Ⓐ The set appears in the Brush menu.

5 Click a brush style to select it.

The mouse pointer changes to the new brush shape.

Ⓑ You can click the slider to adjust the brush size.

Ⓒ You can click the foreground color box to choose a color to apply with the brush. The actual color applied may vary depending on the brush type.

6 Click and drag the brush on the photo.

Photoshop Elements applies the brush to the area.

Customize a Brush

1 Click **Brush Settings**.

The Brush Settings dialog box opens.

D You can limit the length of your brushstrokes with the Fade slider.

E You can randomize the painted color with the Hue Jitter slider.

F You can change the shape of the brush tip by clicking and dragging here.

2 Click and drag the brush on the photo.

Photoshop Elements applies the customized brush to the area.

Note: For more on applying the brush, see the previous section, "Add Color with the Brush Tool."

TIP

How can I make a brush apply dots instead of a line?
In the Tool Options panel, click **Brush Settings** to open the Brush Settings dialog box. Click and drag the slider to increase the Spacing value to greater than 100%. When you click and drag a brush shape, you get dots, patches, or individual shapes (**A**), instead of a line or curve.

Use a Brush to Replace a Color

Y ou can use the Color Replacement tool to paint the foreground color over an existing color. The tool keeps black-and-white detail but replaces colors. You can use this to replace one color with another. If you are skillful, you can repeat the process to repaint an area with a selection of different colors.

Unlike the Brush tool, the Color Replacement tool includes a tolerance setting, which paints matching colors around your brush strokes. Set a low tolerance to match colors precisely, and set a high tolerance to select a wider area. You can also change the brush size.

Using a Brush to Replace a Color

1 In the Editor, click **Expert**.

Note: For more on opening the Editor, see Chapter 1.

2 Click the **Brush** tool (🖌).

3 In the Tool Options panel, click the **Color Replacement** tool (🖌).

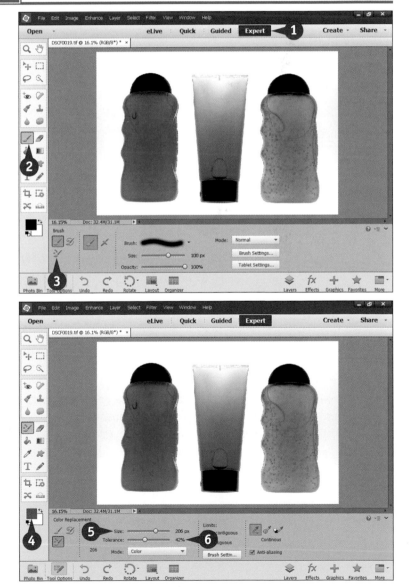

4 Click the foreground color box, and select the color you want to paint with.

5 Click and drag the slider to select a brush size.

Note: You can select a large brush. You do not need to select a tiny brush to paint accurately.

6 Click and drag the slider to set a tolerance from 1% to 100%.

Note: Experiment with the tolerance. Select a value that modifies the color you want to change, but does not spill into surrounding colors.

7 Click and drag in your image.

Photoshop Elements replaces the color.

A If you have set the tolerance correctly, the color does not spill into surrounding areas even if you paint over it.

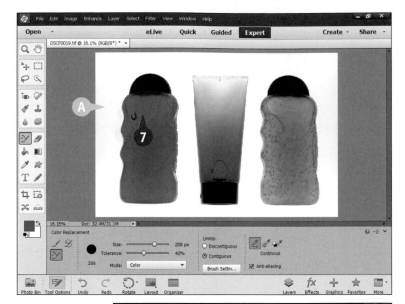

8 Continue painting until the object or area is a new color.

Photoshop Elements replaces more color.

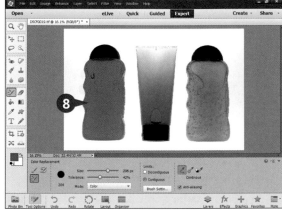

TIP

How do I fill a selection with a color?
Make a selection with a selection tool, and then click **Edit** and **Fill Selection**. In the Fill Layer dialog box that appears, click the menu to select the Foreground Color (Ⓐ) and then set an opacity for the fill color (Ⓑ). Click OK to fill the selection.

Adjust Colors with the Smart Brush

You can paint color adjustments onto objects with the Smart Brush tool. This is a versatile tool. You can use it to increase, decrease, remove, or transform color. You can also darken overexposed areas or brighten areas that are in shadow.

The tool includes effects grouped into categories. Use the effects in the Portrait category to give models a tan, whiten teeth, or change lip color to apply virtual lipstick. Options in the Special Effects category create striking and unusual color effects.

Adjust Colors with the Smart Brush

Select a Smart Brush Effect

1 In the Editor, click **Expert**.

Note: For more on opening the Editor, see Chapter 1.

2 Click the **Smart Brush** tool (🖌).

3 Click the menu to open a list of effect categories.

4 Click the menu, and select a category.

Note: This example selects the Color category.

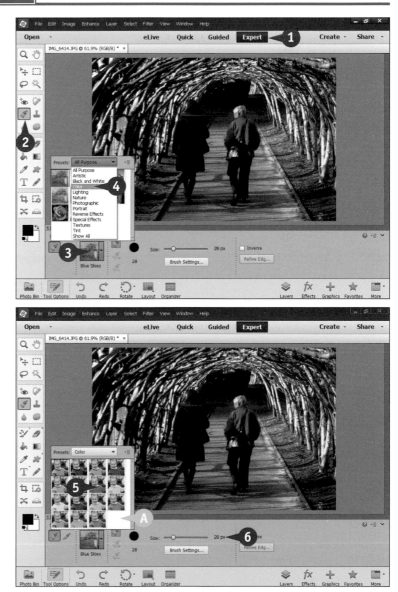

Ⓐ The sub-menu shows a thumbnail for each effect.

5 Click an effect.

Note: This example selects a pink color.

You can click anywhere outside the menu to close it. You can also leave it open to try out different effects.

6 Click the slider to set a brush size.

Note: Make the brush small enough to paint details in the area you want to edit.

7 Click and drag over objects in your image to apply the effect.

Photoshop Elements selects the objects and applies the painting effect.

B You can click **Inverse** (☐ changes to ☑) to invert your selection and apply the effect to the other pixels in your layer.

8 Repeat step **7** until you have painted the object or area you want to edit.

C You can click the add/remove brush variations to paint again, adding or removing areas from the selection.

Apply a Different Effect to a Selected Area

1 Click the menu to open the list of effect categories.

A You can click a different effect to apply it.

Note: You can also click the category menu to select a different category and select a new effect in the new category.

Photoshop Elements changes the Smart Brush effect.

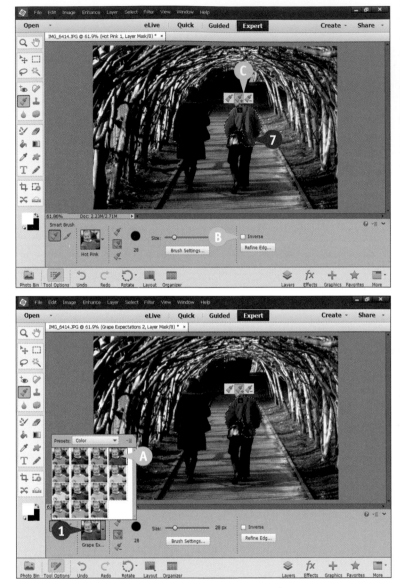

continued ▶

TIP

How do I decrease the effect of the Smart Brush so that it is only partially applied?
Smart Brush effects are applied as *adjustment layers* — floating areas of color that are stored separately from the main image. To change the intensity of a Smart Brush effect, you can change the opacity of its adjustment layer. For more about layers and adjustment layers, see Chapter 13.

You can make a selection bigger or smaller by using the Add to selection and Subtract from selection variations on the Smart Brush.

You can also switch to the Detail Smart Brush tool. Use the Detail Smart Brush to make fine adjustments to the selection. The tool does not try to select pixels with a matching color as you paint. It selects the colors you paint over.

Adjust Colors with the Smart Brush (continued)

Modify a Selection

After applying a Smart Brush effect to one part of the image, you can apply a different effect to another part.

1 Click the **Add to selection** tool ( ).

2 Click and drag over a new area in your image.

Photoshop Elements applies the painting effect.

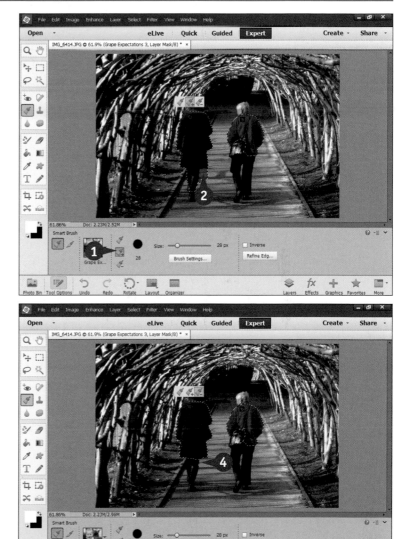

3 Click the **Subtract from Selection** tool ( ).

4 Paint on the image to remove areas from the selection.

You can use this tool to correct color spill.

Photoshop Elements removes the effect from the areas you paint over.

Paint Details

1 In the Tool Options panel, click the **Detail Smart Brush** tool ().

2 Click and drag the slider to adjust the brush size.

Note: Because this tool is more precise, you usually need to select a smaller brush size.

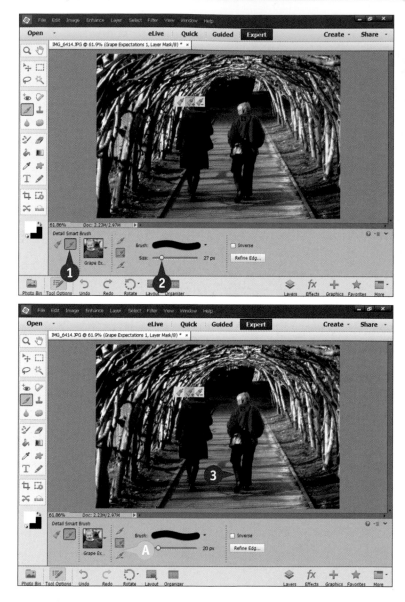

3 Paint on the image to apply the current effect.

Note: This example applies color to a black area.

A You can click the **Add to. . .** and **Subtract from. . .** variations on the Detail Smart Brush to modify the painted area.

Photoshop Elements applies the effect without trying to expand it into areas of matching color around your brush strokes.

TIPS

How can I apply different effects in the same image?
After you apply a Smart Brush effect, click **Select** ⇨ **Deselect** in the main menu. Photoshop Elements deselects the current selection. You can now select the Smart Brush tool in the Tool Options area (🖌), paint a new selection, and apply a different effect to it.

How can I apply Smart Brush textures?
Click **Textures** in the Smart Brush presets menu. Effects include Behind Net, which covers your selection with thin black lines, and Lizard Skin, which applies a scaly look. You can also apply texture effects using one of the Photoshop Elements texture filters. For more about filters, see Chapter 12.

Draw a Simple Shape

You can use the Shape tool to draw shapes on your image. The tool includes rectangles, rounded rectangles, ellipses, polygons, stars, and straight lines.

You can fill a shape with solid color. You can also apply styles — preset graphic effects that draw colors and textures in and around the shape. Because shapes are redrawn when you edit them, you can resize them and try out different fill colors and styles.

Draw a Simple Shape

1 In the Editor, click **Expert**.

Note: For more on opening the Editor, see Chapter 1.

2 Click the **Shape** tool.

Note: The tool defaults to a rectangle shape. But you can select six variations — custom, rectangle, rounded rectangle, ellipse, polygon, and star.

3 Click the menu to select an aspect ratio.

Note: Select **Square** to force the tool to draw a square instead of a rectangle.

4 Click and drag to draw the shape.

Photoshop Elements draws the shape on the photo.

Ⓐ The shape appears on its own layer, so you can edit it and delete it without changing the original photo. See Chapter 13 for more about layers.

C You can click the **Fill Color** menu to view a collection of color presets.

D You can click one of the colors to apply it to the shape.

E You can click the **Styles** menu to view a collection of color presets.

F You can click the sub-menu to view and select different style categories.

G You can click one of the colors to apply it to the shape.

Photoshop Elements applies the style to the shape.

Note: Most styles override and ignore the fill color.

TIPS

How do I apply a simple stroke to the shape?
You can apply plain black strokes by selecting Effects in the toolbar, clicking Styles, and selecting Strokes from the menu. You can now drag preset strokes onto the current shape. To customize the stroke settings, click ⬛ and click the disclosure triangle next to Stroke to see a settings dialog box.

What is the difference between stars and polygons?
Both stars and polygons have a setting for the number of sides. Polygons include that many sides. Stars have an equivalent number of points, but twice as many sides. Stars also have an Indent setting which sets how "pointy" the star is. When the Indent is 0 percent, the star is the same as a polygon. When it is 99%, the lines between points are almost straight lines.

Add an Arrow

You can use the Custom Shape tool in Photoshop Elements to draw complex shapes, including arrows and other graphics. The Custom Shape tool includes a large library of ready-made shapes you can draw on an image.

This example explains how to draw an arrow. You can find various arrow shapes under the Arrows sub-menu.

Add an Arrow

1 In the Editor, click **Expert**.

Note: For more on opening the Editor, see Chapter 1.

2 Click the Shape icon.

Any of the shape tools may be visible.

3 Click the **Custom Shape** tool (▨).

4 Click the shape menu.

5 Click an arrow shape to select it.

Ⓐ For a wider selection of arrows, click the menu and select **Arrows**.

Ⓑ You can use the fill color menu to select an eye-catching color.

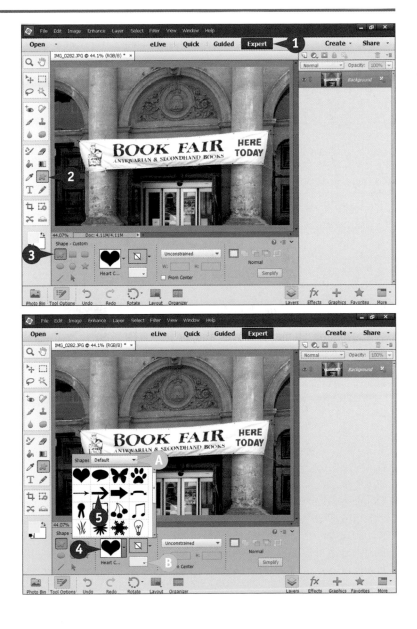

6 Click and drag to draw the arrow.

The arrow is horizontal. You can set the dimensions by dragging the mouse left/right and up/down.

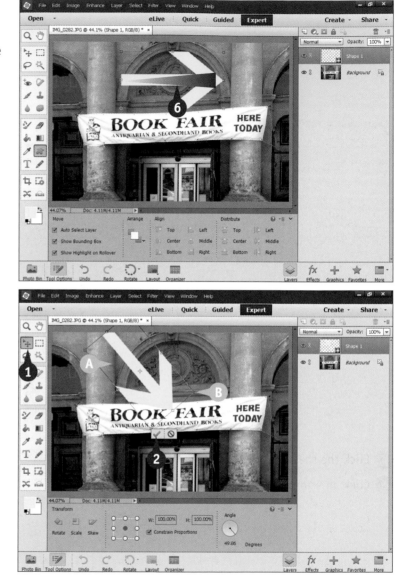

To Rotate or Move the Arrow

1 Click the Move tool (📥).

A You can click and drag in the outline box to move the arrow.

B You can hover the mouse close to the corners of the box and then drag to rotate the arrow.

2 Click ☑ to confirm the edit.

Photoshop Elements moves and/or rotates the arrow.

TIP

Can I draw arrows with the line tool?
Yes. The line tool includes a smaller selection of arrow shapes than the custom shape menu, but you can use the tool to draw an arrow diagonally without having to rotate it. Select the Shape tool, and click **Shape ⇨ Line** to select the line tool. Unlike the other shapes, the line tool includes a special Arrow head menu. Click the menu, and select whether you want no arrow heads, an arrow head at the start or the end of the line, or arrow heads at both ends. Drag to draw the line. Photoshop Elements applies fill colors and styles in the usual way.

Apply the Eraser

You can use the Eraser tool to remove unwanted objects and areas. When you select the standard Eraser tool, it paints with the background color. You can select three modes: Pencil has a hard edge, brush uses a brush preset, and block paints with a rectangular area.

The Eraser tool has two variations. The Background Eraser makes the erased pixels transparent. The Magic Eraser deletes pixels of similar color around the mouse pointer.

Apply the Eraser

Adjust the Eraser Settings

1. In the Editor, click **Expert**.

Note: For more on opening the Editor, see Chapter 1.

2. Click the Erase box in the toolbar.

3. If the standard Eraser (🖉) is not selected, click its icon.

Ⓐ You can click the background color box to select the color painted by the Eraser.

Note: For more, see the section "Set the Foreground and Background Colors."

Ⓑ You can click the **Brush** menu to select a preset eraser size and type.

Ⓒ You can also click and drag the slider to set an eraser size.

Ⓓ You can click one of the **Type** options to control the shape and hardness of the eraser.

Erase the Background

1 Click and drag the mouse pointer.

Photoshop Elements replaces areas of the photo with the background color.

Use the Magic Eraser

1 Click the Magic Eraser ().

2 Click and drag the Tolerance slider to set how aggressively the Magic Eraser erases areas of similar color.

3 Click and drag the mouse pointer.

Photoshop Elements replaces areas of the photo with matching colors with the background color.

A You can select the Background Eraser () to make areas transparent instead of painting them with the background color.

TIP

Why does the standard eraser sometimes make pixels transparent?
When you load a photo and use the Eraser tool on it, the tool paints the background color. But photos can also include layers — independent floating images. If you use the Eraser on a layer, it makes pixels transparent. The Background and Magic Eraser tools convert the photo into a layer and then delete pixels from the layer. If you use the standard Eraser after using these tools, it makes pixels transparent because you are now editing a layer. For more about layers, see Chapter 13.

Apply a Gradient

You can apply a gradient, which is a smooth blend of colors, to create special effects. You can apply a gradient to a selected portion of an image or the entire image. You can use predefined color combinations or create your own blends.

You can also set the shape of the gradient, to control the shape of the color bands in the gradient. For example, in a linear gradient, the lines are parallel. In a radial gradient, they are circular.

Apply a Gradient

1 In the Editor, click **Expert**.

2 Make a selection.

Note: For more on opening the Editor, see Chapter 1. See Chapter 6 for more on making selections.

> If you do not make a selection, the gradient is applied over the image.

3 Click the **Gradient** tool (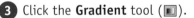).

Ⓐ You can select the gradient shape by clicking these buttons.

4 Click the gradient menu.

Ⓑ You can click the **Gradient** menu to preview more gradient categories.

5 Click a gradient preset to select it.

Ⓒ You can click **Edit** to customize the gradient.

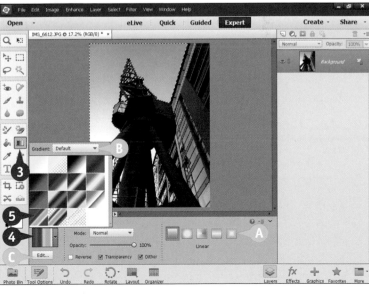

The gradient is defined by arrows called **stops.**

Ⓓ To change the color of a stop, click it and click the color box picker to open the standard color picker.

Ⓔ To change the banding, drag stops left or right.

Ⓕ To add a stop, click the **Color Midpoint** diamond.

Note: The diamond appears either side of the stop you clicked in Ⓓ.

Ⓖ To remove a stop, click it and click the Trash icon (🗑).

Ⓗ Click **OK** to use the custom gradient.

6 Click and drag the mouse pointer inside the selection.

The angle and length of the line define the angle and width of the gradient.

Photoshop Elements paints a gradient inside the selection.

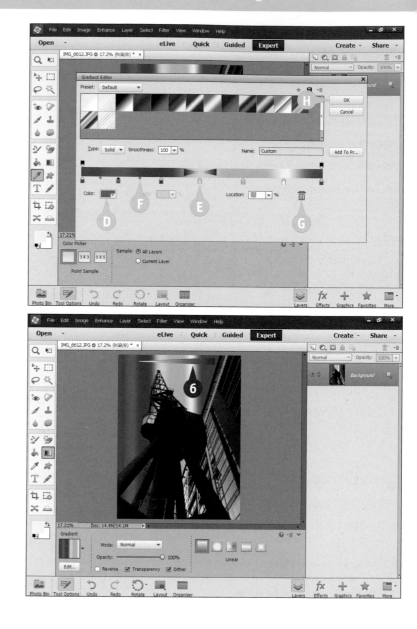

TIP

What do the different gradient shapes do?

The default gradient is **Linear** and paints parallel bands of color. The **Radial** gradient paints concentric circles of color. You can use it to create halo effects. The **Angle** gradient sweeps colors out from a single point, like a radar scan. It creates a 3D effect. The **Reflected** gradient creates a mirrored version of the Linear gradient. To create a good mirror effect, click and drag the mouse across half the target width or height. The **Diamond** gradient creates concentric squares.

Add Content from the Graphics Panel

You can use the Graphics panel to add backgrounds, frames, graphics, and other content to your image. You can move, resize, and transform the content and add more than one element.

The panel includes hundreds of clip art items grouped into categories. Many of the items need to be downloaded the first time you use them, so your computer must be connected to the Internet before you can add them.

Add Content from the Graphics Panel

Add a Transparent Frame

1 In the Editor, click **Expert**.

Note: For more on opening the Editor, see Chapter 1.

2 Click **Graphics**.

Ⓐ The Graphics panel opens.

3 Click the menu, and select **By Type** if it is not already selected.

4 Click the menu, and select **Graphics**.

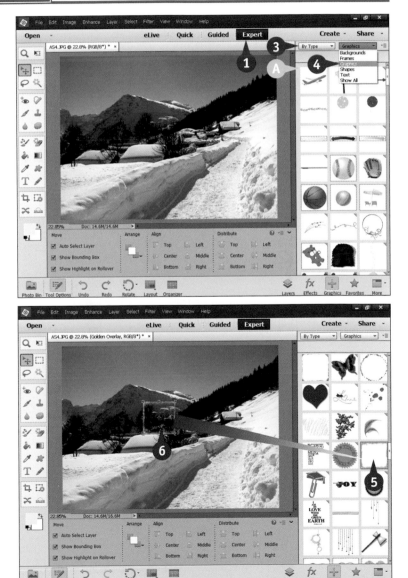

Photoshop Elements displays a selection of clip art.

5 Scroll down to the find the **Golden Overlay** item.

6 Drag it to the window.

7 Drag any corner.

B The **Place** tool options appear.

Note: You can access the Place tool options only by dragging an object into the Editor window and resizing it. The Place tool does not appear in the tool bar.

8 Uncheck the **Constrain Proportions** box (☑ changes to ☐.)

9 Drag the corners of the item again until they cover the edges of the photo.

10 Click 🔧.

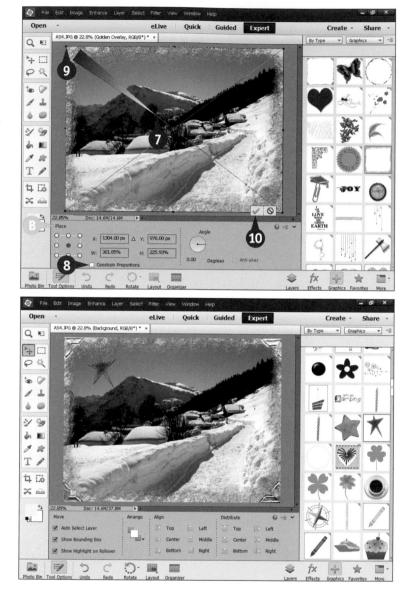

You can add further graphics to the image by repeating steps **5** to **8**.

You can move an item by clicking and dragging its selection box.

You can make the selection box disappear by selecting **Select ⇨ Deselect** in the main menu.

Photoshop Elements combines the graphics with your original photo.

TIP

How can I place a photo over a background?
When you add a background from the Graphics panel, Photoshop Elements puts it into a *layer* — a separate image that floats over your original photo and covers it. To make your photo float over the background, you must change the order in which layers appear. Chapter 13 has more information about layers. See the "Reorder Layers" section for more about changing the layer order. Chapter 13 also explains how to blend layers, so you can use the Shapes in the Graphics panel to create "painted" frames and other effects.

Add Text

You can add text to label your images, add captions, or use letters and words in more creative ways. To add text, use the Type tool. You can add horizontal or vertical text, or make the text follow a selection.

Text appears in its own layer. You can edit text to move it or resize without losing shrpness. For more about layers, see Chapter 13.

Add Text

1 In the Editor, click **Expert**.

Note: For more on opening the Editor, see Chapter 1.

2 Click the **Horizontal Type** tool (⊤).

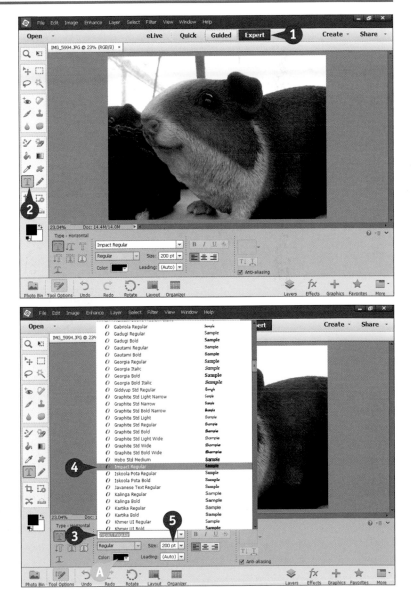

3 Click the menu to open a list of fonts.

4 Click a font to select it.

You can see a preview of each font next to the font name.

5 Type **200pt** into the font box.

This large size creates a readable caption on many recent photos. Use a smaller number on smaller digital images.

Ⓐ You can click this box to open a color picker to select a different font color.

6 Click the image to position the start of the text.

B Photoshop Elements draws a text cursor to show the position and size of the text.

You can also click and drag to define a bounding box to contain your text.

7 Type your text.

To type on the next line, press **Enter**.

8 When you finish typing your text, click ☑ or press **Ctrl**+**Enter** (⌘+**Enter** on a Mac).

You can click ⊘ or press **Esc** to cancel.

Photoshop Elements adds text to the image.

The text appears inside a selection box. To remove the selection box, click any tool except the Move tool (⊕.)

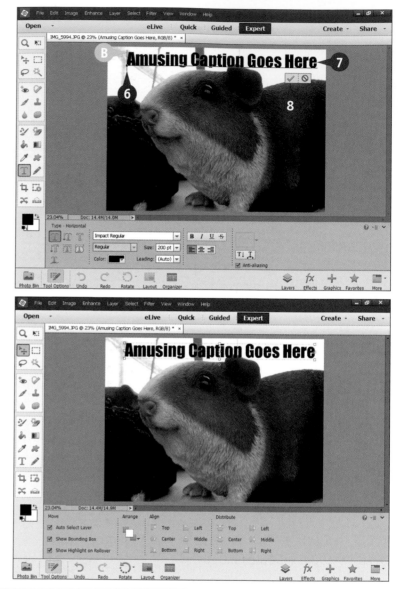

TIPS

Why is my text too small?

Word processors typically use font sizes between 10pt and 30pt. Photos do not have the same physical dimensions or pixel resolution as printed text, so you typically need much bigger letters. Start with a font size of 100pt and up. Adjust the size as needed.

Where can I get other fonts?

Try a web search for "free fonts" to find thousands, or even tens of thousands, of free fonts. Professional designers use expensive, high-quality commercial fonts from sources such as Adobe TypeKit (typekit.com). Fonts are distributed as downloadable files. To install them, copy them to ~/Library/Fonts on a Mac, or to Windows/Fonts on a PC. Not all fonts are compatible. After you install fonts, you must restart Photoshop Elements before you can use them.

Modify Text

Y ou can change the font, style, size, and other characteristics of your text. This can help emphasize or de-emphasize your text.

Photoshop Elements has access to all the fonts on your computer's operating system. A number of fonts are added when you install Photoshop Elements. Available styles for text include italic, bold, and other options that can vary depending on the font being used. The default size measurement is the point, which is 1/72 of an inch. You can enter other units of measurement in the size field in the Tool Options panel, such as 5 cm, and Photoshop Elements converts the value to points.

Modify Text

Move and Rotate Text

1 If you are not already in Expert mode, click **Expert.**

2 Click the **Move** tool (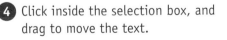.)

3 Click the text you want to move.

Ⓐ If the text was not already selected, a selection box appears around it.

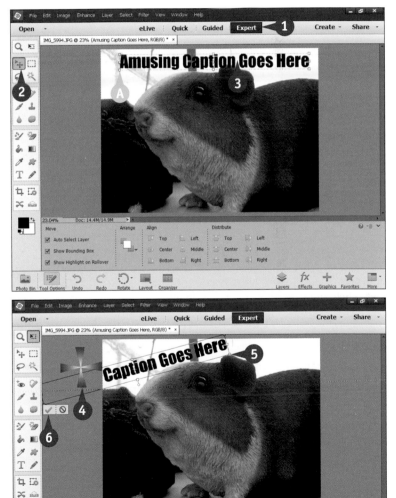

4 Click inside the selection box, and drag to move the text.

5 Hover the mouse just outside a corner, and then click and drag to rotate the text.

Note: You cannot resize the text by dragging the corners. You can make the selection box wider, but you cannot make it taller.

6 Click ☑ to confirm the edit.

You can also click ◯ to cancel the edit.

Change the Text

1 Click the **Horizontal Type** tool (⊤).

2 Click the text you want to change.

3 Drag with the mouse over the text to select it.

Note: You can select some or all of the text.

Photoshop Elements highlights the text you select.

B You can click the font menu to select a new font.

Note: Different fonts have different letter widths, so if you select another font, the text may no longer fit into the selection box.

C You can click the color box and select a new color to change the color of the font.

D You can type a new font size into the **Size** box.

E You can type new text to replace the old text.

Note: Retyping text removes the high-lighting. To apply changes B to D on the new text, click and drag to highlight it again.

F Click ☑ to confirm the edit or ⊘ to cancel the edit.

Photoshop Elements applies the changes to your text.

TIPS

What is anti-aliasing?
Anti-aliasing slightly softens text to smooth its edges. Text without anti-aliasing can look jagged and unprofessional. Leave the anti-aliasing option checked, unless you are using a very small font size and the text looks blurred and difficult to read.

Can I use variations such as bold and italic?
Yes. Photoshop Elements supports bold, italic, underline, and strikethrough text. You can also set left-aligned, center-aligned, and right-aligned text. You can find the standard icons for these, as used on most word processors and notepad apps, to the right of the font menu and font size selection box.

Create Warped Text

You can easily bend and distort layers of text by using the Warped Text feature in Photoshop Elements. This can help you stylize your text to match the theme of your image. For example, text in a sky can be distorted to appear windblown.

Style options include Arc and Arch, which curve text in one direction across the image, and Flag and Wave, which create rippling text. You can warp the text horizontally or vertically to create different effects.

Create Warped Text

1 In the Editor, click **Expert**.

Note: For more on opening the Editor, see Chapter 1.

2 Click the **Horizontal Type** tool (▣).

3 Click the text you want to warp.

Note: You do not need to drag the mouse over the text to highlight it.

4 Click the **Create Warped Text** button (▣).

A The Warp Text dialog box opens.

5 Click the **Style** menu.

6 Click a style to select it.

Note: There are 15 styles. The menu includes a simple preview of each style.

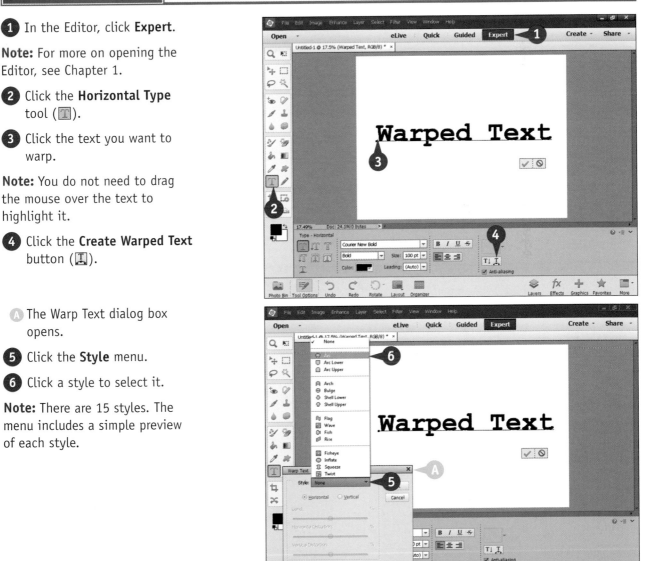

Photoshop Elements applies the warp style to the text.

Ⓑ You can click the radio buttons to select horizontal or vertical warping.

Ⓒ You can click and drag the **Bend** slider to adjust the amount of warping.

Ⓓ You can add further warping with the **Horizontal Distortion** and **Vertical Distortion** sliders.

Ⓔ Photoshop Elements previews the warp effect.

Note: You can click the **Style** menu to select a different warp style.

⑦ Click **OK**, and then click to confirm the edit or ◯ to cancel the edit.

Photoshop Elements warps the text.

TIPS

How do I unwarp text?
In the Warp Text dialog box, click the **Style** menu and select **None**.

When would I use warped text?
This is an artistic effect. You can use it to emphasize the meaning of the text within an image. For example, you could use the vertical arc effect shown in the example to show words coming out of a bull horn. For more ideas, experiment with the presets, explore the settings, and imagine possible applications for each effect.

Draw Text around a Shape

Instead of drawing text on a straight line, you can draw it around any of the standard shapes included in Photoshop Elements, including rectangles, squares, circles, ellipses, stars, and polygons. You can even draw text around the custom shapes.

The simplest shapes are the most useful. Text on a circle usually looks good. Text around a custom shape can be hard to read, although you can sometimes create a good result with text in a small font size.

Draw Text around a Shape

1 In the Editor, click **Expert**.

Note: For more on opening the Editor, see Chapter 1.

2 Click the **Type** box in the tool bar.

3 In the tool options, click the **Text on a Shape Tool** () if it is not already selected, or press **T**.

4 Click a shape to select it.

(A) You can set the font, size, color, and style of the text using these options.

5 Click and drag on the photo to draw the shape.

For details, see the "Draw a Simple Shape" section in this chapter.

This example draws a circle.

Note: You cannot move or resize the shape after drawing it. You can only click 🚫 to cancel it and start again.

6 Click on shape.

The cursor turns into an I-beam. The I-beam is always vertical. It does not rotate to match the shape.

7 Type your text.

Ⓑ Photoshop Elements bends the text around the shape.

8 Click ☑ when you are finished.

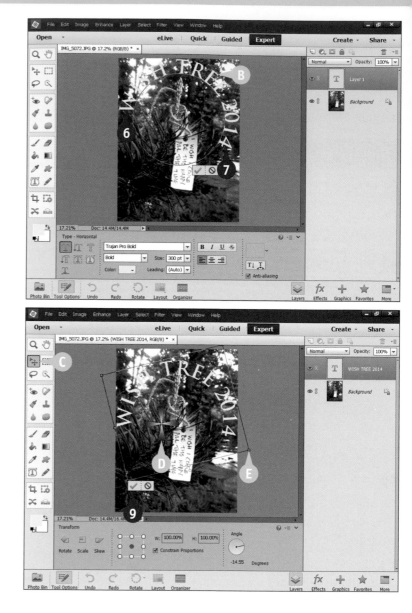

Ⓒ Photoshop Elements selects the Move tool (⊕) automatically.

Ⓓ You can drag in the selection box to move the text.

Ⓔ You can hover near the corners of the selection and click/drag to rotate the text.

9 Click ☑ to confirm when you are finished.

Photoshop Elements adds the text to the image.

TIP

Are there other ways to wrap text around a shape?

You can use the Text on a Path tool (🖳) to draw a freehand line on an image and run text along it. The line — known as a *path* — can be any shape. You can even loop the path over itself. Although this tool is flexible, it can be hard to use, because it is not easy to draw a clean line with the mouse. Simple paths, including simple shapes, often create a more successful result.

Add an Effect to Text

You can add various special effects to text. You can make the characters stand out by adding an outline that contrasts with the background. You can also give text a 3D look by adding a bevel or drop shadow.

To add an effect, click the Effects button and select Styles from the tabs at the top. Click the menu to select a style category. Drag a style onto the text to apply it.

Add an Effect to Text

1 In the Editor, click **Expert**.

2 Select the text you want to enhance.

3 Click **Effects**.

The Effects panel opens.

4 Click **Styles**.

5 Click the menu.

6 Select a category.

In this example, the default Bevels category is selected.

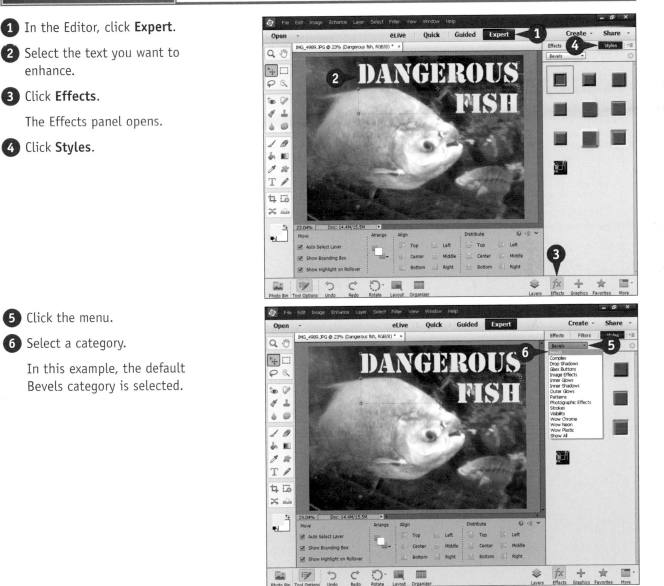

Ⓐ Photoshop Elements displays previews of each effect.

❼ Click and drag a preview to apply it to the text.

Photoshop Elements applies the effect to the text.

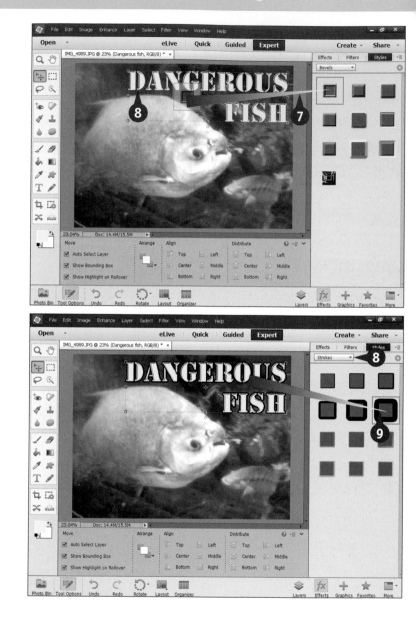

❽ Click the menu, and select another category.

This example selects Strokes, which draws a black outline around text and other shapes.

❾ Drag and drop another style onto the image.

Photoshop Elements combines the two styles to create a custom effect.

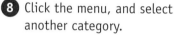

TIPS

How do I remove all effects?

There is no easy way to do this. The simplest option is to use the multiple-undo feature available in the History panel. For details, see Chapter 5.

Can I customize the effects?

Yes. The effects are really layer effects. You can click the Effect Settings icon (▣) and open a dialog box with sliders and other options that control the effects. For more about styles and effects, see Chapter 14.

Add a Bubble Caption

You can add a bubble caption to combine graphics and text. Photoshop Elements includes a selection of bubble text graphics. You can add a bubble as a graphic object and then place text over it. Or you can use one of the preset text bubble frames.

Add a Bubble Caption

1 In the Editor, click **Expert**.

Note: For more on opening the Editor, see Chapter 1.

2 Click **Graphics**.

3 Click the Category menu.

4 Select **By Word**.

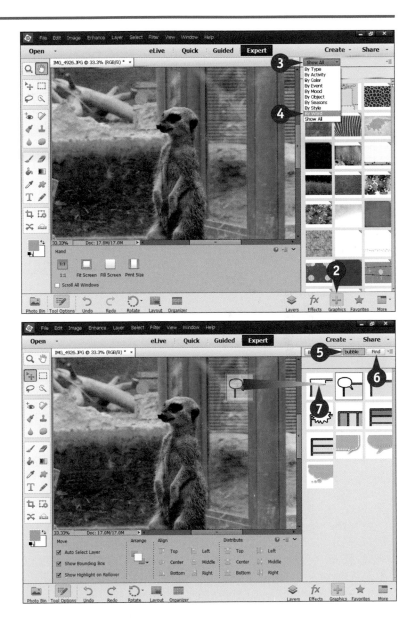

5 Type "Bubble" into the search box.

6 Click **Find**.

Photoshop Elements displays a list of items whose title includes "Bubble."

7 Click and drag the cartoon bubble onto the image.

8 Click and drag the photo within the bubble frame to position the image so the main figure is close to the bubble.

A You can drag the sides to expand or shrink the image.

Note: This distorts the content.

B You can hover over the corners and then click and drag to rotate the content.

9 Click ☑ to confirm when you are finished.

10 Click the **Horizontal Type** tool 🅣.

11 Use the text settings to select the font, size, and color of the text.

12 Click inside the bubble and type your text.

Note: You may need to experiment with the font size to make the text fit.

13 Click ☑ to confirm when you are finished.

Photoshop Elements combines the text with the bubble frame and the photo.

TIP

Why does the text jump around when I drag it?

By default, Photoshop Elements snaps text — aligns it with other objects — to make it easier to place it. This option is helpful when you are placing text in or near objects. But when snapping is on, you cannot align text freely in speech bubbles. To turn it off, select **View ⇨ Snap To. . .** and uncheck Guides, Layers, and Document Bounds. You should now be able to place text anywhere in the bubble.

Applying Filters

You can use the filters in Photoshop Elements to quickly and easily apply enhancements to your image, including artistic effects, texture effects, and distortions. Filters can help you correct defects in your images or enable you to turn a photograph into something resembling an impressionist painting. This chapter highlights a few of the more than 100 filters available in Photoshop Elements. For more on all the filters, see the help documentation.

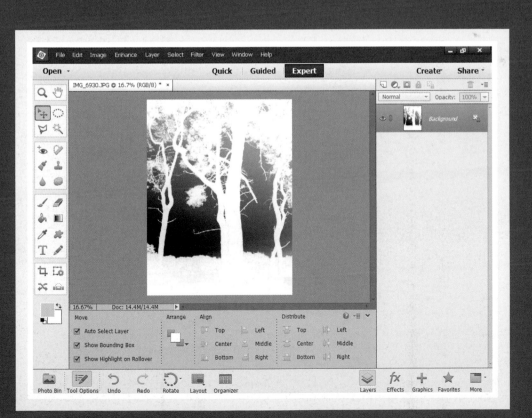

Equalize an Image

You can use the Equalize filter to attempt a quick fix of exposure and lighting. The Equalize filter finds the brightest and darkest areas in an image. Then it makes bright areas as light as possible, and dark areas as dark as possible. This often improves photos with poor exposure or contrast.

The Equalize filter has no settings. The results depend on the quality and composition of the original image. Not all photos look better. Like all filters, you can apply it to an entire image or to a selected area. For more about selections, see Chapters 6 and 7.

Equalize an Image

1 In the Editor, open or select the image you want to correct.

Note: For more on opening the Editor, see Chapter 1.

2 Click **Filter** ⇨ **Adjustments** ⇨ **Equalize**.

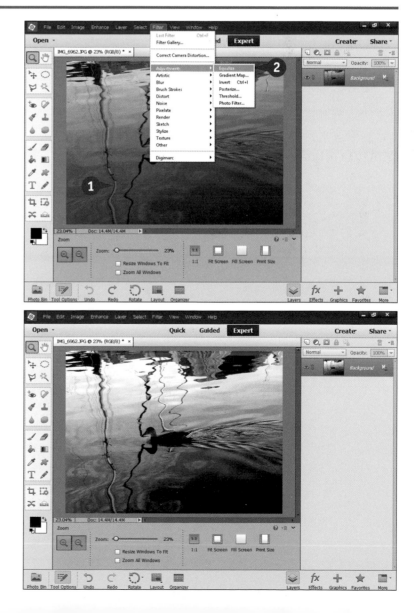

Photoshop Elements equalizes the image.

Note: For a similar effect you can control, use the Levels tool. See Chapter 9 for details.

Create a Negative

You can use the Invert filter to create a negative image. Use this filter to convert scanned film negatives into recognizable photos or as a creative effect. Negative images often look spooky or otherworldly, so you might want to use this effect to help you make Halloween posters.

The Invert filter has no settings. When you select this filter, it converts dark areas into light areas. It also inverts the colors so blues become orange, reds/pinks become green, and vice versa. Like all filters, you can apply it to an entire image or to a selected area. For more about selections, see Chapters 6 and 7.

Create a Negative

1 In the Editor, select and open the image you want to invert.

Note: For more on opening the Editor, see Chapter 1.

2 Click **Filter** ➪ **Adjustments** ➪ **Invert**.

Note: You can also press Ctrl + I .

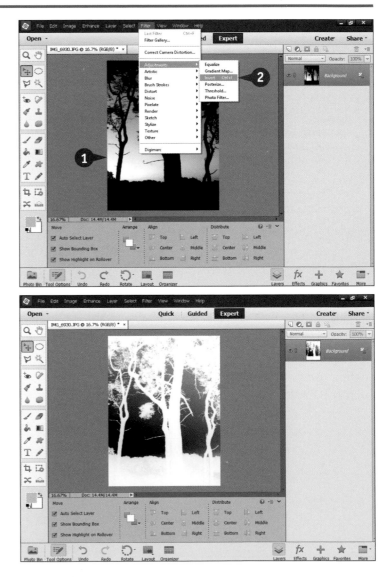

Photoshop Elements converts the image into a negative.

Blur an Image

You can use the Blur filters to apply a variety of blurring effects to your photos. For example, you can use the Gaussian Blur filter to obscure background objects while keeping foreground objects in focus. The Motion Blur filter can create a blur in a single direction or create a spinning blur.

To blur a background behind an object, select the object using one or more selection tools, invert the selection, and apply the filter. This leaves the object sharp, but blurs the area around it. For more details about using selections creatively, see Chapters 6 and 7.

Blur an Image

1 Select the photo you want to blur.

Note: For more on opening the Editor, see Chapter 1.

2 Optionally, select an area to blur. In this example, an elliptical marquee (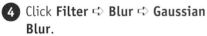) has been drawn around the center of the image.

3 If you want to blur the background instead of the selected object, click **Select** ⇨ **Inverse.**

Note: For a smoother effect, feather the area with a setting of 10% to 25% of the width of your image. For more about feathering, see Chapter 7.

4 Click **Filter** ⇨ **Blur** ⇨ **Gaussian Blur**.

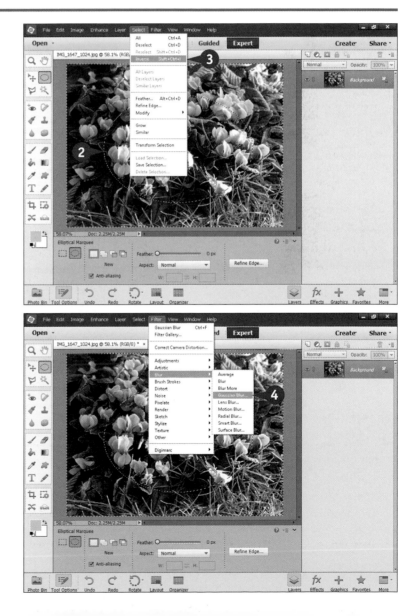

A The Gaussian Blur dialog box opens, displaying a preview of the filter's effect.

Note: Drag the box to one side if it covers the main editor preview window.

Note: You can click the zoom out button () or zoom in button () to change the view in the effect preview window. You do not usually need to do this if you can see the editor preview area.

5 Click and drag the **Radius** slider to experiment with the blur effect.

B You can preview the effect in the main editor window.

Note: The best blur effects keep some detail in the blurred area. If you set the radius value too high, the blur effect turns into gray fog.

6 When you find a setting you like, click **OK**.

Photoshop Elements applies the blur filter.

Note: Click **Select** ➪ **Deselect** to deselect the blurred area.

TIP

How do I simulate a short depth of field in an image?
Short depth of field is a photographic effect where one object in the scene is focused and the rest of the scene is blurred. You can achieve this with a Guided mode feature. Click **Guided** at the top of the Photoshop Elements workspace. On the right, under Photo Effects, click **Depth of Field.** Follow the steps to define an area of focus and to blur the rest of the image. Click **Done** to apply the effect.

Distort an Image

You can use any of the Distort filters to stretch and squeeze your image, creating the appearance of waves, glass, swirls, and more. For example, the Twirl filter twists the image, and the Ripple filter adds wavelike effects. Glass and Ocean Ripple simulate glass distortions. The Shear filter lets you tilt your image at an angle.

You can use the filter settings to control the strength of the effect. Small settings can apply subtle textures. Stronger settings can make an image unrecognizable. The easiest way to learn what the settings do is to play with them.

Distort an Image

① Select the photo you want to distort.

Note: For more on opening the Editor, see Chapter 1.

② Click **Filter** ➪ **Distort** ➪ **Twirl**.

Ⓐ The filter's dialog box opens.

③ Experiment with the filter's settings to fine-tune the effect. All the filters have different settings.

Ⓑ With some filters, you can preview the effect in the filter dialog box.

Note: The distort filters do not display a preview in the main editor area, so you do not need to move the dialog box to uncover the main preview.

Note: You can also click the plus sign (⊞) to zoom in or the minus sign (⊟) to zoom out.

④ Click **OK** to apply the filter, or **Cancel** if you change your mind.

Photoshop Elements applies the filter.

In this example, the Twirl distortion filter is applied.

This example applies the Liquefy filter, which distorts the image as you paint with a "wet pixels" brush.

You can also apply distortion effects with the Reflection tool. To access it, click **Guided**. The tool is located under Photo Play.

TIPS

Does the effect depend on the image size?
Unfortunately, most Photoshop filters do not take into account the size of the image. This means you get different results on small, medium, and large images. For example, on small images ripples look like ripples. On large images they look like fine spray. To compensate for this, experiment with the settings or resize your images before filtering them.

How can I make a water reflection effect?
Select **Guided** mode, click **Photo Play** and select **Reflection**. Work through the stages. Experiment with different settings; you may need to make a few attempts to create an effect that works for you.

Turn an Image into Art

You can use many of the Artistic filters in Photoshop Elements to make your image look as if you created it with a paintbrush or other art media. The Watercolor filter, for example, applies a painted effect by converting similarly colored areas in your image to solid colors. The Palette Knife creates a similar but softer effect. The Colored Pencil filter applies a layer of crosshatched color to your image using the current background color.

To apply a filter to just part of your image, select that portion by using one or more selection tools. For more on selection tools, see Chapter 6.

Turn an Image into Art

① Select the photo you want to turn into art.

Note: For more on opening the Editor, see Chapter 1.

② Click **Filter** ➪ **Artistic** ➪ **Cutout**.

Note: The Cutout filter can simulate a silk-screen print effect.

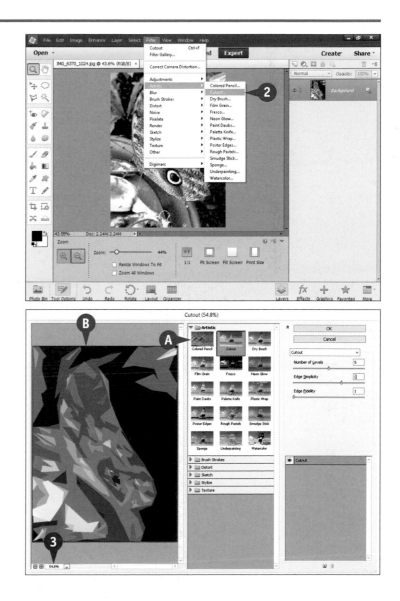

Ⓐ The Filter Gallery dialog box opens with a list of filters showing fixed mini-previews of each effect.

Ⓑ The dialog box displays a "live" preview of the effect you selected.

③ You can type a number into the zoom setting box to select how much of your image you see in the preview.

Note: You can also click the plus sign (⊞) to zoom in or the minus sign (⊟) to zoom out.

Note: Some of the artistic effects are slow and updates can take a while to appear. The more of your image you preview, the longer you must wait.

4 Adjust the filter's settings to fine-tune the effect.

5 Click **OK** to apply the effect, or click **Cancel** to cancel.

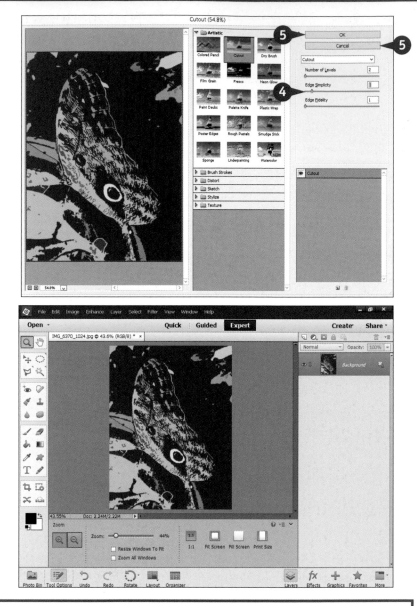

Photoshop Elements applies the filter. This example shows the Colored Pencil effect.

TIPS

What are the Brush Strokes filters?
The filters under the Brush Strokes submenu are another way to give your image a painterly feel. The filters make your image look like its color has been applied with brushes. The Crosshatch filter, for example, adds diagonal stroking across your image. You can boost the strength of the filter to make the crosshatching more noticeable.

How can I make these filters more convincing?
If you are an artist, you may feel that the Artistic filters do not create an accurate simulation of genuine artistic effects. For better results, experiment with the Hue/Saturation tool to introduce color shifts, and/or apply distortions before you work with these filters. Truly artistic results combine many different filters and effects.

Turn an Image into a Sketch

You can use the Sketch filters to make your photo look like a hand-drawn sketch. Most of the Sketch filters "draw" with the foreground color on the background color. Check and set the foreground and background colors before working with these filters. The colors you choose make a big difference. The one exception is the Water Paper filter, which keeps the original colors.

Although you can make a selection and apply the filters to part of an image, the results are rarely successful. It's more usual to apply these filters to a complete image.

Turn an Image into a Sketch

1 Select the photo you want to turn into a sketch.

Note: For more on opening the Editor, see Chapter 1.

2 Check the foreground and background colors, and change them if necessary.

Note: Start with black on white. You can experiment with other combinations later.

Note: For more about setting the foreground and background colors, see Chapter 11.

3 Click **Filter** ➪ **Sketch** ➪ **Stamp**.

A The Filter Gallery dialog box opens with a list of filters showing fixed mini-previews of each effect.

B The dialog box displays a "live" preview of the effect you selected.

4 You can type a number into the zoom setting box to select how much of your image you see in the preview.

Note: You can also click the plus sign (⊞) to zoom in or the minus sign (⊟) to zoom out.

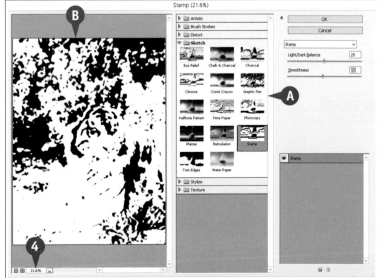

5 Adjust the filter's settings to fine-tune the effect.

6 Click **OK** to apply the effect, or click **Cancel** to cancel.

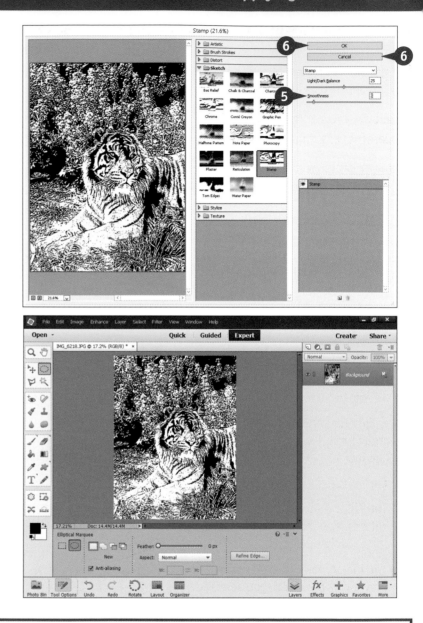

Photoshop Elements applies the filter. This example shows the Stamp effect.

TIPS

How do I know which settings look good?

Mostly, you don't. As you experiment, you can begin to get an intuitive feel for the settings for each filter. But the results depend on the photo and the settings, so you must explore the settings and filters to find good results.

Can I choose any foreground/background colors?

Yes. For example, you can reverse black and white to create negative sketches. But Photoshop Elements allows you to "sketch" with any pair of colors, including lurid and unusual combinations such as hot pink and lime green. The results will not be to everyone's taste, but some artistic styles rely on bright color combinations.

Create a Print Halftone

You can use the Halftone Pattern filter to create an artistic print look. The filter splits an image into four grids of colored dots. When the dots are small, the image looks unchanged. As you make the dots bigger, the image becomes more abstract, creating a look that is popular in certain kinds of art and graphic design.

For example, you can use the Halftone effect to create an image that looks like a field of dots when viewed close up, but becomes a recognizable object or person when viewed from a distance. The settings for this effect are crude. You can type numbers to set the dot size and the grid rotation for each color. You cannot experiment with sliders.

Create a Print Halftone

1 Select the photo you want to turn into a halftone.

Note: For more on opening the Editor, see Chapter 1.

2 Click **Filter** ⇨ **Pixelate** ⇨ **Color Halftone**.

A The settings for the Color Halftone effect appear in a dialog box.

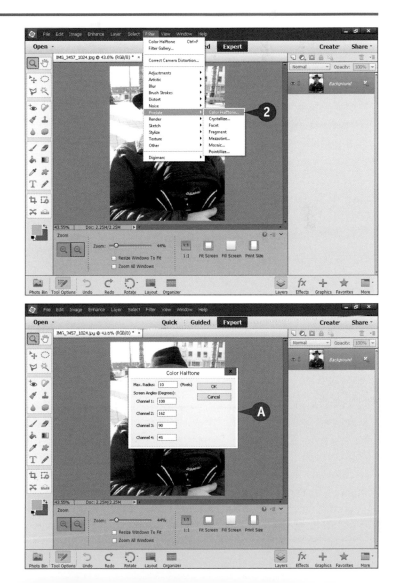

3 Type a number into the Max Radius field to set the dot size.

Note: Larger sizes make the image more abstract. Smaller sizes make it more recognizable.

Note: You can also experiment with changing the grid rotations; you do not usually need to do this.

4 Click **OK**.

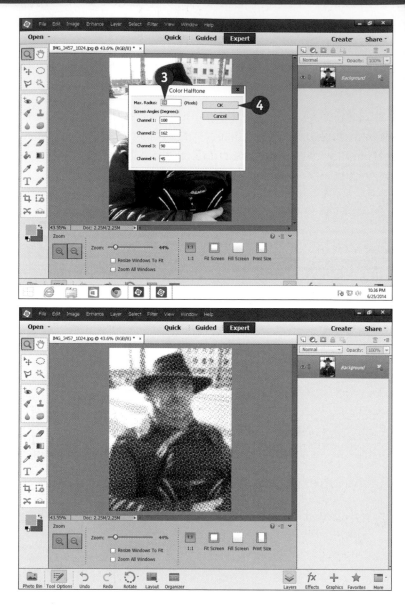

Photoshop Elements applies the Color Halftone filter.

TIPS

What does the Sketch Halftone Pattern filter do?

The Halftone filter in the Sketch submenu is a simpler version of the halftone effect. You can create a single grid of dots in a single color to simulate a newsprint image. You can also apply a line effect to simulate TV lines or a more abstract concentric circle effect. This effect ignores the colors in an image.

What is halftone printing?

The halftone effect was originally invented to print color images in newspapers and magazines. Printing presses cannot print shaded color directly: Ink is either on the page or not. The halftone process makes it possible to print images that appear to have smooth color.

Add Lens Flare

You can use the Lens Flare effect to add a virtual lens flare to any photo. The effect adds a virtual bright light source to your photo. It then simulates the internal reflections created inside various photographic lenses. You do not need to understand the theory to create rainbow halos, sharp white halos, and other effects.

The effect is reasonably realistic. However, it is mathematically perfect. For photo-realistic results, you may want to apply further filters, such as the Diffuse Glow effect, to make it rougher and more convincing.

Add Lens Flare

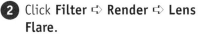

1. Select the photo you want decorate with lens flare.

Note: For more on opening the Editor, see Chapter 1.

2. Click **Filter** ⇨ **Render** ⇨ **Lens Flare**.

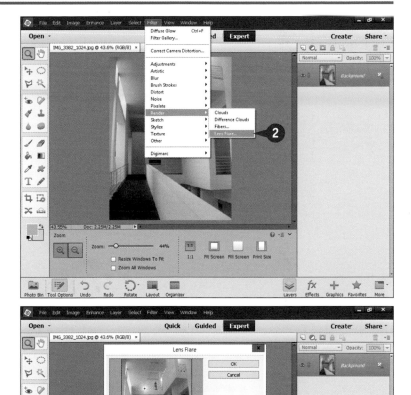

Ⓐ The settings for the Color Halftone effect appear in a dialog box.

Note: Although this dialog box includes a preview window, you cannot zoom in or out.

3 Drag the tiny cross-shaped cursor to change the location of the light source.

A Photoshop Elements moves the reflections to match the position of the light.

4 Use the Brightness slider to set the brightness of the light.

5 Optionally, you can select a different lens type by clicking a radio button.

6 Click **OK** to apply the effect.

Photoshop Elements renders a lens flare effect in your photo.

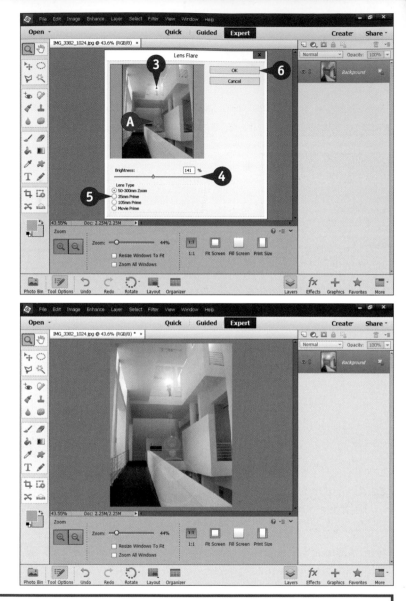

TIPS

What do the different lens types do?
The 50-300mm Zoom lens produces the most obvious and satisfying lens flare, with many reflections. The 35mm Prime Filter creates a starburst effect around the light and adds a couple of tiny reflection dots. The 105mm Prime creates a much fuzzier light with slightly larger reflections. The Movie Prime filter adds diagonal cross-hatch flare.

When would I add lens flare?
Lens flare adds a science-fiction feel to a photo. It can also add atmosphere and improve a photo's production values. If you have a budget camera, you can add lens flare to make a photo look glossier and more sophisticated. For example, if you shoot into the sun with a mobile phone camera, you can place the light source over the sun to add rich and complex reflection effects.

Work with Text

You can use many of the filters in Photoshop Elements to create surprisingly useful and powerful text effects. For example, you can convert block text into outlines, with control over the width and position of the drawn lines. You can also fragment text, rework it into abstract shapes, give it a 3D look, or cover it in spatters or ripples.

To work with text, create it using the instructions in Chapter 11, convert it to a flat image — this is called "simplifying" it — and filter it like any other image. Many effects are possible. This section introduces two, but you can create an almost infinite number by experimenting with single and combined filter effects.

Work with Text

1 Create a new file in the editor, and add a large text banner.

Note: For full instructions on working with text, see Chapter 11.

2 Click **Filter** ➪ **Filter Gallery**.

Note: If you see a warning about simplifying the text layer, select Layer ➪ Flatten Image.

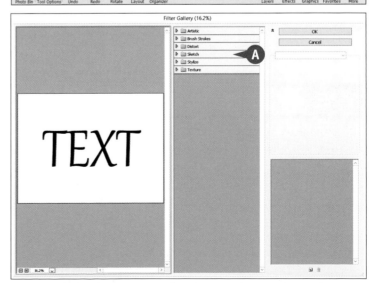

The Filter Gallery dialog box opens.

Note: You can use the Filter Gallery feature for photos as well as text.

3 Click any of the boxes with arrows, folder icons, and named filter groups to view a list of filters.

Note: You can click anywhere in the boxes.

A filter collection opens showing fixed thumbnails of each effect.

 Click any filter thumbnail to select it.

Note: This example uses the Photocopy filter in the Sketch group.

 The Preview Window displays a preview of the effect.

 Experiment with the filter settings.

Note: In this example, the Photocopy effect converts the text into an outline that looks hand-drawn. When Darkness is set to 50, the Detail slider controls the width of the outline.

6 Click **OK**.

Photoshop Elements applies the effect.

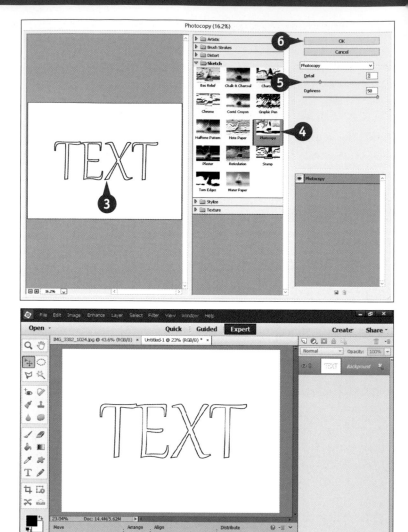

TIPS

Why would I apply filters to text?
Plain text can overpower a photo when you are trying to add captions. Filtered text can look more creative, and more unusual. You can also use it to suggest moods and atmospheres that are not possible with plain text. Text effects are also useful for video titling.

How do I know which filters and settings to use?
The best way to discover the effects you can create is to experiment with all the filters and explore their settings. Some filters create useless results, and others do nothing. A slightly larger number have obvious uses for outlining, embossing, thickening, thinning, distressing, and so on.

Using Layers

You can use layers to work independently with different parts of an image. You can cut items out of an image onto different layers, move the layers independently, filter them separately, and transform them without changing anything else in your image. You can change the order in which layers appear, to control how layers hide other layers. You can combine them visually in different ways without losing their independence. And you can merge layers back into a single image. You can also use special adjustment layers to apply color and lighting effects without making a permanent edit.

Introducing Layers

A Photoshop Elements image can include multiple layers. Each layer can include different objects, adjustments, or color fills. You can use layers to split an image into separate parts. You can then work with the parts independently, so you can try out different edits and ideas without changing the image. You can even save a file with separate layers so you can continue making changes later.

When you open an image in Photoshop Elements, the content appears in a single layer called the *Background Layer*. You can copy or cut items out of the background layer onto new layers as you work, and you can add adjustment layers to modify the image without changing it permanently.

Layer Independence

Layers are like images glued to pieces of transparent plastic. Each layer has its own pixels. You can move and edit it independently. A layer can include a small object, or it can be bigger than the canvas. Complex images can have tens or even hundreds of separate layers. The illustration shows three very simple layers on a plain white background.

Apply Commands to Layers

Most Photoshop Elements commands affect only the layers that you select in the Layers panel. You can move them, rotate them, and transform them independently. Layers are a good way to isolate effects. For example, if you copy a person into a layer in a portrait image, you can improve skin tone without changing the rest of the image. You can also keep different versions of the person in different layers and try them out against the same background to see which works best.

Manipulate Layers

You can combine, duplicate, filter, and hide layers in an image and also shuffle their order. You can also link particular layers so they move in unison, or you can blend content from different layers in creative ways. You manage all of this in the Layers panel. The illustration shows all the layers from the first panel transformed in different ways.

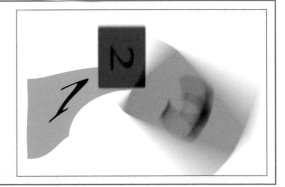

Transparency

Layers can have transparent areas, where the elements in the layers below show through. When you perform a cut or erase command on a layer, the affected pixels become transparent. You can also make a layer partially transparent by decreasing its opacity. Here, layer 1 is partially transparent, and layer 3 has had an area removed so layer 2 shows through.

Adjustment Layers

Adjustment layers are special layers that contain information about color or tonal adjustments. An adjustment layer affects the appearance of the pixels in all the layers below it. You can increase or decrease an adjustment layer's intensity to get precisely the effect you want. Adjustment layers can have any shape you want. Here, an adjustment layer with soft edges and varying intensity shifts colors in parts of the image, and a second adjustment layer inverts the entire image.

Save Layered Files

You can save files with layers using the PSD, PDF, and TIFF file formats. Other formats *flatten* layers back into the background; the layers disappear and you cannot keep working with them. You can also flatten layers in the Editor to save memory and disk space.

File name: IMG_3227 good

Save as type: Photoshop (*.PSD;*.PDD)

Save Options

Organize: ☑ Include in the Elements Organizer

☐ Save in Version Set with Original

Save: ☐ As a Copy

☑ Layers

Color: ☑ ICC Profile: sRGB IEC61966-2.1

Other: ☑ Thumbnail

Create and Add to a Layer

To keep elements in your image independent of one another, you can create separate layers and add objects to them. Typically, you copy and paste elements from one part of your image, or from a different image, and paste them to place them into new layers.

When you create a new layer, the layer appears in a list in the Layers panel. Layers higher in the list appear above and can cover layers lower in the list. To rearrange layers that you have created, see the section "Reorder Layers." To get rid of layers in your image, see the section "Delete a Layer."

Create and Add to a Layer

Create a Layer

1 In the Editor, click **Expert**.

2 Click **Layers** to open the Layers panel.

Note: For more on opening the Editor or panels, see Chapter 1.

3 Click a layer.

Note: Selecting a layer tells Photoshop Elements that you want to create a new layer immediately above it in the layer list.

Note: If you have not yet created any layers there, Photoshop Elements lists a single layer named *Background*.

4 In the Layers panel, click the **Create a New Layer** icon (▣).

Note: Alternatively, you can click **Layer ➪ New ➪ Layer**.

Ⓐ Photoshop Elements creates a new, transparent layer.

Note: To change the name of the layer, see the section "Rename a Layer."

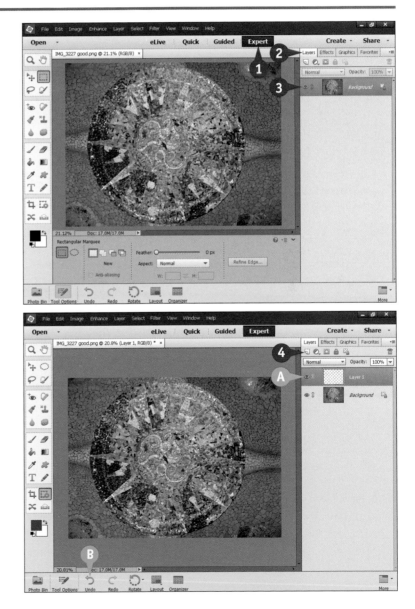

Copy content into a new Layer

1 Open an image.

2 Select an area using any selection tool.

Note: See Chapter 1 for more on opening an image. See Chapter 6 for more on selection tools.

Note: This example uses the Elliptical Marquee tool (⬚) to select the circular mosaic.

3 Right-click (**Ctrl**+click on a Mac) anywhere on the image.

4 Select **Layer via Copy**.

B The selected area appears as a new layer.

Note: The copy keeps its location in the canvas. In the new layer, the pixels outside the selection are transparent. Because the background layer is visible the main image does not look different.

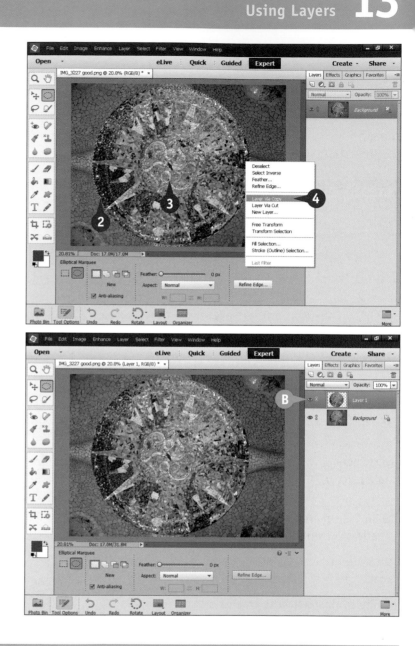

TIPS

What is the Background layer?
The Background layer is the default bottom layer. Photoshop Elements creates it automatically. A Background layer cannot contain transparent pixels and cannot be moved. If you want to move it or delete parts of it, copy it to a regular layer.

How do I turn the Background layer into a regular layer?
Select the Background layer. Click **Layer ⇨ New ⇨ Layer from Background.** You can also press **Ctrl**+**J** (**⌘**+**J** on a Mac) to create an editable copy of the Background layer.

Hide a Layer

You can hide a layer to make it disappear temporarily. Use this option when you want to view or edit the layers under it. You can also use it to check the alignment of objects. Hidden layers remain invisible when you print an image or use the Save for Web command.

You can remove a layer permanently by deleting it. See the section "Delete a Layer" for details. Hiding a layer is different from deleting a layer because you can make a hidden layer visible again.

Hide a Layer

1 In the Editor, click **Expert**.

2 Click **Layers** to open the Layers panel.

Note: For more on opening the Editor or panels, see Chapter 1.

3 Click the visibility icon (👁) for a layer.

Note: You do not need to select the layer first.

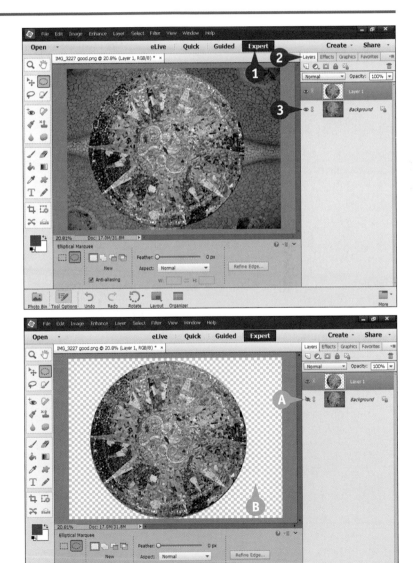

The icon changes to 👁, and Photoshop Elements hides the layer.

Ⓐ The layer remains in the Layer list.

Ⓑ Its content disappears from the Editor window.

To show one layer and hide all the others, press Alt (Option on a Mac) and click the visibility icon (👁) for the layer you want to show.

Move a Layer

Y ou can use the Move tool to move a layer. Select a layer, select the Move tool, and drag the layer to a new location. The other layers remain where they are.

If you make a selection with a selection tool before using the Move tool, Photoshop Elements moves only the selection. The rest of the layer stays where it is. If the selection creates holes in the layer, they become transparent. For more on selection tools, see Chapter 6. To undo a move, click **Undo** or press Ctrl+Z (⌘+Z on a Mac). For more on undoing moves, see Chapter 5.

Move a Layer

 In the Editor, click **Expert**.

2 Click **Layers** to open the Layers panel.

Note: For more on opening the Editor or panels, see Chapter 1.

3 Click a layer to select it.

4 Click the **Move** tool (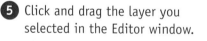).

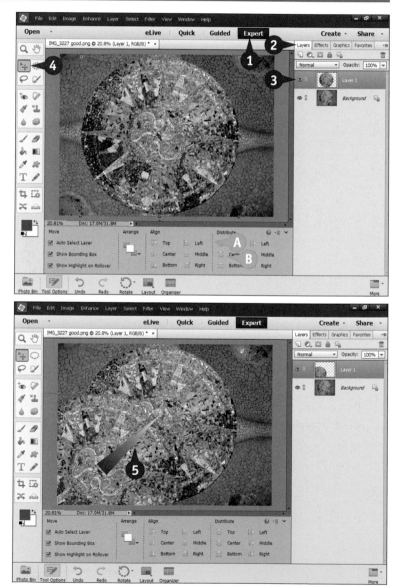

5 Click and drag the layer you selected in the Editor window.

Content in the selected layer moves. In this example, moving the top layer reveals the background layer behind it.

Note: You must click an area with content to move it. In this example, you cannot move the top layer by clicking in the transparent area outside the circle.

Note: You can Ctrl+click (⌘+click) in the Layer list to select multiple layers and move them together.

Duplicate a Layer

You can duplicate a layer when you want to copy its content to a different location. You can also create duplicates to experiment with filtering or transforming a layer without losing the original layer content. If an experiment fails, you can delete the duplicate. You can make as many duplicates as you want.

When you duplicate a layer, it covers identical content in the original layer. The duplicate appears in the Layer list, but you cannot see it in the Editor window unless you move it or edit it.

Duplicate a Layer

1 In the Editor, click **Expert**.

2 Click **Layers** to open the Layers panel.

Note: For more on opening the Editor or panels, see Chapter 1.

3 Click a layer.

4 Right-click (Ctrl+click on a Mac) and select **Duplicate Layer. . .**

Ⓐ You can type a new name for the layer here.

5 Click **OK**.

You can also press Ctrl+J (⌘+J on a Mac) to duplicate a layer after selecting it.

Ⓑ Photoshop Elements duplicates the selected layer. The duplicate appears in the Layer list but does not change the view in the Editor window unless you edit it.

You can now move the layer to a new location. See the previous section Move a Layer for details.

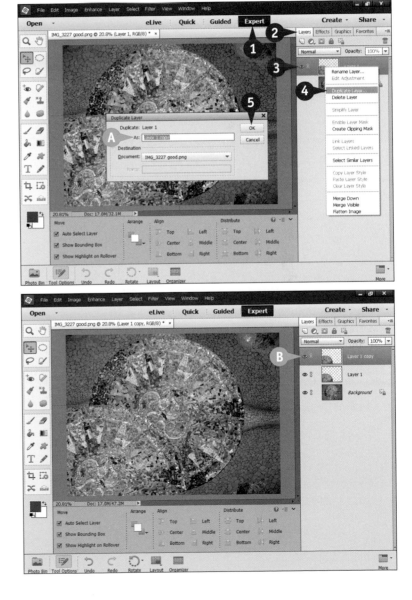

Delete a Layer

You can delete a layer to remove it from your project. Deleting it removes it from the Layer list. Its content disappears from the Editor window. To undo the deletion, you can click **Undo** in the taskbar or press Ctrl+Z (⌘+Z on a Mac).

If you want to make the layer disappear temporarily, you can hide it instead of deleting it. For more details, see the section "Hide a Layer" in this chapter.

Delete a Layer

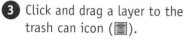

1 In the Editor, click **Expert**.

2 Click **Layers** to open the Layers panel.

Note: For more on opening the Editor or panels, see Chapter 1.

3 Click and drag a layer to the trash can icon (🗑).

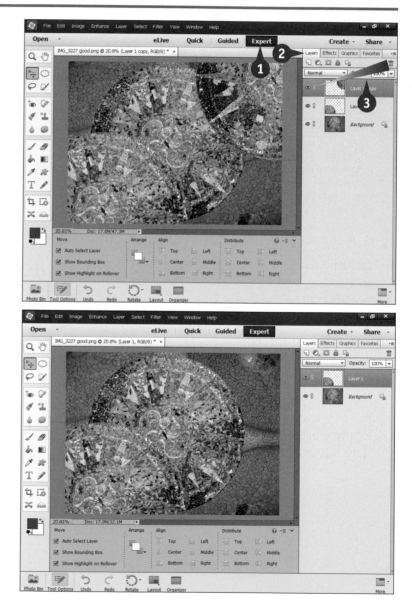

Note: Alternatively, you can click **Layer** ⇨ **Delete Layer** in the main menu; you can select a layer and then click the trash can icon (🗑); you can right-click and select **Delete Layer**.

In all cases, a confirmation dialog box opens unless you check a "Don't Show Again" option.

Photoshop Elements deletes the selected layer, and the content in the layer disappears from the image window.

Reorder Layers

You can change the order of layers in the Layer panel to control how layers overlap. The list is drawn bottom-to-top. Layers at the top cover those lower down. To change a layer's position in the list, drag it up or down and release it. Moving layers changes the order they are drawn in. It does not change their position in the Editor window.

You can drag any layers, including content layers and adjustment layers. Only the background layer is locked. It is always at the bottom of the list, to make sure it works as the image background.

Reorder Layers

Using the Layers Panel

1 In the Editor, click **Expert**.

2 Click **Layers** to open the Layers panel.

Note: For more on opening the Editor or panels, see Chapter 1.

3 Click, drag and release a layer to change its position in the list.

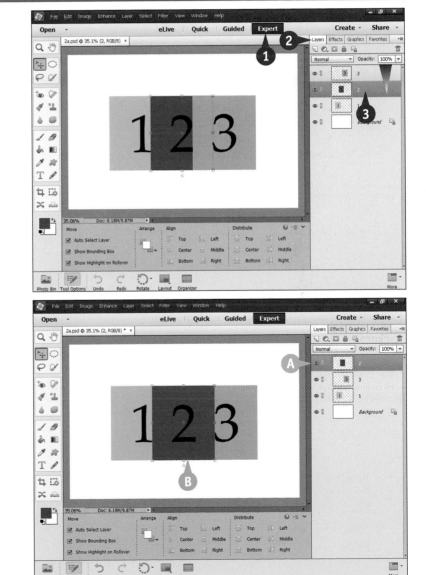

Ⓐ The layer moves up (or down) the list.

Ⓑ In this example, the Red 2 layer is now above the others, so it covers them in the Editor window.

Using the Arrange Commands

1 Click the bottom layer to select it.

2 Click **Layer** ⇨ **Arrange** ⇨ **Bring To Front**.

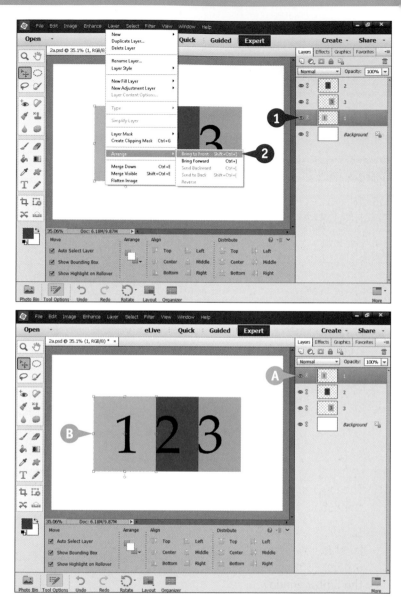

A The layer moves to the top of the list.

B It appears in front of the other layers.

You can choose Bring to Front; Bring Forward; Send Backward; Send to Back; or Reverse. Depending on the layer position, some options are grayed out.

Note: You can use reverse only when you select more than one layer with Ctrl+click (⌘+click) in the Layer list.

Note: You cannot move a layer behind the background layer. To create the same result, duplicate the background layer, hide the original, and move the new layer behind the duplicate.

TIP

Can I use keyboard shortcuts to reorder layers?

You can use the shortcut keys in this table. For Mac, replace Ctrl with ⌘.

Move	Shortcut (Windows)	Move	Shortcut (Windows)
Forward one step	Ctrl+]	To the very front	Shift+Ctrl+]
Backward one step	Ctrl+[	To the very back	Shift+Ctrl+[

Change the Opacity of a Layer

You can adjust the opacity of a layer to allow layers under it to show through. Opacity is the opposite of transparency — decreasing the opacity of a layer increases its transparency.

Layers have opacities between 0 and 100 percent. A layer with 0 percent opacity is completely transparent. You can move it, edit it, and transform it. But you cannot see it in the Editor window. A layer with 100 percent opacity is completely opaque and hides the content under it.

Change the Opacity of a Layer

1 In the Editor, click **Expert**.

2 Click **Layers** to open the Layers panel.

Note: For more on opening the Editor or panels, see Chapter 1.

3 Click the layer whose opacity you want to change.

Note: You cannot change the opacity of the Background layer.

The default opacity is 100%.

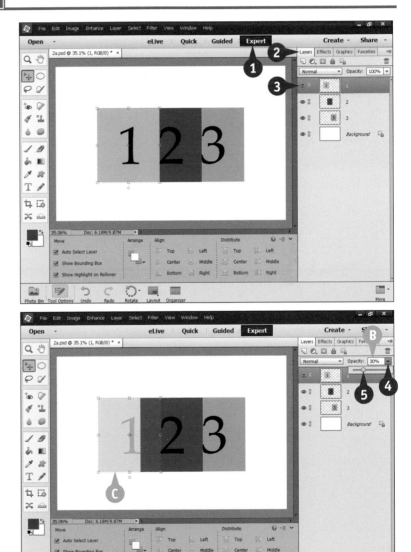

4 Click the .

5 Drag the slider.

Ⓐ You can also type a new value in the Opacity field.

Ⓑ The opacity changes and the layer appears more or less transparent.

If you are using layer blending, changing the opacity may not modify the transparency in a simple way. For details, see the "Blend Layers" section in this chapter.

Link Layers

You can link layers if you want to move them together. Photoshop Elements uses a link icon to show when layers are linked. You can transform linked layers together to change their dimensions or to rotate them. But you cannot filter or enhance them.

Linking is temporary. You can unlink layers at any time if you want to edit them or move them separately. To link layers permanently, you can merge them. See the next section, "Merge Layers," for details.

Link Layers

1 In the Editor, click **Expert**.

2 Click **Layers** to open the Layers panel.

Note: For more on opening the Editor or panels, see Chapter 1.

3 Click a layer you want to link.

4 Click the **Link Layers** icon (⬚) in a different layer to link them.

Note: You can repeat step **4** to link further layers.

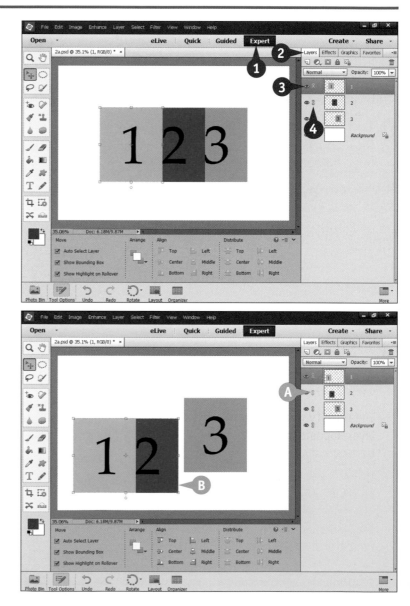

A The layers become linked. The linking icon on each linked layer becomes orange (⬚).

B If you select the **Move** tool (⬚) and drag any linked layer, the other layers move with it.

To unlink a layer, click the ⬚.

Note: You can link layers to the background layer, but this locks them in place.

Merge Layers

You can merge layers to combine them into a single layer. Merged layers are no longer independent, and they appear as a single layer in the Layers list. There are three merge options. **Merge Down** (or **Merge Layers**) merges selected layers. **Merge Visible** merges layers with visibility turned on. **Flatten Image** merges all layers.

If Photoshop Elements is running very slowly, save a safety copy of your project with unmerged layers and merge them together. This often speeds up editing. If you make a mistake, you can reload and re-merge the layers before trying again.

Merge Layers

1 In the Editor, click **Expert**.

2 Click **Layers** to open the Layers panel.

3 Ctrl+click (⌘+click on the Mac) to select two or more layers.

4 Right-click (Ctrl+click on the Mac) the Layer list, and select **Merge Layers**.

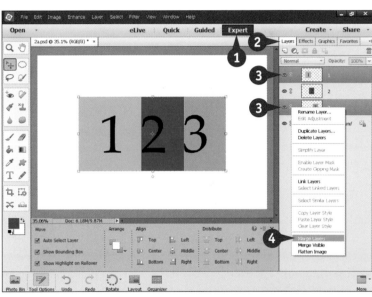

A Photoshop Elements merges the layers.

B The merged layer keeps the name and list position of the top layer.

Note: Layers with 0 percent opacity disappear after merging.

You can also press Ctrl+Shift+E (⌘+Shift+E on a Mac) to merge all visible layers, or Ctrl+Shift+ Alt+E (⌘+Shift+Option+E on a Mac) to merge the visible layers into a new layer without deleting the existing layers.

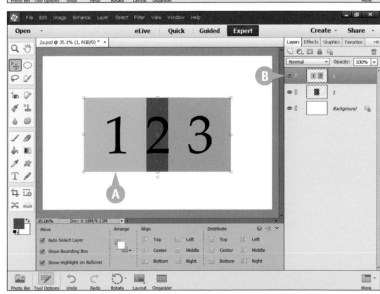

Rename a Layer

You can rename a layer if you want to give it a name to describe its content. For example, in an image that combines flowers on different layers, you can name one layer "red rose" and another "white lily."

When you create a new layer in the Layers panel, Photoshop Elements gives it the generic name "Layer 1." When you duplicate a layer in the Layers panel, the duplicate layer has the same name as the original layer with "copy" added. Text layers include the text. After you create or duplicate a layer, you can rename it.

Rename a Layer

1 In the Editor, click **Expert**.

2 Click **Layers** to open the Layers panel.

Note: For more on opening the Editor or panels, see Chapter 1.

3 Double-click a layer name.

A A small text box opens.

4 Type a new name for the layer and press `Enter`.

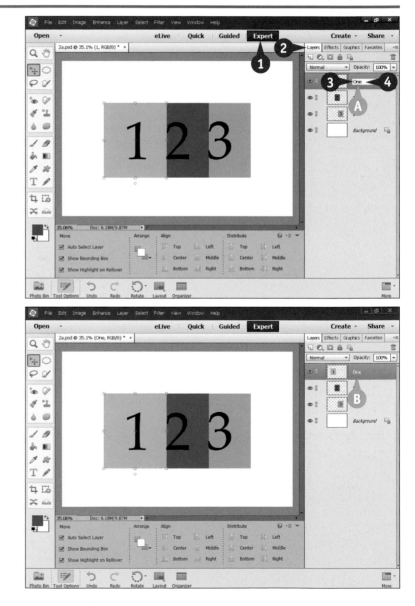

B The name of the layer changes in the Layers panel.

Create a Fill Layer

You can use a fill layer to add a layer or color to your image. Fill layers can create colored backgrounds or filter effects. When you create a fill layer, you select its color using a Color Picker box. You can also add a *gradient*, which creates simple color shadings, or a *pattern*, which creates a repeating texture.

You can move fill layers up and down the Layer list. This can create very dramatic changes. If a fill layer is the top layer, it hides the others and you see a solid color.

Create a Fill Layer

① In the Editor, click **Expert**.

② Click **Layers** to open the Layers panel.

Note: For more on opening the Editor or panels, see Chapter 1.

③ Click the layer above which you want the solid color layer to appear.

This example adds a new colored background layer.

④ Click **Layer ⇨ New Fill Layer ⇨ Solid Color**.

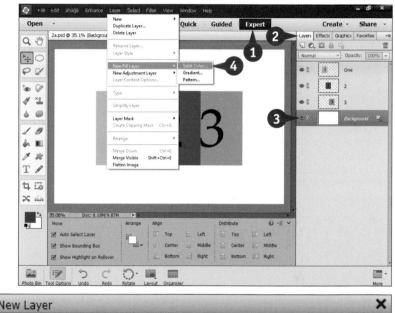

The New Layer dialog box opens.

Ⓐ You can type a name for the layer here, or leave this name unchanged to use the default.

Ⓑ You can click this menu to select a blend mode.

Ⓒ You can click this menu to change the opacity.

Note: See the sections "Blend Layers" or "Change the Opacity of a Layer" for details.

⑤ Click **OK**.

D A Color Picker dialog box opens.

6 To change the base color, drag the slider up or down.

7 To set the lightness and saturation, drag the mouse in this box.

E If the layer is visible, you can preview the color in the Editor window.

8 Click **OK**.

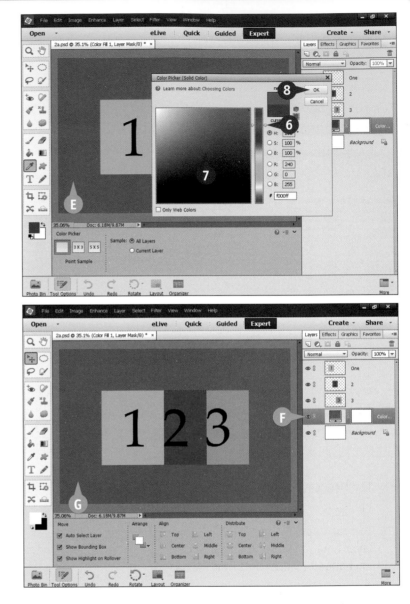

F Photoshop Elements creates a new layer filled with a solid color.

G In this example, a hot pink layer covers the original white background.

TIPS

How do I add solid color to just part of a layer?
Fill layers have two parts. A color or fill control sets the color, fill, or pattern. A white *mask* layer controls the opacity of the color. This mask appears automatically when you add a fill layer. To selectively remove the color, set the foreground color to black, and paint, fill, select and fill, or otherwise edit the white mask. Black areas do not have color. Gray areas have partial color.

Why can I not delete the fill layer?
Because a fill layer has two elements — the fill and the mask — you must delete them both. If you delete only the mask layer, the color/fill/pattern layer remains. To remove a fill layer, repeat the steps in the "Delete a Layer" section twice.

Create an Adjustment Layer

You can use adjustment layers to modify the color, brightness, contrast, and tonal range in an image without making the changes permanent. You can fine-tune the settings in an adjustment layer at any time.

You can also change the opacity of an adjustment layer to lessen its effect, or hide it to turn it off. Adjustment layers are handy for testing editing techniques, colors, or brightness settings. For more about the effects you can apply with adjustment layers, such as levels and curves adjustments, see Chapter 9.

Create an Adjustment Layer

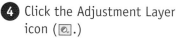

1 In the Editor, click **Expert**.

2 Click **Layers** to open the Layers panel.

Note: For more on opening the Editor or panels, see Chapter 1.

3 Click a layer. Photoshop Elements inserts the adjustment layer above the layer you select.

Note: You can add an adjustment layer to a background layer.

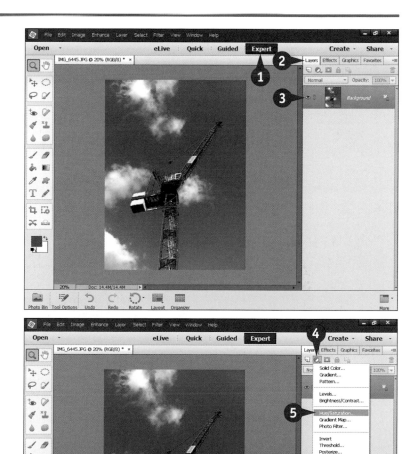

4 Click the Adjustment Layer icon (⬛.)

5 Select **Hue/Saturation**.

🅐 The Hue/Saturation adjustment dialog box appears.

🅑 You can adjust the hue, saturation, and lightness of the image using the sliders.

6 Click the dialog box close icon ✖.

The dialog box closes. The changes remain.

7 Double-click the adjustment icon in the adjustment layer.

🅒 The hue/saturation dialog box appears again.

🅓 You can make more changes to the sliders.

🅔 You can click the Colorize box to apply a uniform color.

8 Click the dialog box close icon ✖.

Photoshop Elements applies the changes.

You can open the adjustment dialog box and make changes as often as you want without permanently editing the background layer.

TIPS

How do I apply an adjustment layer to only part of the image?
Use a *layer mask* to apply the adjustment to part of the image. See the sections "Add a Layer Mask" and "Edit a Layer Mask" for details.

What do the other adjustments do?
Solid Color, Gradient, and Pattern create a fill layer. Levels creates a Levels effect to correct highlights, shadows, and midtones. Gradient Map maps brightness to color through a selection of presets. Photo Filter subtly warms or cools colors to simulate various lens filters. Invert creates a negative. Threshold and Posterize apply standard filters. See Chapter 12 for details.

Blend Layers

Yˉou can use the blending modes in Photoshop Elements to blend layers in creative ways. The range of effects is almost infinite, from subtle enhancements to exotic visual effects. To learn more, experiment with the different modes using many different photos. If you use many layers and many blending modes, the results can be difficult to predict.

When you create a new layer, the default blending mode is Normal, which simply covers one layer with another. You can switch back to Normal mode at any time to turn off blending effects.

Blend Layers

Pop Colors with an Overlay Blend

1 In the Editor, click **Expert**.

2 Load a photo.

For more about loading a photo, see Chapter 2.

3 Duplicate the background layer.

See the "Duplicate a Layer" section for details.

Note: For more on opening the Editor or panels, see Chapter 1.

4 Click the blend mode menu.

5 Select **Overlay**.

A The overlay blend pops the colors.

B If the effect is too exaggerated, you can turn down the opacity to tame it.

Create Unusual Colors with a Difference Blend

1 In the Editor, click **Expert**.

2 Load any photo to create a background layer.

3 Create a single color fill layer.

See the "Create a Fill Layer" section for details. This example uses a bright green fill layer.

4 Click the blend mode menu.

5 Select **Difference**.

A Photoshop Elements subtracts the green color from the colors in the original photo, creating a brightly colored artistic interpretation of the source photo.

Note: You can double-click the fill color icon to adjust the fill color and create many possible color combinations. If the effect is too extreme, you can tone it down by lowering the fill layer's opacity.

Note: Some photo and fill color combinations are more successful than others.

TIP

What are the most useful blending modes?
- **Multiply:** Darkens the colors where the selected layer overlaps layers below it.
- **Screen:** Lightens colors where layers overlap.
- **Color:** Takes the selected layer's colors and blends them with the light and dark details in the layers below it.
- **Luminosity:** Takes the light and dark details and mixes them with colors from the layers below.

Add a Layer Mask

When you change a layer's opacity setting, it affects the entire layer. You can use a *layer mask* to vary opacity across the layer. White areas in the mask have 100 percent opacity. Black areas have 0 percent opacity. Gray areas have in-between values controlled by the darkness/lightness of the gray.

You can use a layer mask to cut out an object from a layer. You can always edit a layer mask, so you can keep fine-tuning the mask until you get the object's edges just right. You can also use masks to create adjustments that vary over the image.

Add a Layer Mask

① In the Editor, click **Expert**.

② Load a photo.

③ Click **Layers** to open the Layers panel if it is not already open.

Note: For details about opening the Editor or panels, see Chapter 1.

④ Click the **Add Layer Mask** icon ().

Note: Alternatively, you can alternatively click **Layer** ⇨ **Layer Mask**, and then **Reveal All** or **Hide All**. This creates an all white or all black layer mask, respectively.

Note: If your project has more than one layer, you can click any layer to select it and then add a mask.

Ⓐ Photoshop Elements adds a layer mask icon to the layer.

The new mask is white, so the entire layer remains visible.

Note: If you add a mask to the background layer, it is "promoted" to a standard layer and is no longer locked.

Note: The mask is selected automatically.

You can now use any of the selection, drawing, painting, fill, and text tools to change the mask.

This example uses the Magic Wand tool to mask out the sky.

5 Click the **Magic Wand** tool ().

Note: In this example, the **Contiguous** check box is turned off to make it easier to select the sky.

6 Click the sky areas repeatedly to select all of the sky.

See the "Select an Area with the Magic Wand" section in Chapter 6 for details.

7 Set the foreground color to black.

See the "Set the Foreground and Background Colors" in Chapter 11 for details.

8 Click the **Paint Bucket** tool (🪣).

9 Click the area you selected in Step **6**.

Ⓑ Photoshop Elements fills the selected area in the mask with black.

Ⓒ The masked area disappears.

Note: The original layer has not changed. You can delete the mask to make it reappear, or you can edit the mask to control how much of it appears.

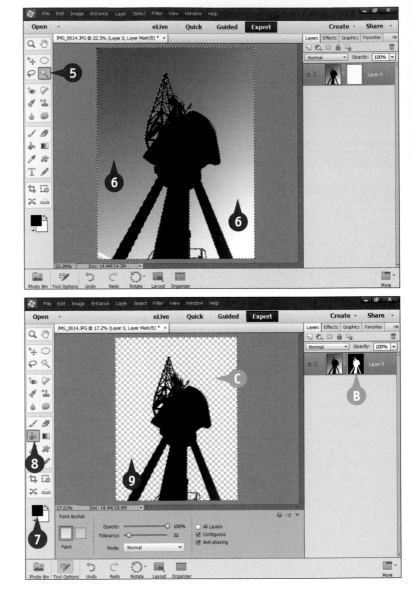

TIPS

How do I edit a masked layer?
Click the layer thumbnail to the left of the mask in the Layers list. You can then edit the layer in the usual way. To go back to editing the mask, click the mask thumbnail.

Can I apply a mask as a permanent edit?
Yes. Right-click (Ctrl+click on a Mac) the layer mask icon in the Layers panel, and select **Apply Layer Mask** from the menu that appears. Photoshop Elements "bakes" the mask opacity into the layer and deletes the mask.

Edit a Layer Mask

After creating a layer mask, you can edit it. You can invert the mask to swap the visible and hidden areas, blur it to soften the mask edges, or paint on it in either black or white to hide or reveal more of the original content.

For more advanced effects, you can apply gradient fills to create a smooth fade over the mask, add type to create text cut out effects, or use the mask to vary the intensity of an effect over the image.

Edit a Layer Mask

Invert the Mask

1. Add a layer mask to a layer in your image. (See the previous section for details.)

Note: See the previous section, "Add a Layer Mask," for details.

2. Click the layer mask thumbnail for the mask you want to edit.

3. Click **Select** ⇨ **All** to make sure the entire mask is selected.

Note: You can also press Ctrl+A (⌘+A on a Mac.)

4. Select **Filter** ⇨ **Adjustments** ⇨ **Invert**.

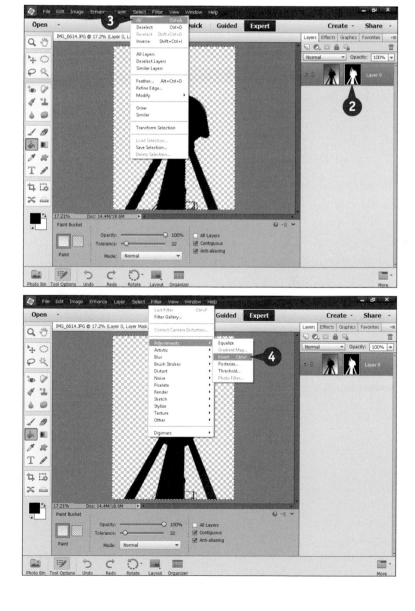

Ⓐ Photoshop Elements inverts the mask, swapping white and black areas.

Ⓑ In this example, inverting the mask hides the object and reveals the background.

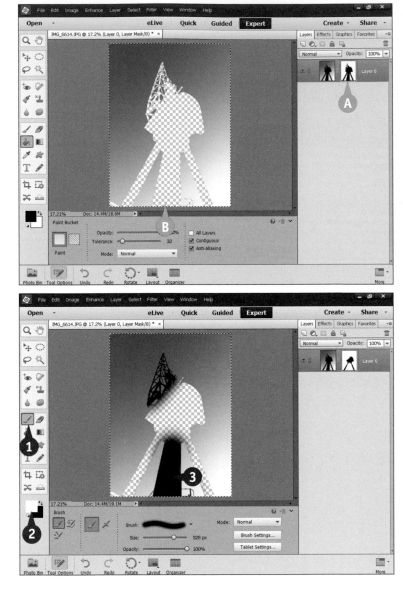

Paint on the Mask

1️⃣ Select the **Brush Tool** (▱).

2️⃣ To reveal more of the original layer, change the foreground color to white. "White to reveal, black to conceal."

See the "Set the Foreground and Background Colors" in Chapter 11 for details.

3️⃣ Paint with the brush in the Editor window to show more of the original layer.

Note: You can use any tool that changes the image, including the text tools, paint bucket, brushes, gradients, and so on.

Note: This is an exaggerated example. In a typical project, you would use a small brush to hide or reveal detail around the edges of an object.

TIP

What happens if I create a selection on a mask?
Often, you use **Select** ➪ **All** to select the entire canvas when editing a mask. But if you select an area on the mask, any changes you make stay within the selection. You can use this option to create precise rectangular or elliptical areas, or to limit mask edits using any of the brushes or selection tools. If you edit the mask and nothing happens, you probably forgot to **Select** ➪ **All**.

Applying Styles and Effects

You can apply special effects to your images by using the built-in styles and effects in Photoshop Elements. The effects enable you to add shadows, glows, and a 3D appearance to your art. You can also add special effects to your layers with layer styles.

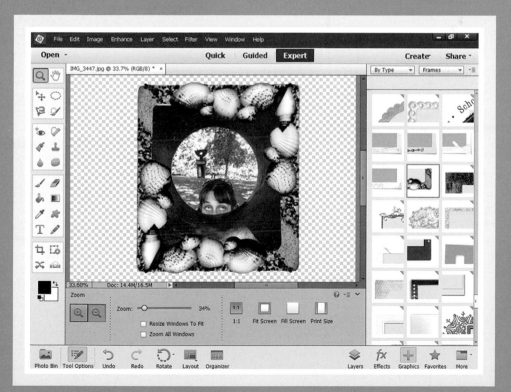

Add a Drop Shadow to a Layer

You can add a *drop shadow* to a layer to create a 3D effect. Photoshop Elements creates a drop shadow by copying the shape of an area, offsetting it slightly, softening it, and placing the shadow under the area. Drop shadows are usually black, but you can use other colors for special effects. They are often used for text, but can also be used with images.

Photoshop Elements includes a selection of predefined drop shadow styles, with varying sizes, opacities, and offsets. You can double-click one of these preset styles to apply it. You can also use a dialog box to create a drop shadow with your own customized settings.

Add a Drop Shadow to a Layer

Apply a Drop Shadow Preset

1 Create a block of text, or copy a selection to a layer.

Note: For more about creating layers from selections, see Chapter 13.

Note: This example shows a new layer on top of a white background layer.

2 Click the new layer to select it.

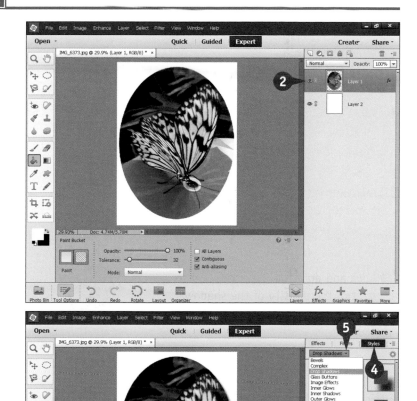

3 Click **Effects**.

4 Click **Styles**.

5 Click the menu selector (▾), and select **Drop Shadows** from the menu.

The Drop Shadow preset styles appear.

6 Double-click one of the style previews.

A Photoshop Elements applies the drop shadow to the layer.

Customize the Drop Shadow

7 Click the settings icon () to open the Style Settings dialog box.

B The Style Settings dialog box opens.

8 Click the Drop Shadow check box if it is not already selected (☐ becomes ☑).

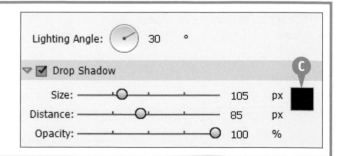

9 Click and drag the **Lighting Angle** dial to specify the direction of the shadowing.

10 Click and drag the **Size** slider to set the size of the shadow.

11 Click and drag the **Distance** slider to set the shadow offset.

12 Click and drag the **Opacity** slider to control the density of the shadow.

13 Click **OK**.

Photoshop Elements applies the style settings.

TIP

How can I select a different color?

In the Style Settings dialog box, click the colored square to the right of the sliders (**C**). Use the standard Photoshop color picker to change the shadow color.

Lighting Angle: 30 °

▽ ☑ Drop Shadow **C**

Size: —○——— 105 px
Distance: ——○——— 85 px
Opacity: ————○ 100 %

Add a Fancy Background

You can add a fancy background to your image with one of several texture effects in Photoshop Elements. The backgrounds include various texture and color combinations and simulations of familiar materials such as brick, denim, and asphalt.

To create a background, select the object you want to place over the background, copy it to a new layer, convert the background to a layer, and apply a pattern effect. For good results, scale the texture. For details, see the tip box.

Add a Fancy Background

1 In the Editor, click **Expert**.

2 Select an object. For good results, use the Rectangular Marquee (▣) or the Elliptical Marquee (▣).

Note: For more about making selections, see Chapter 6.

3 Right-click the selection, and click **Layer Via Copy**.

A Photoshop Elements creates a new layer from the selection.

4 Right-click the background layer, and select **Layer from Background**.

5 Click **OK**.

Photoshop Elements promotes the background to a layer.

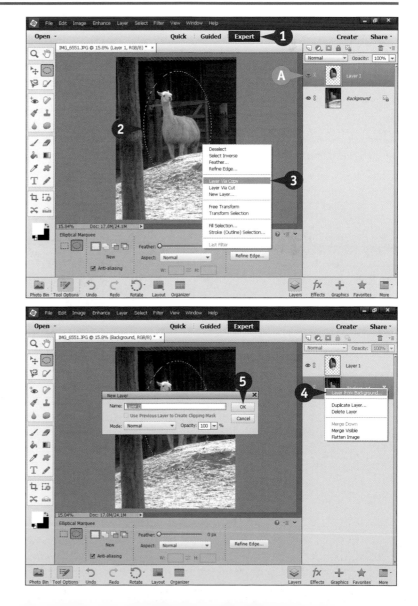

6 Click **Effects**.

7 Click **Styles**.

8 Click the menu selector (), and select **Patterns** from the menu.

The Pattern preset styles appear.

9 Double-click a pattern preset.

B Photoshop Elements applies the pattern to the background layer.

TIPS

What is the difference between color and texture effects?

Photoshop Elements creates a background in two ways. Colors are simple color effects. Some repeat as tiles, while others apply to the image as a whole. Texture effects create a variety of 3D looks, including ripples, creases, bricks, and so on. Color and texture effects are independent. When you select a background with new colors, the texture does not change.

How can I change the size of a layer's background pattern?

To adjust the size of your pattern, click the pattern layer in the Layers panel. Then click **Layer ➪ Layer Style ➪ Scale Effects**. You can adjust the Scale setting in the Scale Layer Effects dialog box to resize the pattern. For example, you can increase the Scale setting to make the bricks in a brick pattern larger.

Create a Beveled Edge

You can add a *beveled edge* to any layer. Beveling creates a chiseled 3D look around the outside of an image or layer, creating an illusion of depth. You can use this feature to create a simple virtual frame around an image. You can also use it to create buttons and other controls for web pages.

Photoshop Elements includes a bevel effect with presets. You can customize the width of the bevel to create a wider frame. You also can improve the effect by adding an *inner glow* around the bevel, which makes it stand out more.

Create a Beveled Edge

1 In the Editor, click **Expert**.

Note: Follow steps **2** and **3** only if your photo has no layers and you want to apply the bevel effects to the background.

2 Right-click the background layer, and select **Layer from Background**.

3 Click **OK**.

Photoshop Elements promotes the background to a layer.

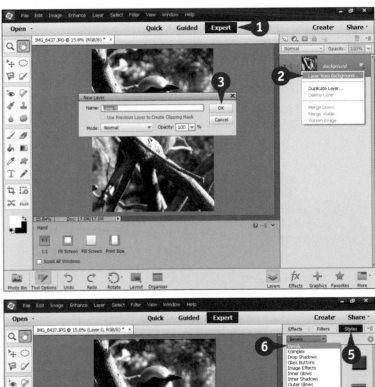

4 Click **Effects**.

5 Click **Styles**.

6 Click the menu selector (⬇), and select **Bevels** from the menu.

The Bevels preset styles appear.

7 Click the settings icon (⚙) to open the Style Settings dialog box.

A The Style Settings dialog box opens.

8 Click the Bevel check box if it is not already selected. (☐ becomes ☑).

9 Adjust the Size slider to set the width of the bevel effect.

B Photoshop Elements displays a live preview of the bevel.

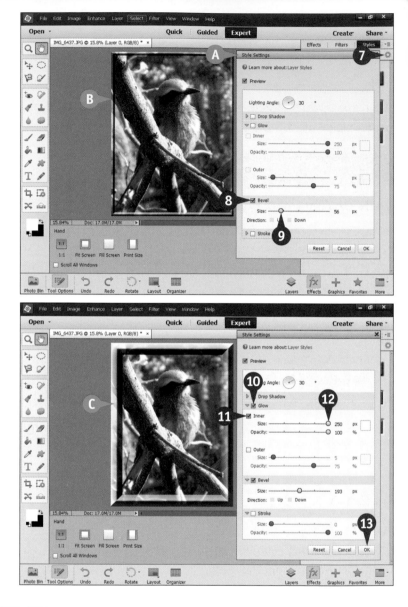

10 Optionally, click the Glow check box (☐ becomes ☑).

11 Click the Inner check box (☐ becomes ☑).

12 Adjust the Size slider to set the width of the glow.

13 Click **OK**.

C Photoshop Elements applies the bevel and glow to the image.

TIPS

Can I change the color of the frame?

Click the color selector box next to the Inner Glow size slider. You can select any color using a standard Photoshop Elements color picker. White and gray create a silver frame. The default light yellow creates a light metallic frame. Other colors are less realistic. For good results, pick a color that matches or complements the photo.

What do the direction radio buttons do?

If you click the Down radio button, Photoshop Elements inverts the bevel effect and chisels the frame into the screen. This is less realistic than the default Up direction, which makes the bevel look like a picture frame around the image.

Apply Image Effects

You can use Image Effects to apply fun, preset image edits. The effects include a vignette feature that places the center of the image in an ellipse and fades out the edges. You can also apply color gradients to remove some of the color around the edges of the photo.

Image Effects are preset. You cannot edit them to create custom effects. Mostly, you cannot change the settings to fine-tune them. However, if a preset applies a texture effect, you can change the size of the texture.

Apply Image Effects

1 In the Editor, click **Expert**.

Note: Follow steps **2** and **3** only if your photo has no layers and you want to apply image effects to the background.

2 Right-click the background layer, and select **Layer from Background**.

3 Click **OK**.

Photoshop Elements promotes the background to a layer.

4 Click **Effects**.

5 Click **Styles**.

6 Click the menu selector (⏷), and select **Image Effects** from the menu.

The Image Effects preset styles appear.

7 Double-click any style.

A Photoshop Elements applies the Image Effect.

Note: This example applies the Sun Faded Photo effect.

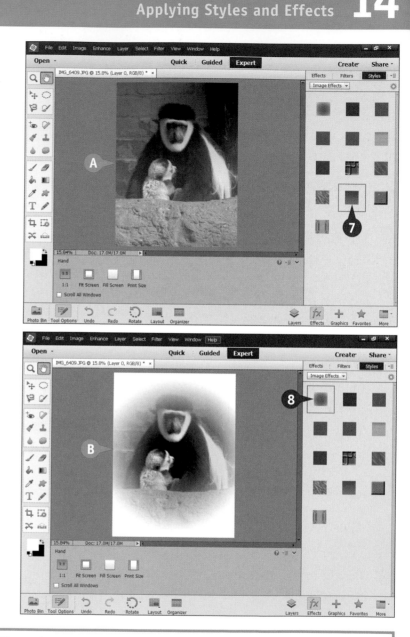

8 Double-click any other Image Effect.

B Photoshop Elements applies the style.

Note: You can apply more than one style. This example adds the Circular Vignette effect to the Sun Faded Photo effect.

TIPS

How can I change the size of a texture effect?
Apply an Image Effect that uses a pattern, such as the Jigsaw effect. Click **Layer** ➪ **Layer Style** ➪ **Scale Effects**. Adjust the Scale setting in the Scale Layer Effects dialog box to resize the pattern. For example, you can increase the Scale setting to make the puzzle pieces bigger.

When would I use Image Effects?
Some effects are more useful than others. The circular vignette and the color effects are all useful. The weather effects — fog, rain, and snow — are less realistic. The abstract effects — night vision, water reflection — are distinctive but unusual. The texture effects — puzzle, tile mosaic — can look realistic if you cut out some of the puzzle pieces or tiles manually after applying the effect.

Add a Watermark

Photoshop Elements can automatically add watermarks to a collection of photos. Watermarks tag your photos with text, such as your name, your website URL, a copyright symbol, and the year, to discourage copying and reuse.

Before you can begin, create a source folder and a destination folder for your images. You can then enter the text you want to use, set the font, size, and color, and control the opacity (transparency) of the text. Pick a color that contrasts with your photos. For best visibility, you may need to use different colors on different photo sets.

Add a Watermark

1 Place the images you want to watermark into a source folder.

2 Create an empty destination folder for the watermarked files.

3 In the Editor, click **File** ⇨ **Process Multiple Files**.

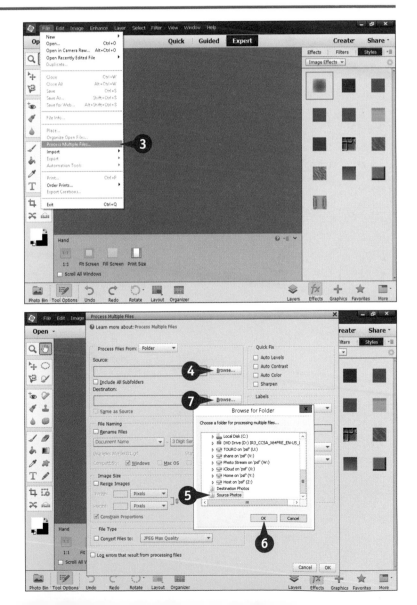

The Process Multiple Files dialog box opens.

4 Click **Browse** next to the Source box.

The Browse for Folder dialog box opens.

5 Navigate to your source folder.

6 Click **OK**.

7 Click **Browse** next to the Destination folder box, and repeat steps **4** to **6** to select the Destination folder.

8 If Watermark is not selected, click the menu selector (▾) and select **Watermark** from the menu.

9 Type your watermark text.

10 Use the text options to set the position, font, and size of your text.

11 Optionally, type a new value into the Opacity box to set the transparency of the watermark.

12 Click the color box, and choose a watermark color.

13 Click **OK**.

A Photoshop Elements adds watermarks to the photos in the source folder and saves them in the destination folder.

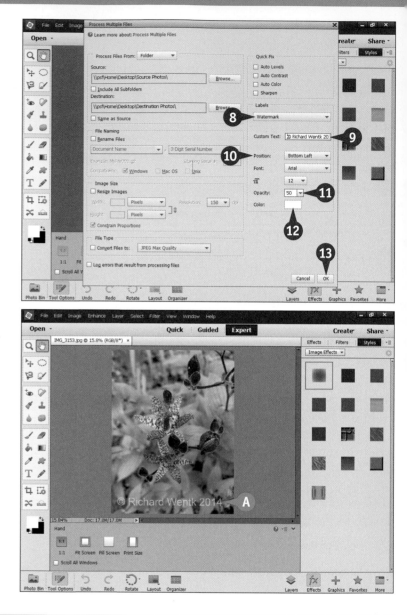

TIPS

Why are my watermarks different sizes?
The font size does not scale to match the dimensions of your photos. To fix this, select the Resize Images check box under the Image Size heading in the Process Multiple Files dialog box. Check Constrain Proportions, and set the target width and height by typing numbers into the corresponding boxes. Now the destination photos are similar sizes, and so are the watermarks.

How do I add a copyright symbol to a watermark?
On a PC, hold down **Alt** and type **0** **1** **6** **9**. You must use the numeric keypad. Release **Alt**. On a Mac, type **Alt**+**G**. Release **Alt**.

Work with Expert Frames

Y ou can use the frames in Expert mode to create more complex effects than are available in Quick mode. More frames are available, and they are almost as easy to add. Optionally, you can use background images to expand the range of effects even more.

Frames and background images must be downloaded before you can use them. You do not have to pay for them, but if you have a slow dial-up connection downloads can take a while.

Work with Expert Frames

1 Open the image to which you want to apply the style.

2 Click **Graphics**.

3 Click the menu selector (▣), and select **Frames** from the menu.

Photoshop Elements displays a set of frame previews.

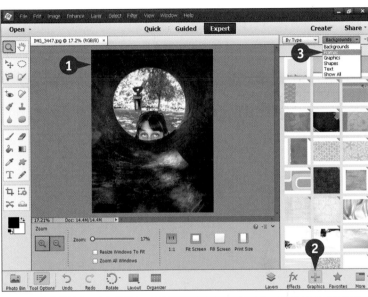

4 Double-click a frame to apply it.

Note: You can also drag the frame and drop it on the photo.

Ⓐ If you have not yet downloaded the frame, Photoshop Elements displays an alert while it downloads it.

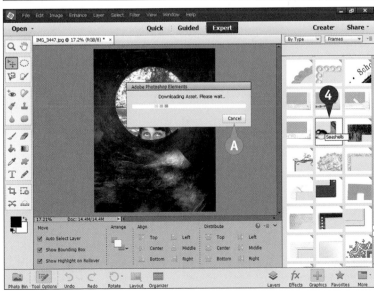

Photoshop Elements applies the frame.

5 Optionally, you can drag the photo within the frame to move it.

6 Optionally, you can drag the slider to resize the in the frame.

7 Optionally, click **Rotate Photo** (⬚) and drag your mouse to rotate the photo in the frame.

8 Optionally, click **Place New Photo** (⬚) to try a different photo in the same frame.

Photoshop Elements applies the frame to the photo.

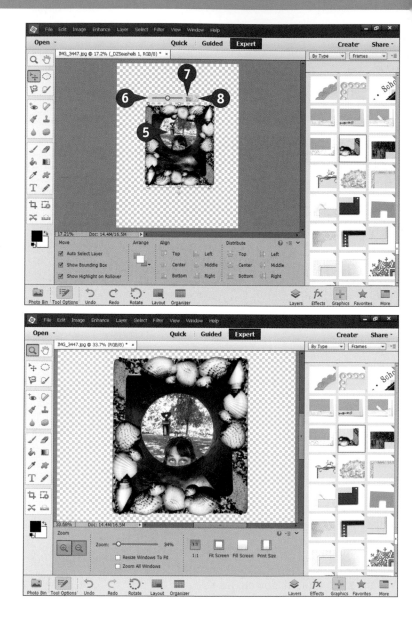

TIP

How do I use a background image with a frame?
Instead of selecting **Frames,** select **Backgrounds.** Double-click a background to copy it to the photo area. It hides your original photo. Select **Frames** again, and select one of the gray graphics without an obvious frame, such as Ripple Edge or Rough Mask 01. Double-click to apply the frame. You can now drag a photo into the gray area. The background remains visible, and the mask frames the photo.

325

Apply an Effect with an Action

You can apply complex effects to an image by playing actions from the Actions panel. An *action* combines several Photoshop Elements commands. Using actions can save time because you can apply multiple edits with a single click. Actions are grouped into sets. There are sets for adding borders, cropping images, and applying special effects.

Note that you cannot undo an action with a single command. You can undo the steps in the action one by one, you can revert the image, or you can save the current state of the image and reload it.

Apply an Effect with an Action

1 Open the image to which you want to apply the action.

2 In the Editor, click **Expert**.

Note: For more on opening the Editor, see Chapter 1.

3 Click **Window** ⇨ **Actions**.

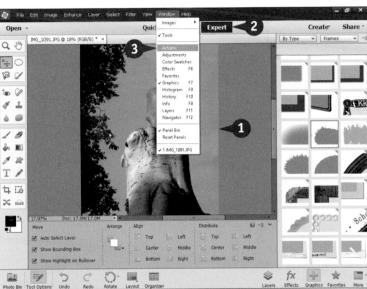

The Actions panel opens.

Ⓐ You can click the folders (📁 changes to 📂) to open different action sets.

 Click to select an action.

 Click the **Play** button (▶).

Photoshop Elements applies the action.

TIPS

Can I change an action or create my own?

This option is not available in Photoshop Elements. If you have the professional version of Photoshop, or if you know someone who does, you may be able to record custom actions and import them into Photoshop Elements. But this is technically challenging, and because of incompatibilities, you may not get the results you expect.

Can I get other actions online?

Yes. Search for "Photoshop Elements Actions" to find free and paid actions you can download and install. To install new actions, click the panel menu (▤) at the top right of the actions list and select **Load Actions**. Navigate to your downloads folder, and click the ATN files.

Add to Favorites

You can save your favorite effects and graphics in a separate Favorites panel. This can save you time because hundreds of effects and graphics are available in their respective panels, most of which you may never use.

Items in the Favorites panel are signified by the same thumbnail image that you see in the other panels. You access the panel via Favorites at the bottom of the workspace.

Add to Favorites

Add an Effect

1 In the Editor, click **Expert**.

2 Click **Effects** to open the Effects panel.

Note: For more on opening the Editor or panels, see Chapter 1.

3 Click the menu, and select an effects group.

4 Right-click an effect.

5 Click **Add to Favorites**.

The effect is added to the Favorites panel.

Add a Graphic

1 Click **Graphics** to open the Graphics panel.

2 Right-click a graphic.

3 Click **Add to Favorites**.

The graphic is added to the Favorites panel.

Apply a Favorite

1 Click **Favorites** to open the Favorites panel.

The favorites appear.

2 Double-click an item.

Photoshop Elements applies the favorite to your image.

Ⓐ You can click **Undo** to undo the edit.

TIPS

How can I remove an item from the Favorites panel?

To remove a favorite, right-click the item and click **Remove from Favorites** from the menu that appears. The item is deleted from the Favorites panel but not from its original place in the Effects or Graphics panel.

How do I change the thumbnail sizes shown in the panels?

You can click the panel menu (▤) in the Effects, Graphics, and Favorites panels and choose a thumbnail view. In the Layers panel, click the panel menu (▤) and then click **Panel Options**.

Saving and Sharing Your Work

You can save your photos in different file formats, print them, store them on CD or DVD, or share them online via Facebook. You can also create slide shows and photo books.

Save a Photo for the Web

You can use the Save for Web. . . dialog box to resize and compress a photo so you can include it in a web page. Uncompressed photos take too much space in the design, and download slowly. You should make your photos as small as you can, without losing impact or detail. As a guide make each web page smaller than 200kb, including all text and images.

Use this tool for your own web pages, but not for photo-sharing sites such as Flickr (www.flickr.com). These sites resize and compress photos for you automatically after you upload them.

Save a Photo for the Web

1 In the Editor, click **Expert**.

2 Click **File** ⇨ **Save for Web**....

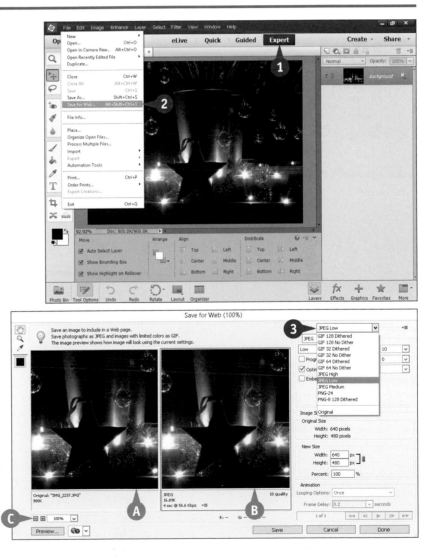

The Save For Web dialog box opens.

Ⓐ The original image appears in the top/left pane.

Ⓑ The compressed image appears in the bottom/right pane.

Ⓒ You can use the zoom factor menu and the zoom buttons (⊞ and ⊟) to zoom into the image and look at fine detail.

3 Click the **Preset** menu, and select a compression preset.

This example shows the Low JPEG preset, which creates very small JPEG files with low image quality.

D You can see the uncompressed file size in the info panel.

E You can compare it with the compressed file size here.

F You can see the estimated download time here.

Note: You can click the panel menu (▤) to select a different download speed. The default uses old modem speeds, which are not a good guide for new site designs.

G You can preview the quality of the compressed image here.

In this example, zooming in shows that the file is too compressed, with blocky details.

H You can check the original image dimensions here.

I You can shrink the image by typing a number smaller than 100% into the **Percent** box, followed by **Enter**.

Note: Shrinking the dimensions lowers image quality. Check the image preview again.

J You can check the new dimensions here.

K You can check the file size and download time of the resized file here.

4 Click **Save** to open a file view, navigate to a save destination, and click **Save** again to save the file. Optionally, you can also type a new name for the file.

Photoshop Elements saves the compressed file to the location you select.

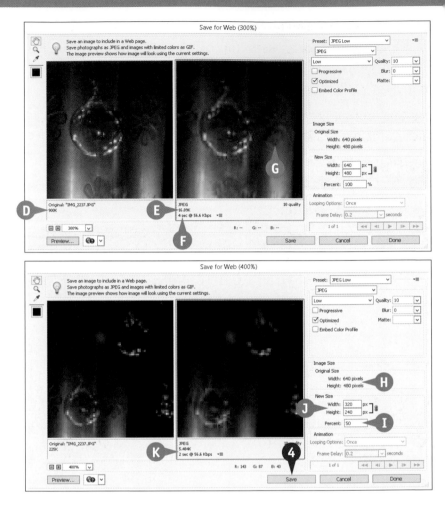

TIP

Which file format should I use?
Use the JPEG (Joint Picture Experts Group) format unless you have a good reason not. Use GIF (Graphic Interchange Format) for small animations. You can make an animation by placing each frame in a separate layer and using the Animation settings at the bottom right of the dialog box to control how quickly the layers play. Use the PNG (Portable Network Graphics) format if you want to save images with transparent or semi-transparent pixels — for example, to make a graphic that floats over the page or has soft edges. Use PNG-24 for photographic objects with many colors, and PNG-8 for simple graphics and clip art with very limited colors.

Convert File Types

You can convert multiple files from one format to another using the Process Multiple Files feature. For example, you can convert a batch of PSD files into JPEG files.

This feature can resize the images as its converts them. It can also rename them with the current date, a serial number, and other details. To use this feature, move or copy the source files to a folder, select a destination folder, and set up the options. Photoshop Elements automatically opens each file in turn, processes it, and saves it.

Convert File Types

1 Copy or move the images you want to convert to an empty folder.

You can also create a separate empty destination folder if you want to keep the processed files separate from the source files.

2 In the Editor, click **File ⇨ Process Multiple Files**.

Note: If a dialog box appears warning about multipage documents and project files, click **OK**.

The Process Multiple Files dialog box opens.

3 Click **Browse**, and navigate to the folder you used in step **1**.

Ⓐ You can check the box (☐ changes to ☑) if you want to include subfolders within the source folders.

4 If you are saving the processed files to a separate destination folder, click **Browse** and select it.

Ⓑ You can check the box (☐ changes to ☑) if you want to save the processed files to the source folder instead of a separate destination folder.

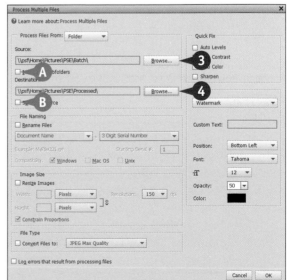

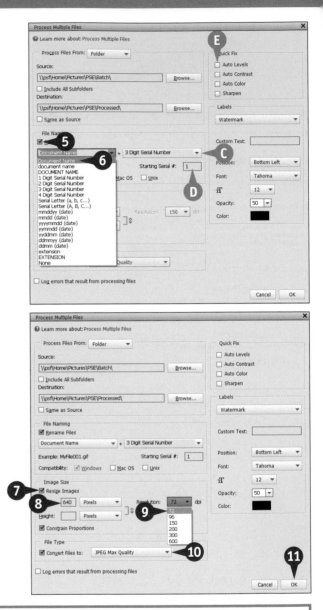

5 To rename the files, check the Rename Files box (☐ changes to ☑).

6 Click the menu, and select the first part of the new name.

C By default the second part of the new name is a serial number. You can click the menu to select a different option.

Note: Both menus include the same list of options.

D You can click this box to type a different initial serial number.

E You can click these check boxes to apply quick fixes to the photos before they are saved.

7 Check the box to resize the images (☐ changes to ☑).

8 Type the new width in pixels into the box.

Note: When **Constrain Proportions** is selected, Photoshop Elements calculates the other dimension, so you do not need to enter it.

9 Click the menu, and select a new resolution.

10 Click the menu, and select the target file format and compression factor.

11 Click **OK**.

Photoshop Elements processes the files and saves the new versions to the folder you selected.

TIPS

Which should I select in the Resolution and File Type menus?
If you are saving files for web use, select 72 dpi. For high-quality printing, select 300 dpi for the best possible quality, or 150 dpi if you want to create smaller files with good but not best-possible quality. For web use, you can select JPEG Max or Medium quality in the File Type menu. If quality is not critical, select JPEG Low Quality. To archive Photoshop Elements projects, select PSD files. Otherwise, select TIFF. Note that there is no PNG option.

Can I resize by a percentage?
Yes. Click the Width and/or Height menus, and select **Percentage**. Type the new percentage size into the adjacent box. Keep percentages between 50% and 200%. Larger percentages are possible, but image quality will be poor.

E-mail Images

You can embed your images in an e-mail message and then send them to others by using the mail feature built into Photoshop Elements. To use the feature, you must set up at least one e-mail account. You can then drag and drop images from the Organizer to an e-mail message.

Previous versions of Photoshop Elements included customized e-mail templates with graphics. This option has been removed from Photoshop Elements 13. But you can still use the Editor to add graphics and frames to images before sending them as e-mails.

E-mail Images

1 In the Organizer, click **Share**.

Note: For more on using the Organizer, see Chapter 3.

2 Click **Email**.

3 If you have not yet set up an e-mail account, click **New**.

4 Type a name into the **Profile Name** box (not shown).

Note: You can use any name. Pick a name that reminds you of your e-mail service.

5 Click the **Service Provider** menu (not shown), and select your e-mail service.

6 Enter your e-mail settings.

7 Click **Validate** to confirm they are correct.

Note: If you do not know the correct settings for some of the options, check with your e-mail provider.

8 Click **OK**.

Click and drag images from the main Organizer window to the Email Attachments pane.

 Click the menu, and select the maximum pixel dimensions.

Note: Use the smallest size possible unless you know that your recipient wants large images.

 Click and drag the slider to set the image quality.

Note: The lower the quality, the smaller the image. Use a minimum of 4 for low-quality images.

B Photoshop Elements shows the estimated size of each photo. Multiply by the number of photos for the total size.

12 Click **Next**.

13 Check the box of each person to whom you want to e-mail the photos (☐ changes to ☑).

Note: If there are no recipients, click the **Edit Recipients in Contact Book** icon (▣) and select **Import** to load the list from your standard Windows or Mac address book. You can also add names manually.

C You can change the default e-mail subject by typing in this box.

D You can change the text of the e-mail message by typing in this box.

14 Click **Next**.

Photoshop Elements e-mails the photos.

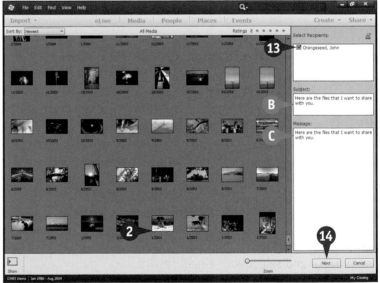

TIP

Can I send images from my usual e-mail software?

Perhaps. Depending on your software, you may be able to drag images from the Organizer directly into an e-mail. There are many e-mail tools and many varieties of web mail. To find out if the tools you use support this option, try it.

Print Photos

You can print your photos on a standard desktop printer. Many printers are compatible with high-quality photo paper, so you can make photo prints at home.

The print feature includes a number of hidden options. You can print single images, a contact sheet with thumbnails of many images, or a picture package with a selection of layout and labeling options. Note that on the Mac, you can select photos for printing in the Organizer, but the print dialog appears in the Editor.

Print Photos

1 In the Organizer, select the photos to print.

Note: For more on using the Organizer, see Chapter 3.

2 Click **File** ➪ **Print**.

You can also print by pressing **Ctrl**+**P** (**⌘**+**P** on a Mac).

The **Prints** dialog box opens.

Ⓐ You can click this menu to select a printer.

Ⓑ You can click this menu to select a paper size.

Note: Select the size you have loaded into your printer.

Ⓒ You can click this menu to select Individual, Contact Sheet, or Picture Package modes.

Ⓓ You can click this menu to select a print size. The default is **Actual Size**.

3 If this option is available, click here to change your printer settings.

A printer settings dialog box appears.

E If you are using special photo-quality paper, you can select it with this menu.

F You can click **Advanced Settings** to access color control and other settings. The settings you see depend on your printer and your operating system.

4 Click **OK** to close the dialog box.

5 Click **More Options** to show further settings.

The More Options dialog box appears.

G You can click items in the list to show further options.

This example shows the Printing Choices dialog box.

H You can click the check boxes to print the date, caption, and filename of the photo.

I You can click the check box and select a number to print more than one copy of each photo.

6 Click **OK** to close the dialog box.

7 Click **Print** to begin printing.

TIPS

What is a contact sheet?

Contact sheets were formerly used by professional photographers to preview thumbnails from a shoot. In Photoshop Elements, you can select photos in the Editor and print preview copies in 1 to 9 columns. You can include details such as the filename and caption under each image. Some photographers use this option to create printed catalogs that they can show or refer to away from the computer.

What is a picture package?

You can use a picture package to create print layouts that use paper efficiently. For example, you can create two horizontal prints on a single sheet of paper in landscape format. This can be more efficient than printing a separate sheet for each photo. You can also print the same photo at different sizes. This option can be useful for creating prints after events such as proms, parties, or weddings. For details, see the online help.

Create a Slideshow

You can use the Organizer to create slideshow that includes photos, music, and text. The slideshow tool has been simplified in Photoshop Elements 13. You cannot add graphics or control transitions — cross fades and other changes — between slides. However, you can select a number of themes for your slideshow with preset backgrounds and complex transitions.

Create a Slideshow

 In the Organizer, Ctrl+click (⌘+click on a Mac) the images you want to put in your slideshow.

Note: For more on using the Organizer, see Chapter 3.

2 Click **Create** ⇨ **Slide Show**.

The Slide Themes dialog box opens.

3 Click and drag the scroll bar to view the themes.

4 Click a theme to select it.

5 Click **Next**.

Note: If you click the **Slide Show** button in the Organizer toolbar, you can skip this step and either use the default theme or select a theme while creating your slideshow.

Photoshop Elements applies the theme, selects a music track, creates a slideshow, and displays it full screen. This can take a few minutes on a slow computer.

 You can click the Pause button to stop the slideshow.

Ⓑ You can click and/or drag the slider to change the play position.

Ⓒ You can click the Save button to save the slideshow.

Note: This option saves the slideshow project to a file and adds it to the Organizer. You can double-click the file in the Organizer later to reload the file into the Slideshow Builder.

❻ Click Edit to open the Slideshow Builder.

The Slideshow Builder dialog box opens.

Ⓓ To add more images, click **Add Media** and select either **Photos and Videos from Elements Organizer** or **Photos and Videos from Folder**.

❼ Drag a photo and release it to move it to a different location in the slideshow.

Ⓔ To delete an item, right-click it and select **Remove item from slideshow**.

❽ Click **Preview** to rebuild the slideshow and preview it.

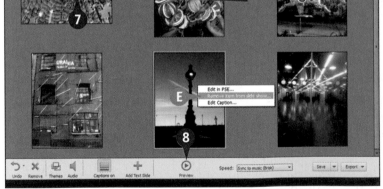

TIPS

How do I create a PDF slideshow?
In earlier versions of Photoshop Elements, you could save a slideshow as a PDF file. In Photoshop Elements 13, this is a separate feature. Click **Share ⇨ PDF Slide Show**. This feature creates an e-mail message with a PDF attachment. Follow the steps in the "E-mail Images" section in this chapter to send the message.

How do I add a title page to my slideshow?
Click a slide thumbnail. Click **Add Blank Slide**. Photoshop Elements adds a blank slide to your slideshow. Click **Add Text**. In the dialog box that opens, type a title for your page and click **OK**. You can click and drag the new title page to reposition it.

continued ▶

You can save the slideshow as a video file in both standard and HD resolutions. You can then share the file by e-mail, or by uploading it to YouTube or your own web pages. You can also import it into a video editing package such as Adobe Premier Elements.

Create a Slideshow (continued)

To Select Different Music

1 Click the **Audio** button.

The Add Audio dialog box appears.

2 Click a file to select it.

3 Click **Play** to preview it.

4 Click **OK** to select the file and add it to your slideshow.

Note: If you have a collection of MP3 files in a folder, you can click **Browse** to open the folder and select a file.

A You can click the **Speed** menu and select **Brisk**, **Normal**, or **No Sync** options to control how quickly items change and whether they follow beats in the music.

To Add a Text Slide

1 Click Add Text Slide.

2 Type your text into the slide.

You can drag and drop the slide to change its position in the list.

Note: You cannot decorate the slide, use a different font, or add a background within the Slideshow Builder.

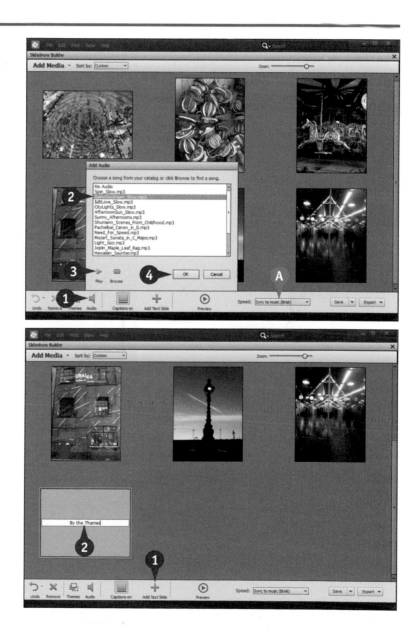

To Select a Different Theme

 1 Click **Themes**.

A The theme list appears.

2 Drag the scrollbar to view all the themes.

3 Click a theme to select it.

4 Click **Apply** to apply the theme and close the theme list.

To Export the Slideshow to a Video File

 1 Click the **Export** button, and select **Export to Local Disk**.

Note: You can also export to Facebook. You typically want to preview the theme from your disk first. You can upload it to Facebook in a separate step.

The Export dialog box appears.

2 Type a filename.

A You can click **Browse** and navigate to a folder to save the file to it.

3 Click the menu, and select a quality preset.

Note: A setting of 640x480 is a small format for custom websites. The other formats work with YouTube and video editors. Select 720p if you have dial-up or slow broadband.

 4 Click **OK**

Photoshop Elements exports the slideshow to a file, including the music you selected.

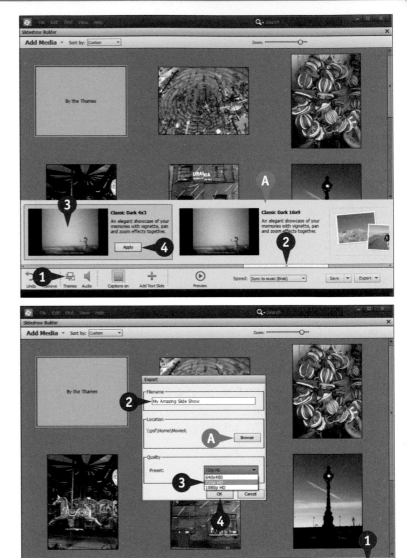

TIP

How can I upload a slideshow to YouTube?
Create a slideshow, and export it as a video file. Use 720p or 1080p resolution for good results. Select the video in the Organizer, and click **Share ⇨ YouTube** from the share menu. Follow the steps to log in to your Google or YouTube account and upload the video.

Create a Photo Book

You can create a photo book to show off your favorite photos in a printed mini-album, with a selection of themes that include page backgrounds, virtual frames, graphics, and styled title text you can edit.

You can add photos from an album, from an Organizer selection, or manually from the Photo Bin or any photo file. You can customize the layout and graphics used in the photo book. The default options often create a good result that does not need to be edited.

Create a Photo Book

Set Up the Book

Ⓐ You can collect the photos into an album and reorder them to set their order in the photo book. See Chapter 3 for details.

① In the Organizer, **Ctrl**+click (⌘+click on a Mac) the images you want to include in your photo book.

② Click **Create** ⇨ **Photo Book**.

The Photo Book dialog box opens in the Editor.

③ Click a book size and printing option.

Note: You can select a size that works with standard U.S. paper sizes or formats the book for a printing partner such as Photoworld in the U.K. or Shutterfly in the U.S.

Note: If you select the local printing partner, an order button appears after you create your book.

④ Drag the scroll bar to view all the available themes.

⑤ Click a theme to preview it.

Ⓑ An animated theme preview showing the page background and virtual frame graphics appears.

⑥ Click **OK** to select a theme.

Photoshop Elements creates the photo book using the photos you selected.

7 If a photo is not selected for editing, double-click it.

C You can click the Move tool () and drag the photo within the frame.

Note: If you drag the frame instead of the photo, right-click the photo and select **Position Photo in Frame**.

D You can drag the slider to change the photo zoom within the frame.

E You can drag the edges of the photo to resize it, or hover at the corners and then click and drag to rotate it.

8 Click ☑ to confirm.

To Change Titles and Text

1 Click the **Horizontal Type** tool (▥).

2 Click a box with dummy text.

3 Drag the mouse to highlight the text.

4 Type new text.

5 Click ☑ to confirm.

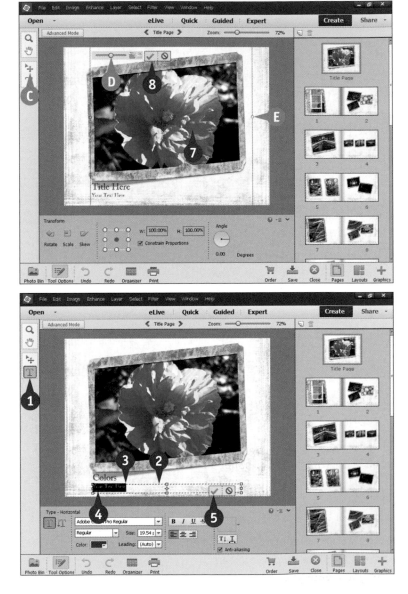

TIP

Can I change choose a different font for title text?

When you click the Horizontal Type tool (▥), Photoshop Elements selects all the usual type options. Click Tool Options in the toolbar if you cannot see the options. You can now select the font, size, color, style, and alignment options in the usual way. You can also apply text warp effects by clicking the Warped Text button (▥).

continued ▶

You can edit and customize the photo book to change the theme graphics and the photo layout. You can also replace individual photos.

After you complete your photo book, you can save it as an Organizer project. You can also print it at home. For better results, with professional binding and high-quality paper, you can use a Printing Partner service.

Create a Photo Book (continued)

To Move, Resize, or Rotate a Frame

1. Click the **Move** tool (⊞).

2. Click a photo to select it, and drag its frame to move it.

3. Drag the edges of the selection box to change the size of the frame.

4. To rotate the frame, hover just outside a corner until the cursor changes to a curved double arrow, and then click and drag.

5. Click ☑ to confirm.

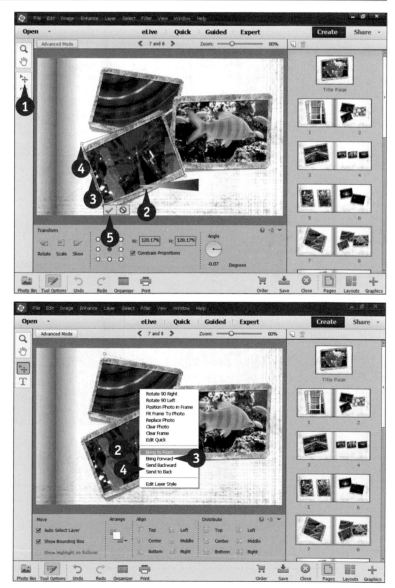

To Place Photos Under or Over Other Photos

1. Right-click a photo.

2. To place it over other photos, select **Bring to Front**.

3. To move it up one level, select **Bring Forward**.

4. To move it under other photos, select **Send Backward** to move it back one level, or **Send to Back** to move it to the back of the layout.

Note: Depending on the photo's position in the layout, some options are grayed out.

To Replace a Photo

 1 Right-click a photo.

2 Select **Replace Photo**.

3 Navigate to the new photo, and click **OK**.

Note: You cannot see the new photo as you select it. You may find it easier to return to the Organizer, rearrange the photos in the source album, and reload the album as a photo book.

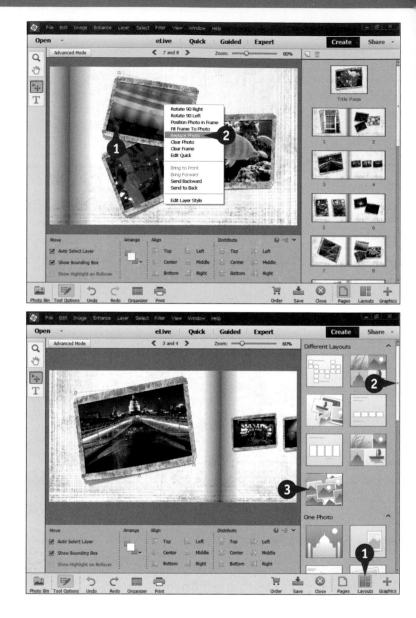

To Change the Layout

 1 Click **Layouts**.

2 Drag the scroll bar to see all the layouts.

3 Double-click a layout to apply it.

Note: Photoshop Elements redistributes the photos on the current page. If you pick a layout with extra frames, you must load them manually.

Note: Currently, Photoshop Elements applies the layout to both pages in a double page spread. This may change in a future update.

TIPS

How can I change the background or frame graphics?
Click Graphics in the toolbar. You can now drag backgrounds and frames onto the layout area.

How do I order a printed photo book?
Click the Order button in the toolbar to see ordering instructions. Different countries have different printing partners.

Share Photos on Facebook

You can select photos in your Organizer catalog and post them to an album on the social network Facebook. You can upload the photos directly to Facebook by giving Photoshop Elements permission to communicate directly with your Facebook account. After the photos are posted, your Facebook friends can view the photos.

This sharing feature requires an Internet connection and a Facebook account. You can visit Facebook at www.facebook.com. Users must be 13 or older.

Share Photos on Facebook

1 In the Organizer, **Ctrl**+click (**⌘**+click on a Mac) to select the photos you want to share.

2 Click **Share** ➪ **Facebook**.

An authorization dialog box appears.

3 Click **Authorize**.

Ⓐ By default, Photoshop Elements downloads your list of friends from Facebook and makes them available when you define people in the Organizer. For more about defining people in your photos, see Chapter 4.

A Facebook login page opens in a web browser.

④ Type the e-mail address for your Facebook account.

⑤ Type your Facebook password.

Ⓑ If you do not have a Facebook account, you can click the link to sign up for one.

⑥ Click **Log In** to sign in to Facebook.

Note: You may see a notice asking you to save the browser you are using. Click **Save Browser** if you are logging in from a private computer at home or work, or click **Don't Save** if you are logging in from a public computer. Then click **Okay**.

Ⓒ A pop-up appears asking you to give the Adobe software access to the information held in your Facebook account.

⑦ Click **Okay**.

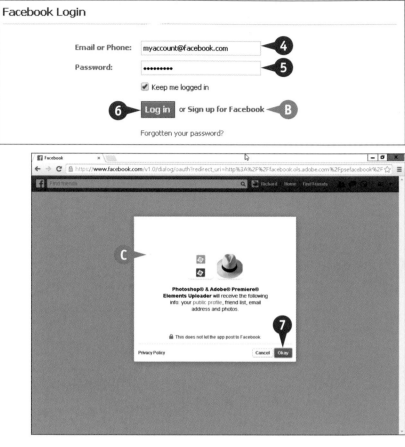

continued ▶

TIP

How can I tag friends on Facebook?
In the Organizer, tag photos with People keyword tags. Follow the steps in this section to share the photos to Facebook. In the Share to Facebook dialog box, make sure **Upload people tags in these photos** is checked (☑). Photoshop Elements automatically tags the photos with the names of your friends as it uploads them.

Share Photos on Facebook (continued)

Facebook organizes your photos into albums, which enables you to keep photos of specific events in one place. You can control who can view the albums that you post. In the Share to Facebook dialog box in Photoshop Elements, you can specify whether just your Facebook friends, friends of your friends, or everyone on Facebook can see the photos.

You can also upload the photos in one of two different resolutions. The higher resolution offers better viewing quality online but takes longer to upload.

Share Photos on Facebook (continued)

Ⓓ A pop-up appears asking you to give permission for Photoshop Elements to post on your account.

⑧ Click **Okay**.

After you give permission, a Thank You page appears.

⑨ Close or hide your web browser to return to Photoshop Elements.

10 Click **Complete Authorization**.

The Facebook dialog box appears.

E You can click the plus sign () to add more photos from the Organizer. To remove a photo from the album, click a thumbnail and then click the minus sign (▬).

F You can click this option (☐ changes to ☑) to add your photos to an existing album on Facebook.

11 If you are uploading to a new album, type a name, optional location, and description for your album.

12 Click the menu to set who can see the photos.

13 Click an option (☐ changes to ☑) to specify normal or detailed (large, high-quality) photos.

14 Click **Upload**.

Photoshop Elements uploads the photos to Facebook.

Click **Visit Facebook** in the confirmation dialog box to view your Facebook account.

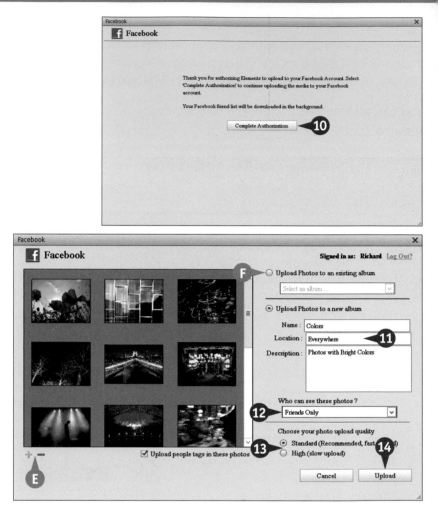

TIP

How do I create a Facebook Cover Photo?

Select three photos in the Organizer, and open the Editor. Click **Create** ➪ **Facebook Cover**. Select a theme. Photoshop Elements places the photos into the theme layout and adds a background. You can think of the cover layout as a single-page Photobook: Most of the editing options are identical. Click **Save** to save the combined image as a Photoshop Elements project. Click **Upload** to set the image as your account cover/ profile image. Click **Close** when you're finished.

Share a Photo on Twitter

Y ou can select a photo in the Organizer and post it to Twitter, adding up to 140 characters of text. Twitter is a microblogging service for short messages or **tweets**. When you post an image with a tweet, a link appears with the text in your Twitter feed. When your followers click the link, they see the photo.

Anyone with an e-mail address can sign up for a Twitter account. You can visit Twitter at www.twitter.com.

Share a Photo on Twitter

1 Click the photo you want to share.

You can share only one photo at a time.

2 In the Organizer, click **Share** ⇨ **Twitter**.

An authorization dialog box appears.

3 Click **Authorize**.

The first time you share via Twitter, a Twitter login page opens in a web browser.

④ Type your Twitter login name.

⑤ Type your Twitter login password.

Ⓐ If you do not have a Twitter account, you can sign up for one.

⑥ Click **Authorize app**.

⑦ Close your web browser when the Thank You page appears.

⑧ In the Twitter dialog box in Photoshop Elements, click **Done**.

A dialog box appears.

⑨ Type the text for your tweet.

Ⓑ Numbers show you how many characters you have left.

Note: The image link in the Tweet uses some of the 140 characters.

⑩ Click **Tweet** to post the photo with your text.

Photoshop Elements sends the tweet and shows a confirmation dialog box. You can click **Done** to close the dialog box or **Visit Twitter** to view your tweet.

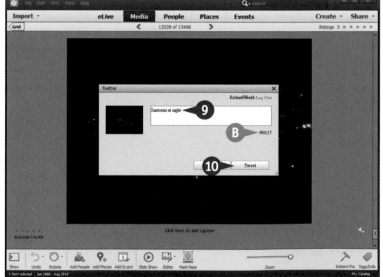

TIPS

What are hashtags?
You can use hashtags as short descriptions to make your tweets easier to follow. Type the hash symbol (#) before any word you want to highlight. Some Twitter users include hashtags as searchable tags. For example, you can include #pet and #germanshepherd when you tweet a photo of your dog. Other users are less literal and use hashtags to describe a mood or feeling.

How can I tell if I have shared a photo on Twitter?
In the Organizer, right-click the photo and click **Show File Info** in the menu that appears. The Information panel opens. Click **History** in the Information panel. When you post a tweet, Photoshop Elements adds Twitter to the Shared With panel.

Export Photos

You can export selected photos from the Organizer to a folder. Use this option if you want to copy the photos to another computer, save them for a feature such as Photomerge Panorama (see Chapter 8), write them to a USB stick or external hard drive, or import them into a blog or custom web gallery.

When you export, you can convert your images to a different file format. If you save the files as JPEGs, you can change the image quality and resize them. PNG and TIFF files do not lose quality and cannot be resized. Save the files as PSDs for use with other Adobe products.

Export Photos

1 In the Organizer, **Ctrl**+click (⌘+click on a Mac) to select the photos you want to share.

Note: For more on using the Organizer, see Chapter 3.

If you do not select any photos, Photoshop Elements exports all the photos in the Organizer.

2 Click **File** ⇨ **Export As New File(s)**.

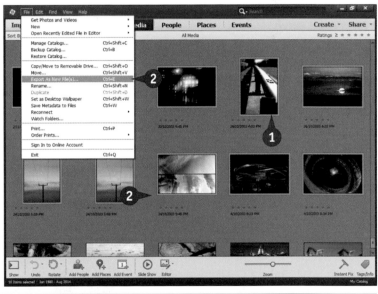

The Export New Files dialog box opens, showing the selected photos listed.

3 Click the radio buttons to select a file type.

Note: Leave **Original Format** selected if you do not want to convert the files.

Ⓐ If you select JPEG, you can click and drag the slider to set the JPEG quality and click the menu to select a new image size.

4 Click **Browse** to choose a destination folder for the images.

5 Click **Add...** to select and add photos from Organizer albums and tag groups.

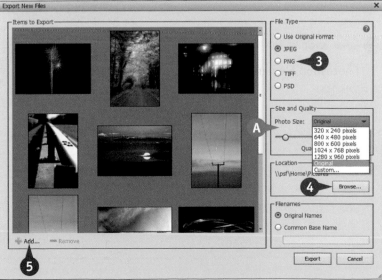

The Add Files dialog box opens.

 6 Click the **Advanced** arrow to show advanced options (▶ changes to ▾).

7 Click a radio button to select photos grouped by albums, keyword tags, people, places, or events.

8 Click a menu to select the media in each group.

Ⓑ You can use the check boxes to show media with star ratings or which are hidden.

Note: This feature shows media with any star rating. You cannot select a rating.

9 Click **Done** to add the media and close the dialog box.

Photoshop Elements adds the photos.

Ⓒ To remove a photo, click the photo then click **Remove**.

10 You can use the radio buttons to keep the original filenames or add a common base name.

11 Type the base name.

12 Click **Export**.

Photoshop Elements exports your images.

TIP

What is the common base name?

If you select **Common Base Name**, you can type a common name for the exported photos — for example, "vacation." When you click Export, Photoshop Elements takes the name and adds a number after it for each photo — "vacation-1.jpg," "vacation-2.jpg", and so on. This option ignores the original filename.

Set up Adobe Revel

You can export photos from Photoshop Elements to Adobe Revel, Adobe's cloud-based photo storage service. Photos in Revel are stored on Adobe's servers.

You can use Revel to keep online copies of your photos and to access your photos from different devices. Your device must be connected to the Internet before you can use Adobe Revel.

Set Up Adobe Revel

1 In the Organizer, click **File** ➪ **Sign In to Online Account.**

A sign-in window appears.

A If you do not have an Adobe ID to sign in with, click **Create an Adobe ID** to create one.

2 Type your Adobe ID. It is the e-mail address you signed up with.

3 Type your password.

4 Click **Sign In**.

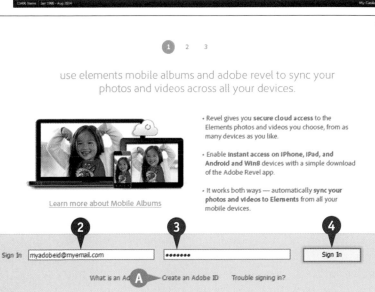

use elements mobile albums and adobe revel to sync your photos and videos across all your devices.

- Revel gives you **secure cloud access** to the Elements photos and videos you choose, from as many devices as you like.

- Enable **instant access on iPhone, iPad, and Android and Win8** devices with a simple download of the Adobe Revel app.

- It works both ways — automatically **sync your photos and videos to Elements** from all your mobile devices.

Learn more about Mobile Albums

Sign In   myadobeid@myemail.com

What is an Ac ... Create an Adobe ID   Trouble signing in?

A welcome screen appears.

5 Click here to upload a selection of media.

B You can click here to share all your media.

Note: You cannot share all your media without a subscription. Fast broadband is essential.

Note: It can take a very long time to upload a large photo collection, even with fast broadband.

6 Click **Next**.

A confirmation screen appears.

7 Click **Done**.

You can now use Revel to share photos and albums.

TIPS

What is eLive?

eLive is a private website for users of Photoshop Elements and Premier Elements. It includes tutorials, news, and inspirational showcases. To use it, click **eLive** in the toolbar at the top of the Organizer. Note that eLive is not a photo-sharing service.

How much does Revel cost?

The first 2GB of photos and videos is free. A subscription with unlimited storage costs $5.99 per month. Casual photographers are unlikely to have more than 2GB of photos. But note that on a typical broadband connection, it will take between three hours and two days to upload 2GB of content. If you use a mobile phone to store content in Revel, be careful of data limits on your account.

Share an Album with Adobe Revel

You can upload photos to Adobe Revel and share them with friends and family. The **Share Private Album** feature in Photoshop Elements uploads the photos and creates a link you can e-mail to friends and relatives.

If you want to upload an album quickly without setting up sharing, you can drag the album icon into the Mobile Library. This option bypasses the Share Private Album dialog box, uploads the photos, and deletes the original Local Album. You can then log in to the Revel website and enable sharing for the album.

Share an Album with Adobe Revel

1 Create or select a local album in the Organizer.

Note: See Chapter 3 for more about working with albums.

2 Click **Share** ⇨ **Private Web Album**.

A dialog box appears.

3 Click **Done** in the dialog box that appears to confirm.

The Private Web Album dialog box appears.

4 Click **Adobe ID** to sign in with your Adobe ID.

A browser window appears.

5 Close or hide the browser window.

6 Click **Complete Authorization** in the Private Web Album dialog box.

The Private Web Album dialog box displays share options.

 Click the ⊞ to create a new album.

Note: This dialog box does not create a new online album automatically when you share a local album.

Note: You can add photos to an existing album by selecting it from the menu.

8 Check **Allow Downloads** (☐ changes to ☑) if you want to allow visitors to download your photos.

9 Click **Start Sharing**.

Photoshop Elements uploads the photos or the album you selected.

The Private Web Album dialog box reappears when the photos have uploaded.

A You can click the link to view the album online.

B You can click **Email Link** to e-mail the link to friends and family.

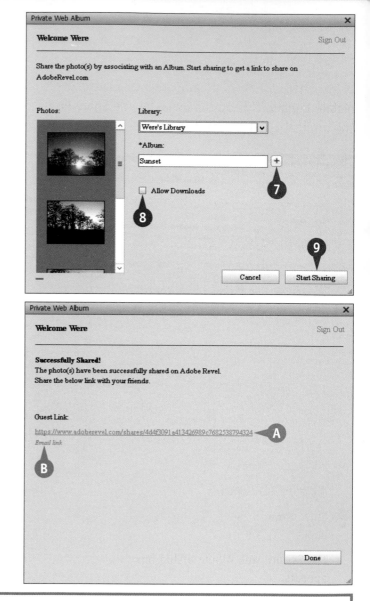

TIPS

How can I view my Revel photos in a web browser?

In your web browser, visit www.adoberevel.com and sign into your Revel account using your Adobe ID and password. From the Revel website, you can access your libraries and see the photos you have exported from Photoshop Elements. You can also export photos directly from your computer to Revel via the website.

How can I view my Revel photos on my mobile device?

You can download the Revel app to your iPhone, iPad, or Android-based device. After you sign into your Revel account on your mobile device, you can view your Revel photos. You can also export photos you take with your mobile device into Revel and then access those photos in Photoshop Elements.

Back Up a Catalog

You can back up your digital photos with the Organizer's backup tool. The tool creates a single backup file. It does not copy the photos to a new folder you can access.

You can use this option to back up files to a CD or DVD. But you should use an external hard drive or USB stick for reliability. Writeable CD and DVD disks can lose their contents after only a few years, especially if left in sunlight.

Back Up a Catalog

1 In the Organizer click **File ➪ Backup Catalog**.

You can also type **Ctrl**+**B** (**⌘**+**B** on a Mac.)

Note: Photoshop Elements may display a warning about missing files. If this happens, click **Reconnect** to perform a check. See the tip for more details.

Photoshop Elements displays a Preparing Files alert. It can take a few minutes to prepare the files for a large catalog.

The Backup Catalog to CD, DVD, or Hard Drive dialog box opens.

2 If this is your first backup, leave **Full Backup** selected.

Ⓐ For subsequent backups, you can click **Incremental Backup** (○ changes to ◉). Incremental Backup backs up files that have changed or been added since the last backup and is faster than a full backup when you have saved a catalog previously.

3 Click **Next**.

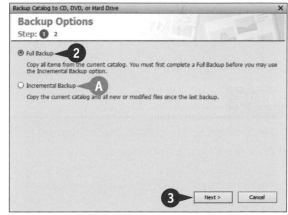

④ Click to select the drive to which you want to copy the backup files.

Ⓑ You can type a name for the backup in this text box.

⑤ Click **Browse**, and create and/or select a folder for the backup.

Ⓒ You can see the estimated size of the backup here.

⑥ Click **Save Backup**.

Photoshop Elements backs up your photos.

Ⓓ An alert confirms the backup. Click **OK** to continue.

TIPS

The Organizer prompts me to find missing files before backing up my photos. What do I do?

If a catalog photo no longer contains a valid link to original file, the backup tool displays a prompt asking you to reconnect any missing files. A file can appear to be missing if you move it after adding the photo to the Organizer or if you rename the file outside the Organizer. Click **Reconnect** to allow Photoshop Elements to look for the missing links and then continue with the backup.

How do I restore my backed-up files?

Click **File** and then **Restore Catalog**. You can restore photos to their original locations or to a new catalog and location.

Index

DISCARD